The Future of Judaism

The Future of Judaism

Dan Cohn-Sherbok

T&T CLARK
EDINBURGH

T&T CLARK LTD
59 GEORGE STREET
EDINBURGH EH2 2LQ
SCOTLAND

First published 1994

ISBN 0 567 29267 3

British Library Cataloguing-in-Publication Data
A catalogue record for this book is available from the British Library

Typeset by Waverley Typesetters, Galashiels
Printed and bound in Great Britain by Redwood Books Ltd, Wiltshire

For Lavinia

Contents

Part II
NON-ORTHODOX JUDAISM

Part III
OPEN JUDAISM

Preface

For over fifteen years I have taught about Judaism to mostly non-Jewish students at the University of Kent at Canterbury, England. In my Introduction to Judaism class, I normally explain that since the Enlightenment at the end of the eighteenth century, Jewry evolved into a number of sub-groups, all espousing divergent approaches to the tradition. On the far right, Orthodoxy has divided into a variety of factions: Hasidism, Traditional Orthodoxy, Neo-Orthodoxy and Liberal Orthodoxy. Yet despite their different orientations, all Orthodox Jews subscribe to the conviction that God gave Moses the Written *Torah* on Mount Sinai – this belief serves as the foundation for the Orthodox adherence to both the Written and the Oral Law. Moving across the religious spectrum, Conservative Judaism offers a traditional interpretation of Jewish observance despite its theological liberalism: for many Jews such a compromise provides a means of harmonizing the demands of the Jewish way of life with contemporary concerns. For others, Reconstructionist Judaism (an offshot of Conservative Judaism) provides a more acceptable alternative. On the far left both Reform and Humanistic Judaism constitute an even-more radical interpretation of the tradition: in both cases, these movements set out to revise the Jewish heritage in the light of modern needs.

Recently, after listening to this catalogue of the various Jewish groups, one of my students raised her hand. 'In the past', she asked, 'wasn't Judaism a unified system of belief and practice?' 'It was,' I said. 'There were, of course, a number of different sects like the Pharisees, the Sadducees, the Essenes. Some like the Karaites were condemned as heretical. But despite their different attitudes, all these sects accepted Scriptural law as binding. In this sense, they subscribed to a common basis of belief and practice. But in the modern world, all this has changed. Never before has there been such a fragmentation of the faith.' 'But', she continued, 'how can Judaism survive if Jews today can't agree any more on the fundamental principles of the Jewish faith. Does Judaism really have a future if there's so much disagreement?'

My student was right to raise this issue, and I began to ponder the implications of the current state of disunity within world Jewry. If Jews are so divided among themselves that they cannot agree on basic questions of belief, practice and identity, is there a future for Judaism as a religious system? Regrettably, few Jewish writers have dealt with this issue: with the exception of such studies as Dov Marmur's *Beyond Survival*, David Vital's *The Future of the Jewish People*, and Jonathan Sacks' *One People?*, there has been little reflection about the nature of Judaism in the third millennium. The purpose of this volume is thus to explore the nature of Judaism in the past, and to chart a new direction for the future. The book itself is aimed primarily for non-Jewish students like those I teach at the University as well as general readers who wish to gain an understanding of the complex nature of contemporary Judaism and the future prospects for the Jewish faith. In addition, the proposals for the future of Judaism are also directed at liberally-minded Jews who are sympathetic to a pluralistic understanding of religion.

Introduction

Does Judaism have a future, and if so, what is it to be? This question is of the utmost importance as Jewry stands on the threshold of the third millennium. Yet surprisingly over the last few decades, Jewish scholars and thinkers have generally not addressed themselves to this vital issue. Instead, there has been an outpouring of books dealing with all aspects of Jewish faith and culture: such investigations of both the Jewish past and present have been undertaken on the assumption that just as Jews and Judaism have existed for millennia, so Jewish civilization will continue to survive despite contemporary secularism and religious scepticism.

In our post-Holocaust world the belief in the continuing existence of Judaism is simply taken for granted, and the future pattern of Jewish life is largely left unexplored. Recently, however, a few Jewish writers have begun to turn their attention to this crucial subject. For example, in *One People? Tradition, Modernity and Jewish Unity* (Littman Library of Jewish Civilization, 1993), Jonathan Sacks, the Chief Rabbi of the United Hebrew Congregations of the British Commonwealth, proposed a new conception of Jewish existence in a future age. According to Sacks, contemporary Jewish life is beset with conflict. No longer is the Jewish people united by a common basis of belief and practice; rather Jews are divided by conflicting religious convictions as the Jewish nation is fractured and fragmented as never before. He wrote:

> Almost all Jewish groups in Israel and the diaspora express a commitment to Jewish survival, peoplehood and unity. But the interpretation of those concepts differ systematically from group to group. Along

religious, ethnic, cultural and national axes, there coexist two deepening senses, of kinship with, and estrangement from, other Jews. Ideology conflicts with empirical reality, and the global vision of peoplehood fragments as soon as the attempt is made to specify it with any precision. (Sacks, 1993, 13)

To overcome this rift, Sacks advanced an inclusivist ideology which would embrace all segments of the Jewish community regardless of their religious orientations. Sacks is critical of those who seek to disparage the various branches of non-Orthodox Judaism (Conservative, Reconstructionist, Reform, Liberal, Humanistic Judaism). Such animosity, he believes, undermines the traditional understanding *Klal Yisrael* (Jewish peoplehood). In its place he endorsed an inclusivist stance which recognizes the positive value of all forms of Judaism while refusing to grant these various branches religious legitimacy. Non-Orthodox Jews are not to be condemned for their departure from tradition, but from an Orthodox perspective non-Orthodox Judaism must not be accepted as a valid interpretation of the Jewish faith. Thus Sacks' notion of Jewish inclusivism is all-embracing, while at the same time firmly rooted in an adherence to the Orthodox way of life.

According to Sacks, the future of the Jewish people can be assured only if they return to the faith of their ancestors. Despite the disintegration of modern Jewish life, it is possible for Jews to regain a love for tradition. Drawing on the biblical narrative, he formulated a vision of the Jewish future in which traditional Jewish life will be renewed:

The primal scene of Jewish history, is of the Israelites in the wilderness, fractious, rebellious, engaged in endless diversion, yet none the less slowly journeying towards the fulfilment of the covenantal promise. No image seems to be more descriptive of contemporary Jewry ... The inclusivist faith is that Jews, divided by where they stand, are united by what they are travelling towards, the destination which alone gives meaning to Jewish history: the promised union of *Torah*, the Jewish people, the land of Israel, and God. (Sacks, 1993, 228)

Here, then, is a modern Orthodox proposal for Jewish survival. Yet, for most Jews, Sacks' endorsement of Orthodox

Judaism as the only viable framework for Jewish life is simply unacceptable. Sacks refuses to grant legitimacy to the majority of religious adherents within the boundaries of modern Judaism. No doubt non-Orthodox Jews would welcome this shift away from previous denunciations of non-Orthodox interpretations of Judaism (even if they reject Sacks' evaluation of non-Orthodox Judaism), but a more realistic conception of Jewish life is needed if Jews, and Judaism, are to continue into the next century and beyond.

The purpose of this book is to offer an alternative view based on an assessment of the nature of contemporary Jewish life. As will be seen, modern Jews are deeply divided on a wide variety of issues – there is simply no way that world Jewry will be able to come to a common view concerning the fundamentals of Jewish belief and practice as Sacks recommends. Moreover, even within each branch of Judaism, individuals consciously choose for themselves which aspects of Judaism they find spiritually meaningful. Given this situation, no uniform pattern of Jewish existence can be imposed from above, nor is it likely to emerge from within the body of Israel. What is required instead, is a philosophy of Jewish autonomy which legitimizes Jewish subjectivity and personal decision-making. This ideology of Judaism – which I believe is the only viable form of Judaism for the future – is referred to as 'Open Judaism'. The intention of this study is to make a case for this new vision.

The book begins with an overview of Jewish history for those unfamiliar with the history of the Jewish people. According to Scripture, God promised Abraham that he would be the father of a multitude. The biblical narrative continues with an account of the patriarchs and the sojourn in Egypt. After escaping from Egyptian bondage, the Hebrew people settled in Canaan after conquering its inhabitants. For nearly a millennium they were ruled over by a series of kings, but in AD 70 the Jewish nation was exiled from its ancestral home. Following this catastrophe, rabbinic scholars engaged in the interpretation of Scripture, and their discussions were recorded in various books of law. The development of rabbinic Judaism continued through the Middle Ages, resulting in the production of a wide variety of works in the areas of Jewish law, philosophy, theology and mysticism. Over the centuries the Jewish tradition continued to evolve, yet despite this development the Jewish people remained loyal to the central teachings of the faith. With the impact of the Enlightenment in the eighteenth century, however, the Jewish community divided into a wide range of groupings with fundamentally different ideologies. Thus, in the modern world, Judaism no longer constitutes a unitary system of belief and practice.

So, throughout Jewish history until the beginning of the nineteenth century the Jewish religious tradition was essentially uniform in character. As Chapter Two illustrates, the ancient Israelites subscribed to a belief in One God who created the cosmos, chose the Jews as his special people, and guides human history to its ultimate fulfilment. In the unfolding of this eschatological scheme, the children of Israel have a major role – they are to be a light to the nations. Despite the absence of a credal formulation of such beliefs in the Bible, Jewish scholars through the centuries attempted to formulate a list of the fundamental principles of the faith. In the Middle Ages there was considerable discussion about this quest, and eventually Maimonides' list of the Thirteen Principles of Judaism became authoritative for Jewry. In consequence, there has been a common core of Jewish belief which has served as the foundation for the development of Jewish life and thought until the modern period.

It might be objected, however, that the emergence of various Jewish sub-groups through the centuries illustrates that such a shared religious basis did not, in fact, exist. Chapter Three demonstrates that this interpretation of Jewish history fails to acknowledge that these different groups – despite their religious orientations – all subscribed to the central principles of the Jewish faith. The Samaritans in ancient times, for example, remained loyal to Scripture. Similarly the Sadducees, Pharisees, Essenes and Rebels of the first century, were faithful to the biblical tradition despite their different interpretations of the Scriptural text. The Karaites of the early Middle Ages also strictly adhered to the tenets of the Bible; even though they rejected the rabbinical understanding of the Written *Torah*, they scrupulously followed the commandments as recorded in the Pentateuch. Likewise, the Shabbateans of the seventeenth century deviated from mainstream Judaism only in their conviction that Shabbetai Tzevi was the long-awaited Messiah. So, too, the Hasidim of the late eighteenth century were loyal to *Torah* Judaism despite their rejection of arid rabbinism.

Until modern times, then, Judaism was essentially a monolithic religious tradition despite the various factions that arose in the course of Jewish history. The Enlightenment, however, had a profound effect on Jewish life. Chapter Four traces the history of this development and the rise and growth of Reform Judaism. Initially, the eighteenth-century German philosopher Moses Mendelssohn, encouraged his co-religionists to integrate into the mainstream of Western society. Subsequently, his followers attempted to reform Jewish education by modifying the traditional Jewish curriculum to include secular subjects. In the wake of these developments, reformers initially called for liturgical change; later they pressed for a re-evaluation of the Jewish tradition and advocated major change in Jewish belief and observance. In order to establish a coherent policy, a series of Reform synods took place in Europe and the United States, resulting in the formulation of a list of Reform principles enshrined in the Pittsburgh Platform of 1886. In the following years Reform Judaism underwent further modification, and new Platforms were propounded by the movement. In all cases, these declarations of Reform principles were far removed from Maimonides' formulation of the Thirteen Principles of the faith. Thus, throughout its history Reform Judaism has distanced itself from the monolithic Jewish religious system of previous ages.

Chapter Five continues this discussion of the fragmentation of the Jewish tradition into various religious groupings, each with its own religious orientation. In the middle of the nineteenth century Zacharias Frankel, an early reformer of a more conservative inclination, formulated a less-radical approach to the Jewish heritage. This development was subsequently known as Conservative Judaism and attracted a

wide following in the United States. Later, under the influence
of the Jewish philosopher Mordecai Kaplan, the Reconstructionist movement broke away from Conservative Judaism.
This new movement rejected supernaturalism even though it
retained many of the traditional elements of the Jewish faith.
More recently, another form of non-supernatural Judaism –
Humanistic Judaism – appeared which espoused a humanistic
ideology rooted in the Jewish tradition. The final form of
modern Judaism – Polydoxy – is a religious ideology which
has emerged from the ranks of Reform Judaism. This new
approach champions personal autonomy as a guiding
principle. Hence, within the Jewish world there currently exist
a variety of interpretations of Judaism, all vehemently
opposed to one another.

The dissolution of the Jewish faith in the modern world is
the result of a number of factors which have affected the
Jewish community. Chapter Six highlights some of the major
forces that have led to this fragmentation of Jewry into a
variey of groups with divergent and conflicting ideologies. For
many Jews, the belief in an all-good, omnipotent deity has
appeared inconceivable in the light of the terrible events of the
Holocaust. Further, it has become increasingly difficult for a
significant segment of Jewry to subscribe to the belief in the
doctrine of *Torah MiSinai* in the light of recent scholarly
investigation of the biblical text. In particular, the findings of
biblical criticism, studies of the history of the Scriptural text,
and the discoveries of archaeology have called into question
the belief that God revealed the Five Books of Moses to Moses
on Mount Sinai. As a result of this altered perspective of the
Jewish heritage, many Jews no longer find it possible to accept
traditional doctrines concerning God's action in the world, the
coming of the Messiah, the resurrection of the dead, and final
judgment; moreover, there has been a growing disenchantment with the system of observance in traditional Orthodoxy.
Thus, the Jewish people has ceased to be a unified nation with
a common heritage and religious vocabulary.

Given this altered state of affairs, there is a pressing need for
the formulation of a new philosphy of Judaism which could
provide a basis for Jewish living for the twenty-first century.

Chapter Seven provides a new vision of Judaism for the future based on a Copernican shift in Jewish consciousness. What is now needed in the Jewish world is a theological framework consonant with a contemporary understanding of Divine Reality. Arguably such a revised Jewish theology should be based on the Kantian distinction between the world-as-it-is and the world-as-perceived. Following this differentiation, the Real-in-itself should be distinguished from the Real as conceived in human thought and experience. From a Jewish standpoint, this shift would call for a radical reconsideration of Jewish claims about Divine Reality. Within this framework, the Jewish understanding of God cannot be viewed as definitive and final. Instead, it should be perceived as only one among many ways in which human beings have attempted to make sense of Ultimate Reality.

In this new philosophy of Judaism, traditional claims about the nature of God and his activity should be viewed as human conceptions based on the religious experience of the ancient Israelites. The implications of the shift from the absolutism of the past to this altered conception of Divine Reality are fundamental in the shaping of Judaism for the future. No longer should Jews proclaim that their religious convictions are universal and absolute. Rather, it must be accepted that since Reality as-it-is-in-itself transcends human comprehension, Jewish beliefs are no different in principle from those found in other religions. Judaism, like all the world's faiths, is ultimately a human construction, and the Jew must in the end remain agnostic about the validity of his own religious opinions.

Such a re-evaluation of Judaism calls for a reinterpretation of both traditional belief and practice. A theology of religious pluralism in which the Jewish faith is perceived simply as one religion among many calls for an attitude of openness. If the Jewish tradition is ultimately a human construct growing out of the experiences of the Jewish nation over four millennia, it must be susceptible to adaptation and change. Conscious of the inevitable subjectivity of religious belief, all Jews should feel free to draw from the past those elements of the tradition which they find spiritually meaningful. The authoritarianism of the past must thus give way to personal autonomy in which all Jews are at liberty to construct for themselves a personal religious system embracing both religious belief and observance. Unlike all the other major branches of contemporary Jewry, this interpretation of Judaism is grounded in an ideology of individual freedom, granting independence of thought and action to each person.

As a radical alternative to the more structured models of the Jewish faith, this approach – which for convenience I have called Open Judaism – provides a non-dogmatic foundation for integrating Jewish belief and practice into modern life. Within this framework, Jews would be encouraged to chart their own path through the Jewish heritage. Such a fluid system also offers a revised orientation to the perplexities regarding Jewish identity. Within Open Judaism, Jewishness can be redefined in terms of an individual's wish to identify as a Jew. Distancing itself from either descent or correct belief and practice, Open Judaism would welcome as Jews all those who, regardless of their ancestry, wish to be identified with the Jewish people. On this basis, Jewish identity would be based only on personal choice rather than the dictates of rabbinical bodies, all of whom set different standards for acceptance into the Jewish fold.

Here, then, is a new foundation for Jewish living in the next millennium. Based on personal autonomy as a fundamental principle of Jewish life, this new philosophy of Judaism provides a basis for religious belief and practice which conforms to the realities of everyday Jewish existence. In modern society Jews across the religious spectrum determine for themselves which features of the Jewish heritage they find spiritually significant. Open Judaism, as portrayed in this book, acknowledges and celebrates this aspect of contemporary Jewish life. Respecting personal liberty and freedom, it offers the adherents of all the branches of Judaism a new perspective on religious faith in our troubled and troubling world.

1

The Historical Background

A vision of Judaism in the future must be grounded in an understanding of the Jewish past. According to the Bible, Abraham was the father of the Jewish people; originally from the Sumerian city of Ur in Mesopotamia, he was commanded by God to travel to Canaan. Breaking with the polytheistic practices of Babylonian society, he worshipped one Lord as did his son Isaac and grandson Jacob. Moving to Egypt, this clan was eventually enslaved by Pharaoh, but escaped from Egyptian bondage and settled in Canaan after conquering its inhabitants. For centuries they were ruled over by a series of kings in both the northern and southern kingdoms, but in AD 70 the Second Temple was destroyed by the Romans and the Jewish nation was exiled from its ancestral home. Following this victory, Pharisaic scholars engaged in the interpretation of Scripture, and their discussions were recorded in the *Mishnah* and the Palestinian and Babylonian *Talmuds*. The development of rabbinic Judaism continued through the Middle Ages; during this period Jewish sages produced a wide variety of works in the fields of Jewish law, philosophy, theology and mysticism. Over subsequent centuries the Jewish tradition evolved and changed, yet despite this development Jews remained loyal to the central tenets of the faith. With the impact of the Enlightenment, however, the Jewish community divided into a wide range of groupings with profoundly divergent ideologies. Thus, in the modern world, Judaism no longer constitutes a unitary system of belief and practice.

Biblical Origins

The history of the Jewish people began in the fertile lowlands alongside the Tigris and Euphrates rivers. It was here in Mesopotamia that successive empires of the ancient world flourished and decayed before the Jews emerged as a separate people. The culture of these civilizations had a profound impact on the Jewish religion: ancient Near Eastern myths and traditions were filtered and refashioned to serve the needs of the faith of the nation. The Hebrew Scriptures are thus an amalgam of elements from neighbouring peoples, and modern archaeology provides a vast array of literary documents preserved on stone and clay tablets which shed light on this development. These sources give an account of the rise and fall of states and empires and the spread of religious ideas, and although not referring to Israel, they indirectly help to clarify the intellectual and religious milieu in which the Bible was formed.

Scholars generally consider that the Jews emerged as a separate people between the nineteenth and sixteenth centuries BC. Some writers maintain that the patriarchs (Abraham, Isaac and Jacob) were real persons – chiefs or founders of tribal units; others argue that the names of the patriarchs refer not to individuals but to families, clans or tribes. In either case, these ancestors of the Jewish nation appear to have been part of a wave of north-western Semitic-speaking people who moved into Canaan in the second millennium BC. They and their descendants were semi-nomadic groups with small bands of sheep and goats coming from the desert in search of pasture and intermingling with the local inhabitants. It has been suggested that these immigrants and sojourners were part of a larger social stratum living on the fringes of settled society, referred to in Near Eastern sources as *Habiru* – a term which resembles the Biblical word 'Hebrew'. The patriarchal clans may have been part of this *Habiru* element in ancient Canaan.

According to the Biblical narrative in Genesis, Abraham was the father of the Jewish nation. Originally known as Abram, he came from Ur of the Chaldaeans – a Sumerian city of Mesopotamia near the head of the Persian Gulf. Together with his father Terah, his wife Sarai, and his nephew Lot, he travelled to Haran, a trading centre in northern Syria. During a famine in Canaan, he went first to Egypt and then proceeded to the Negev, finally settling in the plain near Hebron. Here he experienced a revelation which confirmed that his deliverance from Ur was an act of providence: 'I am the Lord who brought you from Ur of the Chaldaeans to give you this land to possess' (Gen. 15.7).

Eventually when Abram was ninety-nine and Sarai ninety, God granted them a son, Isaac. After Isaac was born, God made a covenant with Abraham symbolized by an act of circumcision: 'You shall be circumcised in the flesh of your foreskins, and it shall be a sign of the covenant between me and you' (Gen. 17.11). Later God tested Abraham's dedication by ordering him to sacrifice Isaac, only telling him at the last moment to refrain. When Isaac became older, Abraham sent a servant to his kinsfolk in Hebron to find a wife; after many years, God answered Isaac's prayers for a son, and twins – Esau and Jacob – were born. Jacob bought his brother's birthright for food, and with his mother's help secured Isaac's blessing. Fleeing from his brother, Jacob went to Haran where he worked for twenty years as a shepherd for his uncle Laban. There he married Laban's daughters, Rachel and Leah. When he eventually returned to Canaan, Jacob wrestled with a mysterious stranger in the gorge of the Jabbok river where God bestowed upon him the new name 'Israel'.

The history of the three patriarchs is followed by a series of stories about Jacob's son, Joseph. As a young boy, Joseph was presented with a special coat as a sign that he was his father's favourite. When he was in Shechem helping his brothers tend his family's flocks, he angered them by recounting dreams in which they bowed down before him. They reacted by plotting his death, but one of the brothers persuaded them to wait and another suggested that they sell him as a slave rather than kill him. Eventually Joseph was taken to Egypt where he subsequently became chief minister of the land. After a famine, he encountered his brothers who came before him to buy grain. He revealed to them his true identity, and urged them to settle in Egypt.

The biblical narrative continues with an account of the deliverance of the Jews from Egyptian bondage. The Book of Exodus relates that a son had been born to Amram of the house of Levi and his wife Jochebed. When he was three months old, his parents concealed him among the reeds growing on the banks of the Nile to save him from Pharaoh's decree. Pharaoh's daughter found the child and adopted him as her son, Moses. Eventually God revealed himself to Moses, commanding that he deliver the chosen people from Pharaoh's harsh bondage. To persuade Pharaoh that he should free the Jewish people, God inflicted ten plagues on the Egyptians culminating in the slaying of every Egyptian first-born son. After this final plague, Pharaoh released the Israelities, but later changed his mind and sent his forces in pursuit. When the Israelites came to an expanse of water, it seemed they were trapped. Miraculously, however, it was converted to dry land.

For forty years Moses led the children of Israel in the wilderness. During this time, God called Moses up to the top of the mountain where he revealed the law. After Moses died, Joshua the son of Nun was commanded by God to lead the people into the Promised Land. After crossing the Jordan, he captured Jericho and went on to take Ai. Subsequently he defeated both the southern and northern kings. To encourage the people, Joshua delivered speeches enjoining them to remain steadfast in their faith. After Joshua's death, the people formed separate tribes – the Book of Judges tells the story of the twelve national heroes who served as judges of the nation. The Judges were tribal rulers attached to particular regions; their fragmented reign continued for more than 150 years during the twelfth and eleventh centuries BC. During quiet periods, the tribes were governed by councils of elders; it was only at times of emergency that the Judges took control. From a religious perspective, the era of the Judges was of central significance in the life of the people. The Covenant between God and the Israelites – first formulated by Moses – was repeatedly proclaimed at gatherings in such national shrines as Shechem. Such an emphasis of covenantal obligation reinforced the belief that the Jews were the recipients of God's loving-kindness: they were his chosen people, a dedicated and separate nation.

In a more settled existence, the Covenant expanded to include additional legislation. Mosaic Law largely comprised unconditional statements of principle, but as time passed provisions for every kind of situation were included within the system. Many of these regulations were needed for an agricultural community, and seem to date back to the time of the Judges. It also became clear to the Jewish nation that the God of the Covenant directed human history: the Exodus and the entry into the Promised Land were seen as the unfolding of a divine plan. Unlike their Canaanite neighbours who worshipped local gods, the people of Israel stressed their detachment from place-related ties by revering a mobile shrine which they carried from place to place. In all likelihood, this tent or tabernacle was the repository of the sacred Ark.

The rejection of Canaanite religions was reinforced by the Israelite disapproval of magic fertility rituals, idol worship, temple prostitution, and the human sacrifice of children. However, the Israelites adapted the three Canaanite agricultural festivals to suit their own religious aims. The spring festival was transformed into *Pesach* (Passover) to commemorate the Exodus from Egypt. The autumn festival became *Sukkot* (Booths), a celebration of the dwelling in tents during the sojourn in the desert. The early summer festival was changed to *Shavuot* (Weeks) to bear witness to the giving of the law on Mount Sinai. These three festivals eventually became occurrences of pilgrimage to remind the Jewish nation of their former suffering, liberation and dedication to the Covenant.

During the period of the Judges, God was conceived as the supreme monarch. When some tribes suggested to Gideon that he deserved a formal position of power, he declared that it was impossible for the nation to be ruled by both God and a human king. None the less, Saul was subsequently elected as king despite Samuel's warnings against the dangers of usurping God's rule. In later years the nation divided into two kingdoms. The northern tribes led by Ephraim and the

southern tribes led by Judah had only been united by their
allegiance to King David. But when King Solomon and his
son Rehoboam violated many of the ancient traditions, the
northern tribes revolted. The reason they gave for this
rebellion was the injustice of the kings, but in fact, they sought
to recapture the simple ways of the generation that had
escaped from Egypt. Then there had been no monarch, and
leadership was exercised on the basis of charisma. What the
north looked for was allegiance and loyalty to the King of
Kings who had brought them from Egyptian bondage into the
Promised Land. It was against this background that the pre-
exilic prophets (Elijah, Elisha, Amos, Hosea, Micah and
Isaiah) endeavoured to bring the nation back to the true
worship of God. Righteousness, they declared, is the standard
by which all people are to be judged, especially kings and
rulers.

During the first millennium BC, the Jews watched their
country emerge as a powerful state only to see it sink into
spiritual and moral decay. Following the Babylonian conquest
in 586 BC, they despaired of their fate – the Temple lay in ruins
and Jerusalem was demolished. This was God's punishment
for their iniquity which the prophets had predicted. Yet
despite defeat and exile, the nation rose anew phoenix-like
from the ashes of the old kingdoms. In the centuries
which followed, the Jewish people continued their religious
traditions and communal life. Though they had lost their
independence, their devotion to God and his law sustained
them through suffering and hardship and inspired them to
new heights of creativity. In Babylonia the exiles flourished,
keeping their religion alive in the synagogues. These institutions were founded so that Jews could meet together for
worship and study; no sacrifices were offered since that was
the prerogative of the Jerusalem Temple. When in 538 BC
King Cyrus of Persia permitted the Jews to return to their
former home, the nation underwent a transformation. The
Temple was rebuilt and religious reforms were enacted. This
return to the land of their fathers led to national restoration
and a renaissance of Jewish life which was to last until the first
century AD.

The period following the death of King Herod in 4 BC was a time of intense anti-Roman feeling among the Jewish population in Judea as well as in the diaspora. Eventually such hostility led to war only to be followed by defeat and destruction, once again, of the Jerusalem Temple. In AD 70 thousands of Jews were deported. Such devastation, however, did not quell the Jewish hope of ridding the Holy Land of its Roman oppressors. In the second century a messianic rebellion led by Simon bar Kosiba was crushed by Roman forces, who killed multitudes of Jews and decimated Judea. Yet despite this defeat, the Pharisees carried on the Jewish tradition through teaching and study at Javneh near Jerusalem.

Rabbinic Judaism

Although all Jews professed allegiance to the *Torah*, the Hellenistic Jewish community was divided into various sects. According to the first century AD Jewish historian, Josephus, the three most important groups were the Sadducees, the Pharisees and the Essenes. The Sadducees consisted of a small group of influential individuals including the hereditary priests who controlled the Temple worship. The second group consisted of the Pharisees; in contrast with the Sadducees who were involved in the Temple cult, they centred their activities on the synagogue. Both Pharisees and Sadducees were involved in the Great Sanhedrin, the central religious and legislative body of the Judean community. The third principal sect were the Essenes who lived near the Dead Sea. Believing that they alone were members of the new Covenant, they congregated in semi-monastic communities.

From the first century BC, Palestinian pharisaic scholars (rabbis) engaged in the interpretation of Scripture. The most important scholar of the early rabbinic period was Judah ha-Nasi, the head of the Sanhedrin, whose main achievement was the redaction of the *Mishnah* (compendium of the Oral *Torah*) in the second century AD. This volume consisted of the discussions and rulings of sages whose teachings had been transmitted orally. According to the rabbis, the law recorded in the *Mishnah* was given orally to Moses along with the written law: 'Moses received the *Torah* from Sinai, and handed it down to Joshua, and Joshua to the Elders, and Elders to the Prophets to the men of the Great Assembly.' This view, recorded in the *Mishnah*, implies that there was an infallible chain of transmission from Moses to the leaders of the nation and eventually to the Pharisees.

The *Mishnah* itself is almost entirely legalistic in content, consisting of six sections. The first section (Seeds) begins with a discussion of benedictions and required prayers and continues with the other tractates dealing with various matters (such as the tithes of the harvest to be given to priests, Levites and the poor). The second section (Set Feasts) contains twelve tractates dealing with the Sabbath, Passover, the Day of Atonement and other festivals, as well as shekel dues and the proclamation of the New Year. In the third section (Women) seven tractates consider matters affecting women (such as betrothal, marriage contacts and divorce). The fourth section (Damages) contains ten tractates concerning civil law: property rights, legal procedures, compensation for damage, ownership of lost objects, treatment of employees, sale and purchase of land, Jewish courts, punishments and criminal proceedings. In addition, a tractate of rabbinic moral maxims (Sayings of the Fathers) is included in this section. In the fifth section (Holy Things) there are eleven tractates on sacrificial offerings and other Temple matters. The final section (Purifications) treats the various types of ritual uncleanliness and methods of legal purification. In addition to the *Mishnah*, the rabbis engaged in the composition of Scriptural commentaries. This literature (known as *midrash*) was written over centuries and is divided into works connected directly with the books of the Bible and those dealing with readings for special festivals as well as other topics.

The Sanhedrin which had been so fundamental in the compilation of the *Mishnah* met in several cities in Galilee, but later settled in the Roman district of Tiberius. Simultaneously other scholars established their own schools in other parts of the country where they applied the *Mishnah* to everyday life together with old rabbinic teachings which had not been incorporated in the *Mishnah*. During the third century the Roman Empire encountered numerous difficulties including inflation, population decline and a lack of technological development to support the army. In addition rival generals struggled against one another for power and the government became increasingly inefficient. Throughout this time of upheaval, the Jewish community underwent a similar decline as a result of famine, epidemics and plunder.

At the end of the third century the emperor Diocletian inaugurated reforms that strengthened the empire. In addition, Diocletian introduced measures to repress the spread of Christianity, which had become a serious challenge to the official religion of the empire. Diocletian's successor, Constantine the Great reversed his predecessor's hostile stance and extended official toleration to Christians. By this stage Christianity had succeeded in gaining a substantial number of adherents among the urban population; eventually Constantine became more involved in Church affairs and just before his death he himself was baptized. The Christianization of the empire continued throughout the century and by the early 400s, Christianity was fully established as the state religion.

By the first half of the fourth century Jewish scholars in Israel had collected together the teachings of generations of rabbis in the academies of Tiberius, Caesarea and Sepphoris. These extended discussions of the *Mishnah* became the Palestinian *Talmud*. The text of this multi-volume work covered four sections of the *Mishnah* (Seeds, Set Feasts, Women and Damages) but here and there various tractates were missing. The views of these Palestinian teachers had an important influence on scholars in Babylonia, though this work never attained the same prominence as that of the Babylonian *Talmud*.

Paralleling the development of rabbinic Judaism in Palestine, Bablyonian scholars founded centres of learning. The great third-century teacher Rav established an academy at Sura in central Mesopotamia; his contemporary Samuel was simultaneously head of another Babylonian academy at Nehardea. After Nehardea was destroyed in an invasion in

AD 259, the school at Pumbeditha also became a dominant Babylonian academy of Jewish learning. The Babylonian sages carried on and developed the Galilean tradition of disputation, and the fourth century produced two of the most distinguished scholars of the talmudic period: Abbaye and Rava who both taught at Pumbeditha. With the decline of Jewish institutions in Israel, Babylonia became the most important centre of Jewish scholarship.

By the sixth century, Babylonian scholars completed the redaction of the Babylonian *Talmud* – and editorial task begun by Rav Ashi in the fourth to fifth centuries at Sura. This massive work parallels the Palestinian *Talmud* and is largely a summary of the rabbinic discussions that took place in the Babylonian academies. Both *Talmuds* are essentially elaborations of the *Mishnah* though neither commentary contains material on every *Mishnah* passage. The text itself consists largely of summaries of rabbinic discussions: a phrase of the *Mishnah* is interpreted, discrepancies are resolved and redundancies are explained. In this compilation conflicting opinions of the earlier scholars are contrasted, unusual words are explained and anonymous opinions are identified. Frequently individual teachers cite specific cases to support their views and hypothetical eventualities are examined to reach a solution on the discussion. Debates between outstanding scholars in one generation are often cited, as are differences of opinion between contemporary members of an academy or a teacher and his students. The range of talmudic exploration is much broader than that of the *Mishnah* itself and includes a wide range of rabbinic teachings about such subjects as theology, philosophy and ethics.

By the sixth century the Jews had become largely a diaspora people. Despite the loss of a homeland, they were unified by a common heritage: law, liturgy and shared traditions bound together the scattered communities stretching from Spain to Persia and Poland to Africa. Though subcultures did form during the Middle Ages which could have divided the Jewish world, Jews remained united in their hope for messianic redemption, the restoration of the Holy Land, and an ingathering of the exiles. Living amongst Christians and

Muslims, the Jewish community was reduced to a minority group and their marginal status resulted in repeated persecution. Though there were times of tolerance and creative activity, the threats of exile and death were always present in the Jewish consciousness during this period.

Within the Islamic world, Jews along with Christians were recognized as Peoples of the Book and were guaranteed religious toleration, judicial autonomy and exemption from the military. In turn they were required to accept the supremacy of the Islamic state. Such an arrangement was formally codified by the Pact of Omar dating from about 800. According to this treaty, Jews were restricted in a number of spheres: they were not allowed to build new houses of worship, make converts, carry weapons or ride horses. In addition, they were required to wear distinctive clothing and pay a yearly poll tax. Jewish farmers were also obligated to pay a land tax consisting of a portion of their produce. Under these conditions, Jewish life nevertheless prospered. In various urban centres many Jews were employed in crafts such as tanning, dyeing, weaving, silk manufacture and metal work; other Jews participated in inter-regional trade and established networks of agents and representatives.

During the first two centuries of Islamic rule under the Ummıyad and Abbasid caliphates, Muslim leaders confirmed the authority of traditional Babylonian institutions. When the Arabs conquered Babylonia, they officially recognized the position of the exilarch who for centuries had been the ruler of Babylonian Jewry. By the Abbasid period, the exilarch shared his power with the heads of the rabbinical academies which had for centuries been the major centres of rabbinic learning. The head of each academy was known as the *gaon* who delivered lectures as well as learned opinions on legal matters.

During the eighth century messianic movements appeared in the Persian Jewish community which led to armed uprisings against Muslim authorities. Such revolts were quickly crushed, but an even more serious threat to traditional Jewish life was posed later in the century by the emergence of an anti-rabbinic sect, the Karaites. This group was founded in Babylonia in the 760s by Anan ben David. The guiding interpretative principle formulated by Anan, 'Search thoroughly in Scripture and do not rely on my opinion' was intended to point to Scripture itself as the source of law. After the death of the founder, new parties within the Karaite movement soon emerged, and by the tenth century Karaite communities were established in Israel, Iraq and Persia. The growth of Karaism provoked the rabbis to attack it as a heretical movement since these various groups rejected rabbinic law and formulated their own legislation.

As early as the eighth century the Muslim empire began to undergo a process of disintegration. When Abbasid caliphs conquered the Ummayads in 750, Spain remained independent under a Ummayad ruler. As the century progressed, the Abbasids began to lose control of the outlying territories. After 850, Turkish troops managed to gain control over the Abbasids and the caliph became essentially a figurehead behind which Turkish generals exerted power. In 909, Shi'ite Muslims (followers of Ali, Muhammad's son-in-law), the Fatimids, took control over North Africa; in 969 they conquered Egypt and Israel. By the end of the tenth century the Islamic world was divided into a number of separate states pitted against one another.

The disappearance of the political unity of the Islamic empire was accompanied by a decentralization of rabbinic Judaism. The rabbinic academies of Babylonia began to lose their hold on the Jewish scholarly world; in many places rabbinic schools (*yeshivot*) were established in which rabbinic sources were studied. The growth of these local centres of learning enabled individual teachers to exert their influence on Jewish learning independent of the academies of Sura and Pumbeditha. The locality in which the local rabbinate asserted itself was the Holy Land. Tiberius was the location of the rabbinical academy there, as well as the centre of the Masoretic scholars such as the families of Ben Asher and Ben Naphtali who produced the standard tradition (*masorah*) of the Bible by adding vowels and punctuation to the Hebrew text. By the ninth century the rabbinic academy moved to Ramleh and then to Jerusalem; this institution was supported by the Jewish communities of Egypt, Yemen and Syria, but due to

Turkish and Christian invations its influence waned in the eleventh century.

Egyptian Jewry also underwent a transformation during this period. Under the Fatimids Jewish life prospered in Egypt, and by the end of the tenth century a *yeshivah* had been established in Cairo. Kairouan had also become a centre of scholarship: at this time academies were established by distinguished Talmudists and affluent Jewish families who supported Jewish scientists and philosophers. The city of Fez also reached a degree of eminence, producing one of the most important rabbinic scholars of the period, Isaac Alfasi who compiled an influential code of Jewish law. But it was in Spain that the Jewish community attained the greatest level of achievement. In tenth-century Spanish royal court the Ummayad caliphs, Abd Al-Rahman III and Hakam II employed the Jewish statesmen Hisdai ibn Shaprut as court physician, administrator and diplomat. In addition he acted as head of the Jewish community and patron of Jewish scholarship. Cordova, the capital of the Ummayad caliphate, became a vibrant centre of Jewish civilization, attracting poets, grammarians and *yeshivah* students from throughout the diaspora.

The Middle Ages

As the Ummayad caliphate began to disintegrate in the eleventh century, small Muslim principalities were often at odds with one another. Several of the rulers of these states used Jewish courtiers, such as Samuel ibn Nagrela of Granada in their administrations. This figure was knowledgeable about mathematics and philosophy, wrote in Hebrew and Arabic, and served as vizier of Granada for thirty years. In commemoration of his own military victories, he composed Hebrew poetry, and he also wrote an introduction to the *Talmud*. Other scholars of the period lived in Seville, Saragossa, Toledo, Calatayud and Lucena, which became renowned for its Jewish academy.

In 1086 the life of Spanish Jewry was shaken when the Almoravides from North Africa were invited to Spain to lead an attack on Christian communities in the north and persecuted the Jewish population as well. Soon, however, Jews were restored to their former secure position and the next generation saw outstanding poets, philosophers, Biblical commentators, theologians and rabbinic authorities. But in the middle of the twelfth century the golden age of Spanish Jewry came to an end. Fearing Christian conquest, the Almohades – a Berber dynasty from Morocco – came to defend the country and simultaneously persecuted the Jewish community. Jews were forced to convert to Islam, and academies and synagogues were closed. Some Jews practised Judaism in secret; others escaped to the Middle East or migrated to Christian Spain. At the beginning of the thirteenth century the dominance of the Almohades came to an end when Christian kingdoms managed to seize control of most of the former Muslim territories in Spain.

In other parts of the Muslim empire, Jews faced changing circumstances during these centuries. In the mid-twelfth century, during the Almohade persecution, some Spanish Jews migrated to Egypt, including the Jewish philosopher Moses Maimonides. In Israel a small Jewish community survived during the Crusades and was augmented by Jewish pilgrims who went to the Holy Land. Babylonian Jewry continued after the death of the last important *gaon*, Hai bar Sherira, in 1038, but the Mongol invasions in the middle of the thirteenth century had devastating consequences for the region. In western North Africa Jewish communities were able to practise their faith as before when the Almohades were removed and many Jews prospered. Some North African Jewish merchants participated in the Saharan gold trade, maintaining links with the kingdom of Aragon in Spain.

The Muslims did not manage to conquer all of Europe in their campaigns in the seventh century – many countries remained under Christian rule as did much of the Byzantine empire. The early Jewish communities in western Europe (Ashkenazic Jewry) lived in small, self-contained communities and engaged in local trades. The Jews in each town constituted a separate unit since there was no equivalent of an exilarch (as in Muslim lands) to serve as the official leader of the Jewish population. Each community (*kahal*) established its own rules (*takkanot*) and administered local courts, in a form of self-government which was the Ashkenazic adaptation to the feudal structure of medieval Christian Europe. In this environment Jewish study took place in a number of important centres such as Mainz and Worms in the Rhineland and Troyes and Sens in northern France and produced such leading scholars as the legal expert Rabbenu Gershom of Mainz and the greatest commentator of the medieval period, Solomon ben Isaac of Troyes (known as Rashi). In subsequent generations, the study of the *Talmud* reached great heights: in Germany and northern France scholars known as the *tosafists* (which included some of Rashi's family) utilized new methods of Talmudic interpretation. In addition, Ashkenazic Jews of this period composed religious poetry modelled on the liturgical compositions (*piyyutim*) of fifth- and sixth-century Israel.

Despite this efflorescence of Jewish learning, Jews in Christian countries were subject to frequent outbursts of anti-Jewish sentiment. In 1095 Pope Urban II proclaimed the First Crusade – an act which stimulated mobs in the Rhineland in 1096 to attack Jews in towns such as Worms and Mainz. Jews in these communities willingly martyred themselves as an act of sanctification rather than convert to the Christian faith. These massacres at the end of the century were not officially authorized by the state, and Jews who had converted under duress were subsequently allowed to return to the Jewish tradition.

In the following two centuries the Jewish community of Christian Europe became increasingly more involved in moneylending as the Christian guilds forced Jews out of trade. The practice of usury intensified anti-Semitism especially by those who were unable to pay back loans. Added to this economic motive, Christians in the Middle Ages persecuted the Jews on religious grounds: the Jew was stereotyped as a demonic Christ-killer and murderer. As early as 1144 in Norwich, England, the Jewish community was accused of killing Christian children at Passover to use their blood in the preparation of unleavened bread. Later the same accusation was made in Blois, France, in 1171 and in Lincoln, England, in 1255. Another frequent charge against the Jews was that they defamed the host in order to torture Jesus's body. Further, Jews were also regarded with enmity since they obtained Church property through defaulted loans. Such factors led the Fourth Lateran Council in 1215 to strengthen the Church's restrictions regarding the Jewish people: 'It is decreed that henceforth Jews of both sexes will be distinguished from other peoples by their garments, as moreover has been prescribed to them by Moses. They will not show themselves in public during Holy Week, for some among them on these days wear their finest garments and mock the Christians clad in mourning. Trespassers will be duly punished by the secular powers, in order that they no longer dare flout Christ in the presence of Christians.'

In the same century Dominican priests were active against the Jewish community. In 1240 they participated in a disputation about the *Talmud* in Paris with leading Jewish scholars. Among the points raised were the following queries: 'Was it true that in the first century after the fall of Jerusalem, Rabbi Simeon bar Yochai proclaimed: "Seize the best of the *goyim* and kill them"? Does the *Talmud* claim that Jesus was an illegitimate child? Is it the *Talmud*'s view that Jesus will suffer the torment of boiling mud in Hell?' In reply the Jewish authorities stressed that many commandments prescribe an equal charity toward Jews and non-Jews. Yet as a result of the debate, the *Talmud* was condemned and all copies were burned.

Expulsion of the Jews from countries in which they lived also became a dominant policy of Christian Europe. In 1182 the king of France, Philip Augustus, expelled all Jews from the royal domains near Paris, cancelled nearly all Christian debts to Jewish moneylenders, and confiscated Jewish property. Though the Jews were recalled in 1198, they were burdened with an additional royal tax and in the next century they increasingly became the property of the king. In thirteenth-century England the Jews were continuously taxed and the entire Jewish population was expelled in 1290, as was that in France by Philip IV some years later. At the end of the thirteenth century in Germany, the Jewish community suffered violent attack. In 1286 the most eminent scholar of the period, R. Meir of Rothenberg was taken prisoner and died in custody; twelve years later mobs rampaged the country destroying about 140 Jewish communities. In the next century Jews were blamed for bringing about the Black Death by poisoning the wells of Europe, and from 1348 to 1349 Jews in France, Switzerland, Germany and Belgium suffered at the hands of their Christian neighbours. In the following two centuries, Jewish massacre and expulsion became a frequent occurrence.

After the Christians had conquered most of the Iberian peninsula in the thirteenth century, Sephardic Jews in Spain combined many features of their life in Muslim lands with aspects of Jewish existence in Christian feudal countries. The Jewish population was employed in a wide range of occupations, including shopkeeping, artisan crafts, medicine and moneylending. The community was stratified into a broad range of social classes: many Jews were poor but a small minority participated in the administration of the country as royal councillors and financial experts.

Legally there were important similarities between the communities of Spanish Jews and their counterparts in northern Europe. Each corporate body (*aljama*) was granted a charter guaranteeing the economic rights of its members as well as their freedom to live according to the Jewish tradition. As a consequence each community was able to regulate its own social services, bureaucratic institutions and judicial system. As under Islamic rule, a number of Spanish Jews studied humanistic and scientific subjects and made notable contributions to a variety of disciplines; the thirteenth century witnessed a flowering of Jewish scholarly activity in the fields of mysticism, theology and halachic studies. Throughout this century Jews were generally secure relative to the plight of their co-religionists in other European lands.

Jewry in the Early Modern Period

By the end of the fourteenth century in Christian Europe

political instability led to the massacre of many Jewish communities in Castile and Aragon. Fearing for their lives, thousands of Jews converted to Christianity in 1391. Two decades later Spanish rulers introduced the Castilian laws which segregated Jews from their Christian neighbours. In the following year a public disputation was held in Tortosa about the doctrine of the Messiah; as a result increased pressure was applied to the Jewish population to convert. Those who became Christian apostates (*Marranos*) found life much easier, but by the fifteenth century anti-Jewish sentiment became a serious problem. In 1480 King Ferdinand and Queen Isabella established the Inquisition to determine whether former Jews practised Judaism in secret. In the late 1480s inquisitors used torture to extract confessions, and in 1492 the entire Jewish community was expelled from Spain. In the next century the Inquisition was established in Portugal.

To escape such persecution many Spanish and Portuguese *Marranos* sought refuge in various parts of the Ottoman empire. Some of these Sephardic immigrants prospered and became part of the Ottoman court, such as Dona Gracia and her nephew Joseph Nasi. Prominent among the rabbinic scholars of this period was Joseph ben Ephraim Caro who emigrated from Spain to the Balkans. In the 1520s he commenced a study of Jewish law, *The House of Joseph*, based on previous codes of Jewish law. In addition he composed a shorter work, the *Shulhan Arukh*, which became the authoritative code of law in the Jewish world.

While working on the *Shulhan Arukh*, Caro emigrated to Safed in Israel which had become a major centre of Jewish religious life. In the sixteenth century this small community had grown to a population of over ten thousand Jews. Here talmudic academies were established and small groups engaged in the study of kabbalistic literature as they piously awaited the coming of the Messiah. In this centre of mystical kabbalistic activity one of the greastest mystics of Safed, Moses Cordovero, collected, organized and interpreted the teachings of earlier mystical authors. Later in the sixteenth century, kabbalistic speculation was transformed by the greatest mystic of Safed, Isaac Luria.

By the beginning of the seventeenth century Lurianic mysticism had made an important impact on Sephardic Jewry, and messianic expectations had also become a central feature of Jewish life. In this milieu the arrival of self-proclaimed messianic king, Shabbetai Tzevi, brought about a transformation of Jewish life and thought. After living in various cities, he travelled to Gaza where he encountered Nathan Benjamin Levi who believed he was the Messiah. In 1665 his Messiahship was proclaimed and Nathan sent letters to Jews in the diaspora asking them to recognize Shabbetai Tzevi as their redeemer. In the following year Shabbetai journeyed to Constantinople, but on the order of the grand vizier he was arrested and put into prison. Eventually he was brought to court and given the choice between conversion and death. In the face of this alternative he converted to Islam. Such an act of apostasy scandalized most of his followers, but others continued to revere him as the Messiah. In the following century the most important Shabbetean sect was led by Jacob Frank who believed himself to be the incarnation of Shabbetai.

During this period Poland had become a great centre of scholarship. In academies scholars collected together the legal interpretations of previous authorities and composed commentaries on the *Shulhan Arukh*. To regulate Jewish life in the country at large, Polish Jews established regional federations that administered Jewish affairs. In the midst of this general prosperity, the Polish Jewish community was subject to a series of massacres carried out by the Cossacks of the Ukraine, Crimean Tartars and Ukrainian peasants. In 1648 Bogdan Chmielnicki was elected hetman of the Cossacks and instigated an insurrection against the Polish gentry. As administrators of noblemen's estates, Jews were slaughtered in these revolts.

As the century progressed, Jewish life in Poland became increasingly more insecure due to political instability; none the less, the Jewish community considerably increased in size during the eighteenth century. In the 1730s and 1740s Cossacks known as Haidemaks invaded the Ukraine, robbing and murdering Jewish inhabitants, and finally butchering the

Jewish community of Uman in 1768. In Lithuania on the other hand, Jewish life flourished and Vilna became an important centre of Jewish learning. Here Elijah ben Solomon Zalman, referred to as the Vilna Gaon, lectured to disciples on a wide range of subjects and composed commentaries on rabbinic sources.

Elsewhere in Europe this period witnessed Jewish persecution and oppression. Despite the positive contact between Italian humanists and Jews, Christian anti-Semitism frequently led to persecution and suffering. In the sixteenth century the Counter-Reformation Church attempted to isolate the Jewish community. The *Talmud* was burned in 1553, and two years later Pope Paul IV reinstated the segregationist edict of the Fourth Lateran Council forcing Jews to live in ghettos and barring them from most areas of economic life. In addition, *Marranos* who took up the Jewish tradition were burned at the stake and Jews were expelled from most church domains.

In Germany the growth of Protestantism frequently led to adverse conditions for the Jewish population. Though Martin Luther was initially well disposed to the Jews, he soon came to realize that the Jewish community was intent on remaining true to its faith. As a consequence he composed a virulent attack on the Jews. None the less some Jews, known as Court Jews, attained positions of great importance among the Germany nobility. A number of these favoured individuals were appointed by the rulers as chief elders of the Jewish community and acted as spokesmen and defenders of German Jewry.

In Holland some Jews had also attained an important influence on trade and finance. By the mid-seventeenth century both *Marranos* and Ashkenazic Jews came to Amsterdam and established themselves in various areas of economic activity. By the end of the century there were nearly ten thousand Jews in Amsterdam; there the Jewish community was employed on the stock exchange, in the sugar, tobacco and diamond trades, and in insurance, manufacturing, printing and banking. In this milieu Jewish cultural activity flourished: Jewish writers published works of drama, theology and mystical lore. Though Jews in Holland were not granted full rights as citizens, they nevertheless enjoyed religious freedom, personal protection and the liberty of participating in a wide range of economic affairs.

From Hasidism to the Enlightenment

By the middle of the eighteenth century, the Jewish community had suffered numerous waves of persecution and was deeply dispirited by the conversion of Shabbetai Tzevi. In this environment the Hasidic movement – grounded in *kabbalah* – sought to revitalize Jewish life.

The founder of this new movement was Israel ben Eleazer known as the Baal Shem Tov (or Besht). According to tradition, Israel ben Eleazer was born in southern Poland and in his twenties journeyed with his wife to the Carpathian mountains. In the 1730s he travelled to Mezibozh where he performed various miracles and instructed his disciples about kabbalistic lore. By the 1740s he had attracted a considerable number of disciples who passed on his teaching. After his death in 1760, Dov Baer became the leader of this sect and Hasidism spread to southern Poland, the Ukraine and Lithuania.

The growth of this movement engendered considerable hostility on the part of rabbinic authorities. In particular, the rabbinic leadership of Vilna issued an edict of excommunication; the Hasidim were charged with permissiveness in their observance of the commandments, laxity in the study of the *Torah*, excess in prayer, and preference for the Lurianic rather than the Ashkenazic prayerbook. In subsequent years the Hasidim and their opponents (the *Mitnagdim*) bitterly denounced one another. Relations deteriorated further when Jacob Joseph of Polonnoye published a book critical of the rabbinate; his work was burned and in 1781 the *Mitnagdim* ordered that all relations with the Hasidim cease. By the end of the century the Jewish religious establishment of Vilna denounced the Hasidim to the Russian government, an act which resulted in the imprisonment of several leaders. Despite such condemnation the Hasidic movement was eventually recognized by the Russian and Austrian governments; in the ensuing years the movement divided into a number of separate groups under different leaders who passed on positions of authority to their descendants.

Hasidism initiated a profound change in Jewish religious pietism. In the medieval period, the *Hasidei Ashkenaz* attempted to achieve perfection through various mystical activities. This tradition was carried on by Lurianic kabbalists who engaged in various forms of self-mortification. In opposition to such ascetic practices, the Besht and his followers emphasized the omnipresence of God rather than the shattering of the vessels and the imprisonment of divine sparks by the powers of evil. For Hasidic Judaism there is no place where God is absent; the doctrine of the *tzimtzum* was interpreted by Hasidic sages as only an apparent withdrawal of the divine presence. Divine light, they believed, is everywhere. As the Besht explained: in every one of man's troubles, physical and spiritual, even in that trouble God Himself is present.

For some Hasidim cleaving to God (*devekut*) in prayer was understood as the annihilation of selfhood and the ascent of the soul to divine light. In this context joy, humility, gratitude and spontaneity were seen as essential features of Hasidic worship. The central obstacles to concentration in prayer are distracting thoughts; according to Hasidism such sinful intentions contain a divine spark which can be released. In this regard the traditional kabbalistic stress on theological speculation was replaced by a preoccupation with mystical psychology in which inner bliss was conceived as the highest aim rather than repair (*tikkun*) of the cosmos. For the Beshtian Hasidim it was also possible to achieve *devekut* in daily activities including drinking, business affairs and sex. Such ordinary acts become religious if, in performing them, one cleaves to God, and *devekut* is thus attainable by all Jews rather than a scholarly elite. Unlike the earlier mystical tradition, Hasidism provided a means by which ordinary Jews could reach a state of spiritual ecstasy. Hasidic worship embraced singing, dancing and joyful devotion in anticipation of the period of messianic redemption.

Another central feature of this new movement was the institution of the *zaddik* (or *rebbe*) which gave expression to a widespread disillusionment with rabbinic leadership. According to Hasidism, the *zaddikim* were spiritually superior individuals who had attained the highest level of *devekut*. The goal of the *zaddik* was to elevate the souls of his flock to the divine light; his tasks included pleading to God for his people, immersing himself in their everyday affairs, and counselling and strengthening them. As an authoritarian figure the *zaddik* was seen by his followers as possessing miraculous power to ascend to the divine realm. In this context *devekut* involved cleaving to the *zaddik*. Give this emphasis on the role of the *rebbe*, Hasidic literature included summaries of the spiritual and kabbalistic teachings of various famous *zaddikim* as well as stories about their miraculous deeds. Foremost among these leading figures was Zusya of Hanipol, Shneur Zalman of Liady, Levi Yitzhak of Berdichev and Nahman of Bratzlav. These various leaders developed their own customs, doctrines and music, and gathered around themselves disciples who made pilgrimages to their courts in the Ukraine and in Polish Galicia. In central Poland Hasidism emphasized the centrality of faith and talmudic study; Lubavich Hasidim in Lithuania, on the other hand, combined kabbalistic speculation and rabbinic scholarship.

In many respects the medieval period extended into the eighteenth century for the Jewish community. Despite the numerous changes taking place in European society, monarchs continued to rule by divine right. In addition the aristocracy was exempt from taxation and enjoyed special privileges; the established Church retained control over religious matters; and merchants and artisans closed ranks against outsiders. At the other end of the social scale peasants continued to be burdened with obligations to feudal masters, and in eastern and central Europe serfs were enslaved and exploited. By 1770 nearly two million Jews lived in this environment in Christian Europe. In some countries such as England and Holland they were relatively free from economic and social restrictions. The English and Dutch governments, for example, did not interfere with the private affairs and

religious life of the Jewish population. Central European
Jewry, however, was subject to a wide range of oppressive
legal restrictions, and Jews were forced to sew signs on their
cloaks or wear special hats to distinguish them from their non-
Jewish neighbours.

By the 1770s and 1780s the treatment of Jews in central
Europe greatly improved due to the influence of such
polemicists as Wilhelm Christian Dohm. In an influential
tract, *Concerning the Amelioration of the Civil Status of the Jews*,
Dohm argued that Jews did not pose any threat and could
become valuable and patriotic citizens. A wise and benevolent
society, he stressed, should abolish restrictions which prevent
the Jewish population from having close contact with
Christians and acquiring secular knowledge. All the occupations he argued, should be open to Jews and educational
opportunities should be provided. The Holy Roman Emperor,
Joseph II echoed such sentiments. In 1781 he abolished the
Jewish badge as well as taxes imposed on Jewish travellers;
in the following year he issued an edict of toleration which
granted Jews of Vienna freedom in trade and industry and
the right of residence outside Jewish quarters. Moreover,
regulations prohibiting Jews from leaving their homes before
noon on Sunday and attending places of public amusement
were abolished. Jews were also permitted to send their
children to state schools or set up their own educational
institutions. In 1784 Jewish judicial autonomy was abolished
and three years later some Jews were inducted into the
Hapsburg army.

As in Germany, reforms in France during the 1770s and
1780s ameliorated the situation of the Jewish population.
Though Sephardic Jews in Paris and in the south and south-
west lived in comfort and security, the Ashkenazic Jews of
Alsace and Lorraine had a traditional Jewish lifestyle and
were subject to a variety of disabilities. In 1789 the National
Assembly issued a declaration proclaiming that all human
beings are born and remain free and equal in rights, and that
no person should be persecuted for his opinion as long as they
do not subvert civil law. In 1790 the Sephardim of south-west
France and Jews from Papal Avignon were granted citizen-

ship. This decree was followed in September 1791 by a resolution which granted citizenship rights to all Jews:

> The National Assembly, considering that the conditions requisite to be a French citizen, and to become an active citizen, are fixed by the constitution, and that every man who, being duly qualified, takes the civic oath, and engages to fulfil all the duties prescribed by the constitution, has a right to all the advantages it ensures – annuls all adjournments, restrictions and exceptions, contained in the preceding decrees, affecting individuals of the Jewish persuasion who shall take the civil oath. (Mahler, 1941, 26)

This change in Jewish status occurred elsewhere in Europe as well – in 1726 the Dutch Jews of the Batavian republic were also granted full citizenship rights and in 1797 the ghettos of Padua and Rome were abolished.

In 1799 Napoleon became the First Consul of France and five years later he was proclaimed Emperor. Napoleon's Code of Civil Law propounded in 1804 established the right of all inhabitants to follow any trade and declared equality for all. After 1806 a number of German principalities were united in the French kingdom of Westphalia where Jews were granted the same rights. Despite these advances the situation of Jews did not undergo a complete transformation, and Napoleon still desired to regulate Jewish affairs. In July 1806 he convened an Assembly of Jewish Notables to consider a number of issues: Do Jewish marriage and divorce procedures conflict with French civil law? Are Jews allowed to marry Christians? Do French Jews consider Frenchmen their compatriots and is France their country?

In reply the Assembly decreed that Jewish law is compatible with French civil law; Jewish divorce and marriage are not binding unless preceded by a civil act; mixed marriage is legal but cannot be sanctioned by the Jewish faith; France is the homeland of French Jews and Frenchmen should be seen as their kin. In the next year Napoleon summoned a Grand Sanhedrin consisting of rabbis and laymen to confirm the views of the Assembly. This body pledged its allegiance to the Emperor and nullified any features of the Jewish tradition that conflicted with the particular requirements of citizenship. In 1808 Napoleon issued two edicts regarding the Jewish community. In the first he set up a system of district boards of rabbis and laymen (consistories) to regulate Jewish affairs under the supervision of a central body in Paris. These consistories were responsible for maintaining synagogues and religious institutions, enforcing the law of conscription, overseeing changes in occupations ordered by the government and acting as a local police force. Napoleon's second decree postponed, reduced or abrogated all debts owed to Jews, regulated Jewish trade and residence rights and prohibited Jewish army conscripts from hiring substitutes.

After Napoleon's defeat and abdication, the map of Europe was redrawn by the Congress of Vienna between 1814 and 1815, and, in addition, the diplomats at the Congress issued a resolution that instructed the German confederation to ameliorate the status of the Jews. Yet despite this decree the German government disowned the rights of equality that had previously been granted to Jews by the French and instead imposed restrictions on residence and occupation. In place of the spirit of emancipation unleashed by the French Revolution, Germany became increasingly patriotic and xenophobic. Various academics maintained that the Jews were 'Asiatic aliens' and insisted that they could not enter into German–Christian culture without converting to Christianity – in 1819 German Jewry was attacked in cities and the countryside (the Hep! Hep! riots). After 1830, however, a more liberal attitude prevailed and various writers advocated a more tolerant approach. The most important Jewish exponent of emancipation, Gabriel Riesser, argued that the Jews were not a separate nation and were capable of loving Germany as their homeland. Jewish converts to Christianity such as Heinrich Heine and Ludwig Boerne also defended the rights of Jews during this period.

Part I

ORTHODOX JUDAISM

2

A Monolithic Religious System

Until the period of the Enlightenment the Jewish religious
tradition was essentially monolithic in character. During the
biblical period the ancient Israelites affirmed their faith in
one God who created the universe; as a transcendent Deity,
he brought all things into being, continues to sustain the
cosmos, and guides humanity to its ultimate destiny. In the
unfolding of this providential scheme, Israel has a central
role – as God's chosen people, the nation is to serve as a light
to all peoples. Although Scripture does not contain a
dogmatic formulation of such beliefs, Jewish scholars from
early rabbinic times to the late Middle Ages attempted to
establish the underlying tenets of Judaism. While this quest
gave rise to serious dispute, Maimonides' formulation of the
Thirteen Principles of the Jewish Faith – (1) God's existence;
(2) God's unity; (3) God's incorporeality; (4) God's eternity;
(5) God alone is to be worshipped; (6) prophecy; (7) Moses
is the greatest of the prophets; (8) the divine origin of the
Torah; (9) the *Torah* is immutable; (10) God knows the
thoughts and deeds of human beings; (11) reward and
punishment; (12) the Messiah; (13) resurrection of the dead
– became authoritative for Jewry and were incorporated
into the prayerbook. These principles as formulated by
Maimonides as well as parallel dogmatic formulations by
other medieval thinkers served as the basis for theological
speculation through the centuries. Thus underlying the
development of Jewish life and thought through the ages
until the modern period there has been a common core of
religious belief, variously interpreted by Jewish sages.

The Biblical View

Although the Bible contains no formal list of dogma, God's nature and activity are depicted through the *Tanakh*. According to Scripture, the universe owes its existence to the one God, the creator of heaven and earth. Jewish biblical teaching emphasizes that he alone is to be worshipped. As Isaiah declared:

> I am the Lord, and there is no other,
> besides me there is no God . . .
> I form the light and create darkness,
> I make weal and create woe,
> I am the Lord, who do all these things (Isa. 45.5–7).

For Jews, God is the creator of the universe. Thus, in Genesis 1.1–2, he is described as forming heaven and earth:

> In the beginning God created the heavens and
> the earth. The earth was without form and void,
> and darkness was upon the face of the deep;
> and the spirit of God was moving over the face of the waters.

Throughout Scripture this theme of divine transcendence is repeatedly affirmed. Hence the prophet Isaiah proclaimed:

> Have you not known? Have you not heard?
> Has it not been told you from the beginning?
> Have you not understood from the foundations of the earth?
> It is he who sits above the circle of the earth,
> and its inhabitants are like grasshoppers;
> who stretches out the heavens like a curtain,
> and spreads them like a tent to dwell in (Isa. 40.21–2).

Despite this view of God's remoteness from his creation, he is also viewed as actively involved in the cosmos. In the Bible his omnipresence is repeatedly stressed. As the Psalmist proclaimed:

> Whither shall I go from thy Spirit?
> Or whither shall I flee from thy presence?
> If I ascend to heaven, thou art there!
> If I make my bed in *Sheol*, thou art there!
> If I take the wings of the morning
> and dwell in the uttermost parts of the sea,
> even thy hand shall lead me (Ps. 139.7–12).

Further, Scripture states that God has neither beginning nor end. In the words of the Psalmist:

> Before the mountains were brought forth,
> Or ever thou hadst formed the earth and the world,
> from everlasting to everlasting thou art God (Ps. 90.2).

In the Bible the term *olam* is most frequently used to denote the concept of God's eternity. In Genesis 21.33 he is described as the eternal God; he lives for ever (Deut. 32.40), and reigns for ever (Exod. 15.18; Ps. 10.16). He is the living God and everlasting king (Jer. 10.10); his counsel endures for ever (Ps. 33.11) as does his mercy (Ps. 106.1). For the biblical writers, God's eternal existence is different from the rest of creation – he exists permanently without beginning or end.

The Bible also affirms that God is omnipotent. Thus in Genesis when Sarah expressed astonishment at the suggestion she should have a child at the age of ninety, she was criticized: 'The Lord said to Abraham, "Why did Sarah laugh, and say, 'Shall I indeed bear a child, now that I am old?' Is anything too hard for the Lord?"' (Gen. 18.13–14). Similarly in the Book of Jeremiah when the city was threatened by the Chaldeans, God declared: 'Behold I am the Lord the God of all flesh; is anything too hard for me?' (Jer. 32.27). On such a view their is nothing God cannot do: what appears impossible is within his power. Paralleling the doctrine of God's omnipotence, Jews throughout the ages have affirmed that God is all-knowing. In the Bible the Psalmist stated:

> The Lord looks down from heaven,
> he sees all the sons of men . . .
> he who fashions the heart of them all,
> and observes all their deeds (Ps. 33.13–15)

The Bible also depicts God as controlling and guiding the cosmos. The Hebrew term for such divine action is *hashgagah*, derived from Psalm 33.14: 'From where he sits enthroned he looks forth (*hishgiah*) on all the inhabitants of the earth.' Such a view implies that the dispensation of a wise and benevolent providence is found everywhere – all events are ultimately foreordained by God. According to the biblical tradition there are two types of providence: (1) general providence – God's

provision for the world in general, and (2) special providence –
God's care for each individual. In Scripture God's general
providence was manifest in his freeing the ancient Israelites
from Egyptian bondage and guiding them to the Promised
Land. The belief in the unfolding of his plan for salvation is a
further illustration of such providential care for his creatures.
Linked to this concern for every person is God's providential
concern. In the words of Jeremiah: 'I know, O Lord, that the
way of man is not in himself, that it is not in man who walks to
direct his steps' (Jer. 10.23).

The Bible further maintains that God is the all-good ruler of
the universe. In the Psalms he is described as good and
upright (Ps. 25.8); his name is good (Ps. 52.9; 54.6); he is good
and ready to forgive (Ps. 86.5); he is good and does good (Ps.
119.68); he is good to all (Ps. 145.9). Yet although God is
concerned with all of humanity, he has a special role for the
Jewish people. In the Bible the Hebrew root 'bhr' (to choose)
denotes the belief that God selected the Jewish nation from all
other peoples. As the Book of Deuteronomy declares, 'For you
are a people holy to the Lord your God; the Lord your God
has chosen you to be a people for his own possession out of all
the peoples that are on the face of the earth' (Deut. 7.6).
According to Scripture, this act was motivated by divine love:
'It was not because you were more in number than any other
people that the Lord set his love upon you and chose you, for
you were the fewest of all peoples; but it is because the Lord
loves you' (Deut. 7.7–8).

Through its election Israel has been given an historic
mission to bear divine truth to humanity. Before God
proclaimed the Ten Commandments on Mount Sinai, he
admonished the people to carry out this appointed task (Exod.
19.4–6). God's choice of Israel, therefore, carries with it
numerous responsibilities. As Genesis proclaims: 'For I have
chosen him, that he may charge his children and his
household after him to keep the way of the Lord by doing
righteousness and justice' (Gen. 18.19). Divine choice
demands reciprocal response. Israel is obligated to keep God's
statutes and observe his laws as revealed to Moses. In doing
so, the Jewish people will be able to persuade the nations of

the world that there is only one universal God. Israel is to be a prophet to the nations in that it will bring them to salvation. Yet despite this obligation, the Bible asserts that God will not abandon his chosen people even if they violate the Covenant. The wayward nation will be punished, but God will not reject them: 'Yet for all that, when they are in the land of their enemies, I will not spurn them, neither will I abhor them so as to destroy them utterly and break my covenant with them; for I am the Lord their God' (Lev. 26.44).

Such a reciprocal agreement with Israel involves the fulfilment of God's promise to Abraham that he would provide them with a land of their own. In Genesis, God called Abraham to travel to Canaan where he declared that he would make him the father of a multitude: 'Go from your country and your kindred and your father's house to the land that I will show you. And I will make of you a great nation' (Gen. 12.1–2). This same declaration was repeated to his grandson Jacob who, after wrestling God's messenger, was renamed 'Israel'. After Jacob's son Joseph became vizier of Egypt, the Israelite clan settled in Egypt for several hundred years – eventually Moses led them out of Egyptian bondage, and the people settled in the Promised Land. In the Bible the covenant with Israel is conceived as an essential element in the unfolding of God's plan for all people. Thus the Book of Samuel declares that the Lord chose David and his descendants to reign over Israel to the end of time (2 Sam. 1, 3, 5). In addition, it was held that this figure had been granted dominion over all nations. Thus 2 Samuel 22.50 states:

> For this I will extol thee, O Lord, among the nations,
> and sing praises to thy name.
> Great triumphs he gives to his king
> and shows steadfast love to his anointed,
> to David, and to his descendants for ever.

In this passage David is the anointed in the sense that he was consecrated for a divine purpose – this early biblical doctrine presupposed that David's position will be inherited by a series of successors with the task of carrying out God's will. With the fall of the Davidic empire after Solomon's death, there arose the view that the house of David would eventually rule over the two divided kingdoms as well as neighbouring peoples. In the words of Amos:

> In that day I will raise up
> the booth of David that is fallen
> and repair its breaches
> and raise up its ruins,
> and rebuild it as in the days of old;
> that they may possess the remnant of Edom
> and all the nations that are called by my name. (Amos 9.11–12)

Eventually Isaiah shifted the emphasis for the perpetuity of the Davidic dynasty to the nature of the future king; the foundation of his throne would be justice, and he would be endowed with the capacity to exact judgment:

> Of the increase of his government and of peace
> there will be no end,
> upon the throne of David, and over his kingdom,
> to establish it, and to uphold it
> with justice and with righteousness
> from this time forth and for evermore. (Isa. 9.7)

Such expectations paved the way for the vision of a transformation of earthly life. During the Second Temple period, the idea of eschatological salvation became an animating force in Jewish consciousness; in this regard, the Book of Daniel prophesized the coming of the messianic Son of Man:

> I saw in the night visions,
> and behold, with the clouds of heaven
> there came one like a son of man,
> and he came to the Ancient of Days
> and was presented before him.
> And to him was given dominion
> and glory and kingdom,
> that all peoples, nations, and languages
> should serve him;
> his dominion is an everlasting dominion,
> which shall not pass away,
> and his kingdom one
> that shall not be destroyed. (Dan. 7.13–14)

During this epoch there was intense speculation about the nature of the Messiah. In the Book of Zachariah, for example, two messianic figures – the high priest and the messianic king – are depicted. Later these two figures were joined by a third personage, the prophet of the last days; these three messianic roles correspond to the three major functions of a future Jewish state where kingship, priesthood and prophecy will exist side by side.

Yet despite such a proliferation of messianic figures, it was the Davidic Messiah who came to dominate Jewish thought. According to tradition, this king-Messiah will put an end to all wars on earth; he will make a covenant with the righteous and shall slay the wicked in accordance with God's decree. Such a conception served as the basis for subsequent reflection about messianic redemption, the ingathering of the exiles, and salvation in the world to come.

Principles of the Jewish Faith

Although the Bible does not contain a dogmatic formulation of the central tenets of the Jewish faith, it makes numerous claims about the nature and activity of God. In the first century BC, however, the Jewish philosopher Philo outlined what he considered the central doctrines of Judaism. After discussing the first few chapters of Genesis, he listed five central teachings of the Jewish faith:

> By his account of the creation of the word of which we have spoken, Moses teaches us among many other things five that are fairest and best of all.
>
> 1. Firstly that the Deity is and has been from eternity. This with a view to atheists, some of whom have hesitated and have been of two minds about eternal existence, while the bolder sort have carried their audacity to the point of declaring that the Deity does not exist at all, but that it is a mere assertion of men obscuring the truth with myth and fiction.
>
> 2. Secondly, that God is one. This with a view to propounders of polytheism, who do not blush to transfer from earth to heaven mob rule, that worst of evil policies.

3. Thirdly . . . that the world came into being. This because of those who think it is without beginning and eternal, who thus assign to God no superiority at all.

4. Fourthly, that the world too is one as well as its maker, who made his work like himself in its uniqueness, who used up for the creation of the whole all material that exists . . . For there are those who suppose that there are more worlds than one, while some think that they are infinite in number.

5. Fifthly that God exercises forethought on the world's behalf . . . (Philo, 1949, 135–7)

Paralleling Philo's formulation, rabbinic sources contain various discussions about the underlying tenets of Judaism. The third-century Palestinian teacher R. Simlai, for example, stated that Moses received 613 commandments, but King David reduced them to eleven:

O Lord, who shall sojourn in thy tent?
(1)   Who shall dwell on thy holy hill?
(2)   He who walks blamelessly, and does what is right,
(3)   and speaks truth from his heart;
(4)   who does not slander with his tongue,
(5)   and does no evil to his friend,
(6)   nor takes up a reproach against his neighbour;
(7)   in whose eyes reprobate is despised,
(8)   but who honours those who fear the Lord;
(9)   who swears to his own hurt and does not change;
(10) Who does not put out his money at interest,
(11) and does not take a bribe against the innocent.
      He who does these things shall never be moved. (Ps. 15)

Similarly, Isaiah reduced them to six:

(1)   He who walks righteously
(2)   and speaks uprightly,
(3)   who despises the gain of oppressions,
(4)   who shakes his hands, lest they hold a bribe,
(5)   who stops his ears from hearing of bloodshed
(6)   and shuts his eyes from looking upon evil.
      he will dwell on the heights;
      his place of defence will be the fortresses of rocks;
      his bread will be given him, his water will be sure.
      (Isa. 33.15–16)

Again, Micah reduced them to three:

> He has showed you, O man, what is good;
> and what does the Lord require of you
> (1) but to do justice,
> (2) and to love kindness,
> (3) and to walk humbly with your God? (Mic. 6.8)

Again, Isaiah reduced them to two principles:

> Thus says the Lord:
> (1) Keep justice,
> (2) and do righteousness,
> for soon my salvation will come,
> and my deliverance be revealed. (Isa. 56.1)

Finally, Habakkuk reduced them to one:

> Behold, he whose soul is not upright in him shall fail
> (1) but the righteous shall live by his faith. (Hab. 2.4)

Here R. Simlai was concerned primarily with principles of action rather than theological dogma. In all these examples, the assumption is that by keeping these precepts, one will fulfil all the other commandments.

Another example of rabbinic speculation about the central teachings of the Jewish faith is contained in Sanhedrin 10.1 in the *Mishnah*. According to the *Mishnah* the following individuals have no share in the world to come:

> (1) He that says there is no resurrection of the dead in the *Torah*;
> (2) and he that says that the *Torah* is not from Heaven;
> (3) and the Epicurean.
> (4) R. Akiva says: 'Also he that reads the external books' (books not included in Scripture),
> (5) or that utters a charm over a wound and says: 'I will put none of the diseases upon thee which I have put upon the Egyptians: for I am the Lord that healeth thee' (Exod. 15.26).
> (6) Abba Saul says: 'Also he that pronounces the Name (the Tetragrammaton) with its proper letters.'

In this formulation there is an emphasis on both belief and deed – the intention is to warn against false opinions as well as religiously harmful practices.

These early attempts to define the central teachings of the Jewish faith were superseded by more elaborate formulations made by Jewish theologians in response to philosophical thought as well as Christianity and Islam. These thinkers were compelled to isolate the central features of Judaism and emphasize their merits. The most important compilation of the central tenets of Judaism was delineated by Moses Maimonides (twelfth century) in his commentary of the *Mishnah*. Commenting on the previous passage in Sanhedrin, he declared that there are thirteen fundamental principles of the Jewish faith:

1. Belief in the existence of God.
2. Belief in God's unity.
3. Belief in God's incorporeality.
4. Belief in God's eternity.
5. Belief that God alone is to be worshipped.
6. Belief in prophecy.
7. Belief in Moses as the greatest of the prophets.
8. Belief that the *Torah* was given by God to Moses.
9. Belief that the *Torah* is immutable.
10. Belief that God knows the thoughts and deeds of men.
11. Belief that God rewards and punishes.
12. Belief in the advent of the Messiah.
13. Belief in the resurrection of the dead.

Concluding this formulation, Maimonides wrote:

> When all these principles are in the safe keeping of man, and his conviction of them is well established, he then enters 'into the general body of Israel', and it is incumbent upon us to love him, to care for him, and to do for him all that God commanded us to do for one another in the way of affection and brotherly sympathy. And this, even though he were to be guilty of every regression possible, by reason of the power of desire or the mastery of the base natural passions. He will receive punishment according to the measure of his perversity, but he will have a portion in the world to come, even though he be of the 'transgressors in Israel'. When, however, a man breaks away from any of these fundamental principles of belief, then of him it is said that 'he has gone out of the general body of Israel', and 'he denies the root truth of Judaism'. And he is then termed 'heretic' (*min*) and 'unbeliever' (*epiqoros*) and 'hewer of the plants', and 'it is obligatory upon us to hate him and cause him to perish'. (Jacobs, 1988, 14–15)

Here Maimonides stressed the importance of correct belief – in his view the unbeliever is excluded from *Klal Yisrael* (the Community of Israel).

In his *Code*, Maimonides elaborated this earlier opinion. The unbeliever, he asserted, is not only excluded from the body of Israel, but also from the Hereafter. 'The following', he wrote, 'have no share in the world to come but are cut off and destroyed and punished for ever for their great wickedness and sin':

> The *Minin*, the *epiqorsim*, those who deny the *Torah*, who deny the Resurrection, the coming of the Redeemer, the apostates, those who cause many to sin, those who separate themselves from the ways of the community, those who sin with a high hand like Jehoakim, the informers, those who terrorize the public for purposes other than the sake of Heaven, those who shed blood, the slanderers, and those who remove the sign of circumcision.

Commenting on the five types of *Minim*, he continued:

> Five are called *Minim*: One who says there is no God; that the world has no controller; one who agrees that the world has a controller but believes that there are two or more; one who says that there is no Lord but the first and the rock of all, also one who worships a star or planet and so forth as an intercessor between him and the Lord of the universe. Each one of these is called a *Min*.

Concerning the *Epiqorsim*, he declared that they consist of:

> One who says that there is no prophecy at all and that there is no knowledge which reaches to the hearts of men from the creator; one who denies the prophecy of Moses our teacher; and one who says that the creator does not know men's deeds. Each one of these three is an *Epiqoros*.

Finally, he listed three who are deniers of the *Torah*:

> One who says that the *Torah* is not from God, even if he refers to no more than one verse or one word, saying that Moses spoke of it of his own accord, he is a denier of the *Torah*. The same applies to one who denies its explanation, namely the Oral *Torah*, or like Zadok and Boethus, denies its teachers. The same applies to one who says that the creator changed one precept for another so that even though the *Torah* did once come from God it is no longer valid, like the Christians and the Muslims. Each one of these three is a denier of the *Torah*. (Jacobs, 1988, 16)

In conclusion, Maimonides stated that 'each one of the twenty-four persons we have counted, even if he is an Israelite, has no share in the world to come'.

Alternative Formulations

In the subsequent centuries, a number of medieval thinkers proposed different formulations of the central tenets of Judaism. The fourteenth-century Jewish theologian Hasdai Crescas, for example, argued in his *Light of the Lord* that there is one fundamental belief in Judaism: that God exists, is a unity, and is incorporeal. In addition to this primary belief, he argued, there are five fundamental beliefs without which Judaism is inconceivable:

1. Providence.
2. Divine power.
3. Prophecy.
4. Freewill.
5. The *Torah* is humanity's true hope.

Added to these tenets are beliefs which Crescas termed 'true opinions' which can be divided into two types. The first are beliefs which are independent of any precept:

1. Creation
2. Immortality of the soul.
3. Reward and punishment.
4. Resurrection.
5. The immutability of the *Torah*.
6. Moses.
7. The High Priest had the oracle of the *Urim* and *Thummim*.
8. Messiah.

The second type consists of beliefs dependent on particular precepts:

1. Beliefs implied in prayer and the blessing of the high priest.
2. Beliefs implied in repentence.
3. Beliefs implied in the Day of Atonement and other festivals.

According to Crescas, any individual who denies one of these fundamental beliefs or true opinions is an unbeliever. However, there is another category of beliefs which are not religiously obligatory; here there is scope for personal opinions:

1. Is the world eternal?
2. Are there many worlds?
3. Are the spheres living creatures?
4. Do the stars have an influence over human destiny?
5. Is there any efficacy to charms and amulets?
6. Do demons exist?
7. Is the doctrine of metempsychosis true?
8. Is the soul of an infant immortal?
9. Do heaven and hell exist?
10. Are the doctrines of 'Works of Creation' and the 'Works of the heavenly chariot' identified with 'physics' and 'metaphysics'?
11. What is the nature of comprehension?
12. Is there a First Cause?
13. Can the nature of God be comprehended?

Another formulation of the central principles of the Jewish faith was propounded by the fifteenth-century theologian, Simeon ben Zemah Duran. According to Duran, there are three central principles of the Jewish faith:

1. The existence of God
2. The Divine origin of the *Torah*
3. Reward and punishment

These principles, Duran argued, are explicitly denoted in the *Mishnah* which refers to three persons who are denied a share in the world to come – one who states that the *Torah* is not from heaven; one who denies resurrection; and the *epiqoros*. For Duran the denial of these three central beliefs implicitly involves the denial of other basic beliefs:

> The foundation of faith is to believe in God, blessed be he, that he is one, that he is eternal, that he is incorporeal and that it is fitting to worship him alone. All these included in the term *epiqoros*. Next, one must believe in the predictions of the prophets and of Moses, in the *Torah* and that it is eternal. These are included in the term '*Torah* from Heaven'. Next, one must believe in reward and punishment and their offshoots, which is included in the term 'the resurrection of the dead'. (Jacobs, 1988, 20)

Thus, in this interpretation of the *Mishnah*, Duran managed to include in his three fundamental beliefs Maimonides' thirteen principles of the Jewish faith.

Another formulation of the central beliefs of the Jewish faith was proposed by the fifteenth-century theologian Joseph Albo in his *Book of Principles*. Criticizing Maimonides; he argued that an unbeliever should be defined as one who knows the *Torah* lays down a principle but denies its truth. Such rebellion against the teaching of the tradition constitutes unbelief. But, a person who upholds the law of Moses and believes in principles, he wrote,

> when he undertakes to investigate these matters with his reason and scrutinizes the texts, is misled by his speculation and interprets a given principle otherwise then it is taken to mean at first sight; or denies the principle because he thinks that it does not represent a sound theory which the *Torah* obliges us to believe; or erroneously denies that a given belief is a fundamental principle, which however he believes as he believes the other dogmas of the *Torah* which are not fundamental principles; or entertains a certain notion in relation to one of the miracles of the *Torah* because he thinks that he is not thereby denying any of the doctrines which it is obligatory upon us to believe by the authority of the *Torah* – a person of this sort is not an unbeliever; his sin is due to error and requires atonement. (Jacobs, 1988, 21)

According to Albo, there are three basic tenets of the Jewish faith: belief in God, in revelation, and in reward and punishment. Like Duran, he subdivided these principles into subordinate beliefs. In Albo's view the three benedictions incorporated in the additional service for New Year represent these three principles. The 'Kingdom' benediction which consists of Scriptural verses dealing with God's reign corresponds to the principle of reward and punishment; the 'Memorial' benediction containing verses dealing with God's remembrance corresponds to the principle of reward and punishment; the benediction 'Trumpets' corresponds with the principle of revelation. These blessings, he believed, were ordained in order to emphasize the significance of the central teachings of Judaism at the beginning of the Jewish year, that by properly believing in these principles together with the dogmas derived from them we shall win a favourable verdict in the divine judgment.

In conclusion, Albo stated that the number of fundamental principles and those derived from them is eleven:

1. The existence of God
2. Unity
3. Incorporeality
4. God's independence from time
5. Freedom from defect
6. Prophecy
7. Authenticity of prophecy
8. Revelation
9. God's knowledge
10. Providence
11. Reward and punishment

In addition, Albo stated that there are six dogmas which everyone who professes Mosaic law is obliged to accept – whoever denies them, he believed, is a heretic who has no share in the world to come.

1. *Creatio ex nihilo*
2. The superiority of Moses' prophecy
3. The immutability of the *Torah*
4. Human perfection can be attained by fulfilling even one of the commandments of the *Torah*
5. Resurrection of the dead
6. The Messiah

Again, in the fifteenth century the preacher Isaac Arama formulated three fundamental principles of the Jewish faith:

1. *Creatio ex nihilo*
2. Revelation
3. Belief in the world to come

In Arama's view the Sabbath is the foundation of the Jewish faith, since all these principles are expressed in its observance: the Sabbath reminds human beings of creation; on the Sabbath Jews have the leisure to engage in *Torah* study; Sabbath bliss indicates the state the righteous will attain in the world to come.

In *Pinnacles of Faith*, the fifteenth-century philosopher Isaac Abrabanel discussed Maimonides' formulation of the principles of Judaism. Although he defended Maimonides from criticism, he argued that since every part of the *Torah* is of divine origin, the attempt to formulate principles of the Jewish faith is misguided. He wrote:

> I am convinced that it is improper to postulate principles or foundations with regard to the *Torah* and we are not permitted to doubt the smallest matter therein that it should be necessary to prove its truth by reference to principles or root ideas. For whoever denies or doubts any matter, small or great, of the beliefs or narratives contained in the *Torah* is a heretic and an unbeliever. Since the *Torah* is true no single belief or narrative in it can be superior to any other. (Jacobs, 1988, 24)

A similar view was advanced by the sixteenth-century thinker David ben Solomon ibn Abi Zimra who refused to distinguish between parts of the *Torah* as principles of the faith. In one of his responses, he wrote 'You ask me with regard to the matter of principles of faith, whether I accept the formulation of Maimonides or Crescas or Albo'. In response, he declared:

> I do not agree that it is right to make any party of the perfect *Torah* into a 'principle' since the *Torah* is a 'principle' from the mouth of the Almighty. Our sages say that whoever states that the whole of the *Torah* is from heaven with the exception of one verse is a heretic. Consequently, each precept is a 'principle' and a fundamental idea. Even a light precept has a secret reason which is beyond our understanding. How then dare we suggest that this is inessential and that fundamental? In short, Rabbi Isaac Abrabanel of blessed memory, wrote correctly in his work '*Rosh Amanah*'; consult this work. My opinion is the same as his that every detail and inference of the *Torah* is a 'principle', a foundation and a fundamental belief and whoever denies it is an unbeliever and has no share in the world to come. (Jacobs, 1988, 24–5)

Despite these alternative formulations of the central tenets of the Jewish faith as well as the criticisms of such dogmatic systems, Maimonides' thirteen principles eventually became authoritative for Jewry: as a result they are included in most traditional prayerbooks in two versions. The first is the *Yigdal* hymn composed in Italy at the beginning of the fourteenth century, probably by Daniel ben Judah of Rome. The second is a prose formulation *Ani Maamin* (I believe) which first appeared in 1517:

1. I believe with perfect faith that the creator, blessed be his name, is the author and guide of everything that has been created, and that he alone has made, does make, and will make all things.

2. I believe with perfect faith the creator, blessed be his name, is a unity, and that there is no unity in any manner like unto his, and that he alone is our God, who was, is, and will be.

3. I believe with perfect faith that the creator, blessed be his name, is not a body, and that he is free from all the accidents of matter, and that he has not any form whatsoever.

4. I believe with perfect faith that the creator, blessed be his name, is the first and the last.

5. I believe with perfect faith that to the creator, blessed be his name, and to him alone it is right to pray, and that it is not right to pray to any being besides him.

6. I believe with perfect faith that all words of the prophets are true.

7. I believe with perfect faith that the prophecy of Moses our teacher, peace be unto him, was true, and that he was the chief of the prophets, both of those who preceded and of those that followed him.

8. I believe with perfect faith that the whole law, now in our possession, is the same that was given to Moses our teacher, peace be unto him.

9. I believe with perfect faith that this law will not be changed, and that there will never be any other law from the creator, blessed be his name.

10. I believe with perfect faith that the creator, blessed be his name, knows every deed of the children of men, and all their thoughts, as it is said, it is he that fashioneth the hearts of them all, that giveth heed to all their deeds (Ps. 33.15).

11. I believe with perfect faith that the creator, blessed be his name, rewards those that keep his commandments, and punishes those that transgress them.

12. I believe with perfect faith in the coming of the Messiah, and though he tarry, I will wait daily for his coming.

13. I believe with perfect faith that there will be a resurrection of the dead at the time when it shall please the creator, blessed be his name, and exalted be the remembrance of him for ever and ever.

The Nature of God

In line with various formulations of the central principles of the Jewish faith, rabbinic sages through the ages concurred in conceiving God as a divine unity who is transcendent, immanent, eternal, omnipotent, omniscient, and all-good. In rabbinic sources scholars stressed that the *Shema* implies that there is only one God. For a number of medieval theologians, the concept of God's unity implies that there can be no multiplicity in his being. Thus the tenth-century philosopher Saadiah Gaon insisted in *The Book of Beliefs and Opinions* that the creator is a single incorporeal being who created the universe out of nothing. Like the Islamic Mutazilite theologians, he asserted that if God has a plurality of attributes he must be composite in nature. Thus, such terms as 'life', 'omnipotence', and 'omniscience' should be understood as implications of the concept of God as creator rather than attributes of the Deity. According to Saadiah, the reason why we are forced to describe God by means of these descriptions is because of the limitations of language, but they do not in any way involve plurality in God.

Another thinker of this period, Solomon ben Joseph ibn Gabirol, argued that God and matter are not opposed as two ultimate principles – instead matter is identical to God. It emanates from the essence of the creator, forming the basis of all subsequent emanations. For ibn Gabirol the universe consists of cosmic existences flowing out of the superabundant light and goodness of the creator; it is a reflection of God, though God remains in himself and does not enter his creation with his essence. In a poem, 'Religious Crown', ibn Gabirol used neo-Platonic images to describe God's nature:

> Thou art One, the beginning of all computation
> the base of all construction,
> Thou art One, and in the mystery of thy
> Oneness the wise of heart are astonished,
> for they know not what it is.
> Thou art One, but not as the one that is counted
> or owned, for number and chance cannot reach thee,
> not attributed, nor form.

This insistence on God's unity was a theme of the twelfth-century philosopher Abraham ben David Halevi ibn Daud, who in *The Exalted Faith* derived God's absolute unity from his necessary existence. For ibn Daud this concept of divine oneness precludes the possibility of any positive attributes of God. Similarly, Moses Maimonides in the same century, argued in the *Guide for the Perplexed* that no positive attributes can be predicated of God since the Divine is an absolute unity. Hence, when God is described positively in the Bible, such ascriptions refer to his activity. The only true attributes are negative ones; they lead to a knowledge of God because in negation no plurality is involved. Each negative attribute excludes from God's essence some imperfection.

In addition to such speculation about the concept of God's unity, the rabbis also theorized about his transcendence and immanence. In rabbinic literature, Jewish scholars formulated the doctrine of the *Shekhinah* to denote the divine presence. The indwelling presence of God, the *Shekhinah* is compared to light. Thus the *midrash* paraphrases Numbers 6.25 ('The Lord make his face to shine upon you, and be gracious to you'): May he give thee the light of the *Shekhinah*. In another *midrash* the 'shining' of the *Shekhinah* in the Tent of Meeting is compared to a cave by the sea. When the sea rushes in to fill the cave, it suffers no diminution of its waters. Likewise the divine presence filled the Tent of Meeting, but simultaneously filled the world.

In the medieval period the doctrine of *Shekhinah* was further elaborated by Jewish scholars. According to the tenth-century Jewish thinker Saadiah Gaon, the *Shekhinah* is identical with the glory of God, which serves as intermediary between God and man during the prophetic encounter. Following Saadiah, the eleventh-century scholar Judah Halevi argued in the *Kuzari* that it was the *Shekhinah* rather than God himself who appeared to the prophets. However, unlike Saadiah he did not describe the *Shekhinah* as a created light; rather he identified the *Shekhinah* with the divine influence. In his *Guide*, however, Maimonides embraced Saadiah's belief that the *Shekhinah* is a created light identified with glory. In addition, he associated the *Shekhinah* with prophecy. According to Maimonides, prophecy is an overflow from God which passes through the mediation of the active intellect and then to the faculty of imagination. It requires perfection in theoretical wisdom, morality and development of the imagination.

In kabbalistic teaching the *Shekhinah* also played an important role. In early kabbalistic thought the *Shekhinah* was identified as the feminine principle in the world of the *sefirot*. Later the *Shekhinah* was understood as the last in the hierarchy of the *sefirot* – as the divine power closest to the created world, it is the medium through which the divine light passes. Further, in kabbalistic thought the *Shekhinah* is the divine principle of the Jewish people. Everything that happens to Israel is reflected upon the *Shekhinah* which grows stronger or is weakened with every meritorious or sinful act of each Jew and of the people as a whole.

The rabbis were also concerned to stress that God would endure for ever. In the Middle Ages, for example, Moses Maimonides in his *Guide* argued that time itself was part of creation. Therefore, when God is described as existing before the creation of the universe, the notion of time should not be understood in its normal sense:

> In the beginning God alone existed and nothing else; neither angels nor spheres, nor the things that are contained within the spheres existed. He then produced from nothing all existing things such as they are, by his will and desire. Even time itself is among the things created; for time depends on motion . . . We say that God existed before the creation of the universe, although the verb existed appears to imply the notion of time; we also believe that he existed in an infinite space of time before the universe was created. (Guide II, 13)

This concept of time as part of creation was later developed by the fifteenth-century Jewish philosopher, Joseph Albo. In his *Ikkarim* he maintained that the concepts of priority and perpetuity can only be applied to God in a negative sense. That is, when God is described as being 'before' or 'after' some period, this only means that he was non-existent before or after that time: measured time which depends on motion, and time in the abstract. The second type of time has no origin – it is the infinite space of time before the universe was created.

Although it is difficult to conceive of God existing in such a duration, it is difficult to imagine God outside space. For this reason, Albo argued, the rabbis state that one should not seek what it above, what is below, what is before and what is behind.

According to other Jewish thinkers God is outside time altogether – he is in the 'Eternal Now'. Hence in the thirteenth century, Bahya ibn Asher ibn Halawa in his commentary on the Pentateuch discussed the verse, 'The Lord will reign for ever and ever' (Exod. 15.18): All times, past and future, are in the present so far as God is concerned, for he was before time and is not encompassed by it. Likewise the sixteenth-century scholar Moses Almosnino commented on, 'For now I know' (Gen. 22.12). According to Almosnino, God is in the Eternal Now and he used this notion to explain how God's fore-knowledge is not incompatible with human free will.

For the rabbis the belief in God's omnipotence was also an essential feature of their faith. As a consequence, in the Middle Ages Jewish thinkers wrestled with the concept of divine omnipotence. Pre-eminent among their concerns was the question whether God can do absolutely everything. According to Saadiah Gaon in his *Beliefs and Opinions*, the soul will not praise God for causing five to be more than ten without further addition, nor for being able to put the world through the hollow of a signet ring without making the world narrower and the ring wider, nor for bringing back the day which has passed in its original state. These would be absurd acts. Subsequently Moses Maimonides stated that although God is all-powerful there are certain actions that he cannot perform because they are logically impossible:

> That which is impossible has a permanent and constant property which is the result of some agent, and cannot in any way change, and consequently does not ascribe to God the power of doing what is impossible. (Maimonides, 1881, 59)

Such medieval reflections were not intended to impose restrictions on God's power; rather these theologians were preoccupied with defining those acts which are logically incoherent. Since they are inherently absurd, they argued, it is impossible to believe that God could perform them.

Paralleling the doctrine of God's omnipotence the rabbis were anxious to stress that God is all-knowing. According to rabbinic Judaism, God's knowledge is not limited by space and time. Rather nothing is hidden from him. Further, the rabbis declared that God's foreknowledge of events does not deprive human beings of free will. Thus in the *Mishnah*, the second-century sage Akiva declared: 'All is foreseen, but freedom of choice is give.' Maimonides in his *Guide* similarly claimed that God knows all things before they occur; none the less human beings are unable to comprehend the nature of God's knowledge because it is of a different order from that of human beings: on this account it is similarly not possible to understand how divine foreknowledge is compatible with human freedom. Other medieval thinkers, however, were unconvinced by such an explanation. In his *Wars of the Lord*, the fourteenth-century philosopher Gersonides argued that God only knows things in general. The world is thus constituted so that a range of possibilities is open to human beings. Since human beings are able to exercise free will, these possibilities are open to them, since they are only possibilities. According to Gersonides, such a view does not undermine God's providential plan. Even though God does know all future events, he is cognizant of the outcome of the whole process. In the same century the Jewish theologian Hasdai Crescas, however, held a radically different position in *The Light of the Lord*. For Crescas human beings only appear to be free, but in reality all their deeds are determined by virtue of God's foreknowledge. Thus rather than attempting to reconcile free will and omniscience, he asserted that God's knowledge is absolute and free will is an illusion.

For the rabbis, God is the all-good ruler of the universe. In the Middle Ages such a view gave rise to speculation about the existence of evil. In the twelfth century, for example, Abraham ibn Daud argued that both human reason and the Jewish tradition teach that God cannot be the cause of evil. Reason demonstrates that this is so because God is wholly good; it would be self-contradictory for him to be the source of evil. Because God does not have a composite nature, it is logically impossible for him to bring about both good and evil. But why then does evil exist? Poverty, for example, is the absence of wealth; darkness the absence of light; and folly the absence of understanding. It is a mistake to think that God made elephants in Spain. Such a lack of elephants is not divinely willed. Similarly evil is not divinely created. It occurs when goodness is not present. The absence of good is not inherently evil: instead imperfections in the world exist so that God can benefit a multitude of creatures of different forms. In his *Guide* Maimonides argued along similar lines. All evils, he asserted, are privations. For this reason God is not responsible for evil – he is liable only for the privation of good.

By defining evil as a privation of good, ibn Daud and Maimonides were anxious to demonstrate how apparent evil could exist in a universe created by a wholly good omnipotent God. Since evil does not, in fact, exist, it is incorrect to assume that God is responsible for its occurrence. What is called evil is a corruption of nature. If it were not corrupt, it would be good. It is bad only so far as it is corrupted. Thus everything that exists is good, and those things which are now less good or no longer good at all have merely fallen away from their original state.

For the kabbalists, the existence of evil constitutes a central problem for the Jewish faith. According to one tradition evil has no objective reality. Human beings are unable to receive all of the influx from the *sefirot*, and it is this inability which is the origin of evil. Created beings are therefore estranged from the source of emanation and this results in the illusion that evil exists. Another view depicts the *sefirah* of power as 'an attribute whose name is evil'. On the basis of such a teaching the thirteenth-century mystic Isaac the Blind concluded that there must be a positive root of evil and death. During the process of differentiation of forces below the *sefirot* evil became concretized. This interpretation led to the doctrine that the source of evil was the supra-abundant growth of judgment – this was due to the separation and substitution of the attribute of judgment from its union with compassion. Pure judgment produced from within itself 'the other side' (*Sitra Ahra*). The *Sitra Ahra* consists of the domain of emanations and demonic powers. Though it originated from one of God's attributes, it is not part of the divine realm.

In the *Zohar* there is a detailed hierarchial structure of this emanation in which the *Sitra Ahra* is depicted as having ten *sefirot* of its own. The evil in the universe, the *Zohar* explains, has its origins in the leftovers of worlds that were destroyed. Another view in the *Zohar* is that the Tree of Life and the Tree of Knowledge were harmoniously bound together until Adam separated them, thereby bringing evil into the world. This is referred to as 'the cutting of the shoots' and is the prototype of sins in the Bible. Evil thus originated through human action. Both these views concerning the origin of evil were reconciled in another passage where it is asserted that the disposition towards evil derives from cosmic evil which is in the realm of the *Sitra Ahra*.

Divine Action

Through the ages the rabbis affirmed that God exercises his providence over creation, revealed himself to Israel, and has a plan for all humanity. With regard to divine providence, the *Mishnah* declares: 'Everything is foreseen.' In the *Talmud* we read: 'No man suffers so much as the injury of a finger when it has been decreed in heaven.' Such a conviction became a central feature of the *Rosh Hashanah* service. According to the New Year liturgy, God, the judge of the world, provides for the destiny of individuals as well as nations on the basis of their actions. In the medieval period Jewish theologians were preoccupied with this doctrine. In his *Guide*, Maimonides defended both general and special providence. The latter, he argued, extends only to human beings and is in proportion to a person's intellect and moral character. Such a view implies that God is concerned about each non-human species, but not with every individual. Only humans come under divine care as they rise in intellectual and moral stature. The fifteenth-century thinker Hasdai Crescas, however, maintained that God created human beings out of his love for them – thus his providential care is not related to their personal characteristics. All persons enjoy God's special providence.

The kabbalists were also concerned with this subject. In his *Shomer Emunim*, for example, the eighteenth-century scholar

Joseph Ergas explained that there are various types of providence:

> Nothing occurs by accident, without intention and divine providence, as it is written: 'Then will I also walk with you in chance' (Lev. 21.24). You see that even the state of 'chance' is attributed to God, for all proceeds from him by reason of special providence.

None the less, Ergas limited special providence to human beings:

> However, the guardian Angel has no power to provide for the special providence of non-human species; for example, whether this ox will live or die, whether this ant will be trodden on or saved, whether this spider will catch this fly and so forth. (Jacobs, 1973, 115)

Such a view caused offence to a number of Hasidic teachers – divine providence, they insisted, is exercised over all things. Thus the eighteenth-century Hasidic scholar, Phineas of Kortez stated: 'A man should believe that even a piece of straw that lies on the ground does so at the decree of God. He decreed that it should lie there with one end facing this way and the other end the other way' (*Peer la-Yesharim*, No. 38). Again, Hayim of Sanz contended: 'It is impossible for any creature to enjoy existence without the creator of all worlds sustaining it and keeping it in being, and it is all through divine providence. Although Maimonides has a different opinion in this matter, the truth is that not even a bird is snared without providence from above' (*Divre Hayim to Mikketz*).

In the Middle Ages Jewish theologians also wrestled with dilemmas concerning God's foreknowledge as it relates to human freedom. If God knows everything which will come to pass, how can human beings be free? According to Maimonides, human beings are free despite God's knowledge of future events because God's knowledge is not our knowledge. Thus he wrote in his *Guide*:

> You may ask: God knows all that will happen. Before someone becomes a good or bad man God either knows that this will happen or he does not know it. If he knows that the person will be

good it is impossible for that person to be bad. You must know that the solution to this problem is larger than the earth and wider than the sea. God does not 'know' with a knowledge that is apart from him, like human beings. God's knowledge and his self are one and the same though no human being is capable of clearly comprehending this matter. (Guide III, 20)

Other scholars, such as the twelfth-century Jewish theologian Abraham ibn Daud, disagreed. For ibn Daud God's foreknowledge is not determinative or causative. Thus human beings are able to act freely: his knowledge is not in the nature of a compelling decree but is comparable to the knowledge of the astrologers who know, by virtue of some other power, how a certain person will behave.

As an act of special providence God chose Israel from all nations as his special people. In explaining this act the rabbis argued that their election was due to an acceptance of the *Torah*. According to tradition the *Torah* was offered first to other nations of the world, but they all rejected it because its precepts conflicted with their way of life. Only Israel accepted it. On one account this occurred only because God suspended a mountain over the Jewish people, threatening to destroy the nation if they refused. The dominant view, however, was that the Israelites accepted God's law enthusiastically. For this reason, Scripture states that the Jewish people declared: 'All that the Lord has spoken we will do' (Exod. 24.7), showing a willingness to obey God's decrees without knowledge of its contents.

The concept of Israel's chosenness was also a major theme of medieval kabbalistic thought. According to the *kabbalah*, the Jewish people on earth has its counterpart in the *Shekhinah* in the sefirotic realm – the *sefirah* '*Malkhut*' [Kingdom] is known as the 'community of Israel' which serves as the archetype of the Israelite people on earth. For the kabbalists, Israel's exile mirrors the cosmic disharmony in which the *Shekhinah* is cast into exile from the Godhead. The drama of Israel's exile and its ultimate restoration reflects the dynamic of the upper worlds. In later *Habad* mysticism, the Jew has two souls: the animal soul and the divine soul. The divine soul is possessed only by Jews, and even the animal soul of Israel is derived from a source which is a mixture of good and evil. The animal souls of gentiles, on the other hand, derive from an unclean source. For this reason no gentile is capable of acting in a completely good fashion.

Turning to the nature of God's revelation, the tradition distinguished between the revelation of the *Torah* and the prophetic writings. This was frequently expressed by saying that the *Torah* was given directly by God, whereas the prophetic books were given by means of prophecy. The remaining books of the Bible were conveyed by means of the holy spirit rather than through prophecy. None the less, all these writings constitute the canon of Scripture. The Hebrew term referring to the Bible as a whole is *Tanakh*. This word is made up of the first letters of the three divisions of Scripture: *Torah* (Pentateuch): *Neviim* (Prophets); and *Ketuvim* (Writings). This is the Written *Torah* (*Torah She-Bi-Ketav*).

According to the rabbis, the expositions and elaborations of the Written Law were also revealed by God to Moses on Mount Sinai; subsequently they were passed from generation to generation, and through this process additional legislation was created, referred to as the Oral *Torah* (*Torah She-Be-Al Peh*). Thus traditional Judaism affirms that God's revelation is two-fold and binding for all time. Committed to this belief, Jews pray in the synagogue that God will guide them to do his will as recorded in their sacred literature:

> O our Father, merciful Father, ever compassionate, have mercy upon us: put it into our hearts to understand and to discern, to mark, learn, and teach, to heed, to do and to fulfil in love all the words of instruction in the *Torah*. Enlighten our eyes in thy *Torah*, and let our hearts cling to thy commandments, and make us single-hearted to love and fear thy name, so that we be never put to shame.

In the Middle Ages this traditional belief was continually affirmed. Like Maimonides, the thirteenth-century thinker Nahmanides argued in his Commentary to the Pentateuch that Moses wrote the Five Books of Moses at God's dictation. It is likely, he observed, that Moses wrote Genesis and part of Exodus when he descended from Mount Sinai. At the end of the forty years in the wilderness he completed the rest of the

Pentateuch. Nahmanides observed that this view follows the rabbinic tradition that the *Torah* was given scroll by scroll. For Nahmanides, Moses was like a scribe who copied an older work. Underlying this conception is the mystical idea of a primordial *Torah* which contains the words describing events long before they happened. This entire record was in heaven before the creation of the world. In addition, Nahmanides maintained that the secrets of the *Torah* were revealed to Moses and are referred to in the *Torah* by the use of special letters, the numerical values of words and letters, and the adornment of Hebrew characters.

Paralleling Nahmanides' mystical interpretation of the *Torah*, the *Zohar* asserts that the *Torah* contains mysteries beyond human comprehension. As the *Zohar* explains:

> Said R. Simeon: 'Alas for the man who regards the *Torah* as a book of mere tales and everyday matters! If that were so, even we could compose a *Torah* dealing with everyday affairs, and of even greater excellence. Nay, even the princes with everyday affairs, and of even greater worth which we could use as a model for composing such *Torah*. The *Torah*, however, contains in all its words supernal truths and sublime mysteries . . . Thus, had the *Torah* not clothed herself in garments of this world, the world could not endure it. The stories of the *Torah* are thus only her outer garments, and whoever look upon this garment as being the *Torah* itself, woe to that man – such a one has no portion – in the next world.

According to tradition God revealed 613 commandments to Moses on Mount Sinai which are recorded in the Five Books of Moses. These prescriptions, which are to be observed as part of God's covenant with Israel, are classified in two major categories: (1) statutes concerned with ritual performances characterized as obligations between human beings and God; and (2) judgments consisting of ritual laws that would have been adopted by society even if they had not been decreed by God (such as law regarding murder and theft). These 613 commandments consist of 365 negative (prohibited) and 248 positive (duties to be performed) prescriptions.

Traditional Judaism maintains that Moses received the Oral *Torah* in addition to the Written Law. This was passed down from generation to generation and was the subject of rabbinic debate. This first authoritative compilation of the Oral law was the *Mishnah* composed by Judah ha-Nasi in the second century AD. This work is the most important book of law after the Bible; its purpose was to supply teachers and judges with an authoritative guide to the Jewish legal tradition. In subsequent centuries sages continued to discuss the content of Jewish law; their deliberations are recorded in the Palestinian and Babylonian *Talmuds*. After the compilation of the *Talmuds* in the sixth century AD, outstanding rabbinic authorities continued the development of Jewish law by issuing answers to specific questions. These responses touched on all aspects of Jewish law and insured a standardization of practice. In time, various scholars felt the need to produce codes of Jewish law so that all members of the community would have access to the legal tradition.

In kabbalistic thought the observance of the *mitzvot* takes on cosmic significance. For the mystic, deeds of cosmic repair (*tikkun*) sustain the world, activate nature to praise God, and bring about the coupling of the tenth and sixth *sefirot*. Such repair is accomplished by keeping the commandments which were conceived as vessels for establishing contact with the Godhead and for enduring divine mercy. Such a religious life provided the kabbalist with a means of integrating into the divine hierarchy of creation – the *kabbalah* was able to guide the soul back to its infinite source.

For the rabbis, divine providential concern embraces all humanity. Drawing on messianic conceptions found in Scripture, they foresaw a future redemption when earthly life would be transformed and all peoples would convert to the worship of the true God. Such ideals animated rabbinic speculation about the eschatological unfolding of history. According to a number of scholars, such a process of salvation would be brought about by charity, repentance and the observance of the law. None the less, prior to the coming of the Messiah, the world would endure serious tribulations (the birth pangs of the Messiah). These would be followed by the appearance of Elijah, the forerunner of the Messiah. Subsequently a second messianic figure – the Messiah ben Joseph – would engage in battle with Gog and Magog (the enemies of the Israelites). Although he would be slain in this war, the king Messiah – Messiah ben David – would eventually prevail.

With the coming of the Messiah ben David the dispersion of Israel would cease and all exiles would return to Zion; during this period of messianic redemption, earthly life would be utterly transformed. Finally, at the end of the messianic age, all human beings would be judged and either rewarded with heavenly life or condemned to eternal punishment. This eschatological scheme, which was formulated over the centuries by innumerable rabbis, should not be seen as a flight of fancy. Rather it was a serious attempt to explain God's ways. Israel was God's chosen people. The nation had been driven from their homeland, but the Messiah would come to deliver them from exile and redeem the world. The period of messianic redemption would unfold in numerous stages, culminating in a final judgment with reward for the righteous and punishment for the wicked; in this way the vindication of the righteous was assured in the hereafter.

3

Unity and Diversity

Over the centuries the development of Orthodox Judaism rested on a common core of shared belief and practice – biblical and rabbinic teaching about the nature of God and his action in the world constituted the foundation of the faith. Yet, from biblical times the Jewish community divided into a variety of sub-groups all of whom espoused different approaches to the tradition. Such diversity could be construed as illustrating the absence of such shared religious convictions. However, this interpretation fails to recognize that these different groups adhered to the principles of the faith.

The Samaritans of ancient Israel, for example, remained loyal to biblical teaching; holding fast to the faith of their ancestors, they strictly adhered to the Jewish way of life. Similarly, the Sadducees, Pharisees, Essenes and Rebels of the first century were faithful to the biblical inheritance despite their different understanding of the tradition. So too, the Karaites in the early Middle Ages strictly adhered to the tenets of biblical Judaism; although they rejected the rabbinic understanding of Scriptural law, they remained loyal to biblical teachings about God and conscientiously observed the law as set forth in Scripture.

Likewise the Shabbeteans of the seventeenth century deviated from mainstream Judaism only in their belief that Shabbetai Tzevi was the true Messiah. Even those who continued to believe in Shabbetai after his conversion to Islam utilized kabbalistic categories drawn from traditional sources to make sense of this act of apostasy. The Hasidim of the late eighteenth century also remained loyal to the *Torah* despite their rejection of the arid scholasticism of rabbinic Judaism. In all cases these various sects despite their different teachings, subscribed to the central tenets of the Jewish faith. Thus, although various sub-groups emerged within the Jewish community through the course of history, they did not sever themselves from the central body of shared tradition. In this respect Judaism remained monolithic in character until the advent of the Enlightenment.

The Samaritans

In ancient times the Samaritans constituted a separate people originating from within the Jewish community. This Jewish sect occupied Samaria after the conquest of the Northern Kingdom by the Assyrians in 722 BC. Intermingling with the resident non-Jewish population, this mixed population continued to follow Jewish laws and customs while simultaneously adopting pagan practices. When Cyrus of Persia conquered Babylon in the sixth century, he allowed the Jews to return from Babylonia to their homeland. When the Samaritans offered to help these returning exiles to rebuild the temple, Zerubbabel, who supervised the repair and restoration of the Temple, refused their offer since he regarded them as of uncertain racial origin and was suspicious of their worship. Recognizing that they would be excluded from the state which these exiles were intent on creating, the Samaritans persuaded the Persian officials responsible for the western empire that the plans for restoration were illegal, thereby delaying work on the Temple for ten years or more. This was the beginning of the emnity between the Jewish and Samaritam peoples which continued for hundreds of years.

Despite their rejection from the Jewish community, the Samaritans remained loyal to traditional beliefs and practices. In its earliest form, the Samaritan creed consisted of a simple belief in God and the Pentateuch. For the Samaritans, God is the wholly other – he is manifest in all things, all powerful, and beyond comprehension. His purposes for Israel and all peoples were communicated to Moses on Mount Sinai; according to Samaritan tradition, Moses was 'God's man' who wrote the Pentateuch and authorized Mount Gerizim as the place which God chose for sacrifice. In addition, the Samaritans subscribed to a belief in resurrection and anticipated the arrival of a restorer who would restore all things prior to the Final Judgment.

Given that the Samaritans possessed only the Pentateuch as the sole source of authoritative source, the Five Books of Moses served as the basis of their religious practices. Frequently the Samaritans were stricter about the interpretation of biblical law than the rabbis because of their adherence to the letter of the law; in other cases Samaritan law deviated from rabbinic traditions because of a different interpretation of the biblical text.

Regarding the Sabbath, for example, the Samaritans held four prayer services. The first, on the Sabbath eve, lasted for about an hour before the setting of the sun. This was followed on the Sabbath morning by the second service which began between three and four a.m. The afternoon service was held only on regular Sabbaths and those that fall during the counting of the *Omer*; it began at noon and lasted for about two hours. The fourth prayer service took place at the end of the Sabbath and continued for about half an hour until the sun set. On Sabbaths the Samaritans wore special clothing consisting of a long-sleeved white *tallit* over a striped robe. In the synagogue which points toward Mount Gerizim, worshippers removed their shoes before entering, wore head coverings, and stood on rugs spread on the floor. After the service a portion of the law was read at home by the head of the household. On the Sabbath, Samaritans did not light fires or travel; their meals were prepared beforehand on the Sabbath eve when they lit the Sabbath candles. The priests in the communities wore white mitres, as opposed to red ones which were worn during the week; they also led services and religious rites and opened the reading of the *Torah* portion.

In addition to Sabbath observance, Samaritans also celebrated the other festivals recorded in Scripture. For the Samaritan community the Passover, which takes place on the fifteenth day of the first month of the Samaritan calendar, was of central significance. On the eve of the festival, the

Samaritans carried out the sacrifice of the pascal lamb on Mount Gerizim. At twilight on the fourteenth day of the first month all members of the community gathered at the site of the altar in two groups; the first carried out the sacrifice and the second engaged in prayer. The High Priest then climbed on a large stone and gave the signal to slaughter the sheep while reading the account of the Exodus from Egypt. Then a number of sheep corresponding to the families present was slaughtered.

Another festival of major significance is *Shavuot*, when the Samaritans made a pilgrimage to Mount Gerizim. This holiday was celebrated on the fiftieth day of the counting of the *Omer*. The period is divided into seven weeks, on each the Samaritans devoted the Sabbath to one of the places that children of Israel passed on the Exodus from Egypt before arriving at Mount Sinai. On the first day after the sixth Sabbath, the Samaritans celebrated the day standing on Mount Sinai – there they prayed and read from the Pentateuch from the middle of the night until the following evening. The seventh Sabbath is called the celebration of the Ten Commandments. The pilgrimage itself began early in the evening and all places holy to the Samaritans were visited.

The Samaritan community also celebrated the Day of Awe which took place on the first day of the seventh month; at the close of the day the prayers of the Ten Days of Repentance were recited each evening and morning until the Day of Atonement which began during the late afternoon; the fast continued for twenty-five to twenty-six hours accompanied by prayer and there was continuous reading from the Pentateuch as well as the recitation of *piyyutim*. This festival was followed by *Sukkot* when the Samaritans cut palm branches, hung citrus fruit from the net roof, and suspended willow branches from the roof. The *sukkah* itself was located inside the house – the eve of *Sukkot* was devoted to building this structure, and on the morning of the holiday the Samaritans made a pilgrimage to Mount Gerizim. *Shemini Azeret* commenced on the twenty-second day of the seventh month and is also referred to as *Simhat Torah*. After prayers which took place from midnight and continued for more than ten hours, the priest carried the *Torah* around the synagogue.

In addition to these biblically based festivals, the Samaritans scrupulously followed the numerous practices outlined in Scripture. Regarding circumcision, for example, the Samaritans were obliged to circumcise their sons at the age of eight days. The High Priest officiated at this ceremony which took place following morning prayer. Laws of ritual purity were also followed rigorously within the Samaritan community. After a woman's menstrual period, she was obliged to separate herself from her family and was forbidden to touch utensils; anything she sat on was to be rinsed with water. On the seventh day she was to bathe in water, thereby becoming clean at sundown. Men who become unclean through a nocturnal emission were obligated to wash their bodies in water. During this period such individuals were to sit during prayers in a special place outside the worshipper's hall and were forbidden to raise their voice or touch holy articles until evening. Samaritan law also decreed that a woman who gives birth to a son was unclean for forty days or eighty days for a daughter. The redemption of a circumcised first born son took place only after the mother was cleansed of impurity.

In accordance with Samaritan law, the Samaritan's coming of age ceremony was dependent on education and ability. Only after a boy had learned the entire Pentateuch could the ceremony be arranged. In anticipation of this event, the father took his son to the scholar of the community or to one of the priests for schooling in the Samaritan traditions. The child studied the Pentateuch in ancient Hebrew script and in the Samaritan pronunciation; in addition he learned to write. Some children were able to complete the reading of the Pentateuch by the age of six; others continued until the age of ten. When completing the reading, the child learned the blessing of Moses (Deut. 33–4) by heart. The father then gathered all the Samaritans to the place of rejoicing; the child stood in the centre on a high chair, recited the blessing of Moses, and delivered a speech. He then descended from the chair, kissed the priests and other dignitaries' hands, and received gifts. Having completed this ritual, he was regarded as one of the quorum needed for communal prayer. On the following Sabbath after prayers he read a portion of the Pentateuch after the high priest – this was followed by a feast.

Another major life-cycle event regulated by Samaritan law was betrothal and marriage. The proposal (*kiddushin*) was the first of the three stages in marriage. When a Samaritan girl was certain whom she would marry, she asked the youth to request his parents ask her parents for her hand. Once asked, the girl's parents reply 'We will call the damsel and inquire at her mouth' (Gen. 24.57). The girl then appointed a guardian to perform the betrothal ceremony which took place in the girl's home. The second stage, *erusin*, occurred a short time after *kiddushin*. At this ceremony representatives took the place of the girl. The participants clasped right hands as a sign of the bond. The high priest placed his right hand upon their clasped hands and pronounced the *erusin* blessings. He then received a tied handkerchief containing six shekels from the young man and handed them to the girl's representatives as a symbol of the dowry. Marriage (*nissuin*) then took place as the final stage of this process. A week of rejoicing was followed by the wedding. During the day the bridegroom and guests awaited the coming of the bride. On her arrival, the groom handed the marriage contract to the high priest and kissed his right hand. The priest read it; the groom then turned to the bride, lifted her veil, kissed her, and placed a ring upon the finger of her hand. Sometimes they strengthened the bond by drinking wine from the same cup. During the following Sabbath prayers, songs referring to marriage were added, and the groom read the weekly portion of the law. This was followed by a meal which concluded the week of marriage.

In the Samaritan community, divorce was permitted. Three causes were recognized as valid: (1) abominable practices committed by either party or together; (2) quarrelling that makes life intolerable; (3) immorality. In any of these cases the cause had to be confirmed by two or three witnesses. The high priest then imposed upon applicants a period of appeasement of at least a year; if all efforts failed, the couple went to the house of the high priest with several relatives. The high priest then read the bill of divorce before the couple, tore the marriage contract, and removed their rings. A divorced woman was not allowed to remarry her husband if either party married after the divorce. The guilty party was obliged to pay any damages as fixed by the high priest.

Mourning and burial were also regulated by Samaritan law. The Samaritans buried their dead in the cemetery on Mount Gerizim. After death, the mourners read the Pentateuch all night; on the next morning they washed the corpse. They then placed the body in a coffin and transported it to the burial ground. The high priest recited a eulogy over the dead person (without making himself ritually unclean by touching the body). When the burial party returned from the cemetery, a family unrelated to the dead hosted a meal of consolation. Samaritans mourned for the dead for seven days, but they did not stay indoors for this period. Instead they visited the grave and delivered memorial addresses every morning and evening. On the seventh day the mourning was completed, and at the end of thirty days the relatives of the dead invited the Samaritans to a memorial meal. On the Sabbath the entire Pentateuch was recited in the home of the relatives of the dead; this was repeated daily in order to purify the soul of the departed. For a year after the death, no festivity was to take place in the deceased's house. At the recital of the *piyyutim* of the festival when the prayers were completed, the high priest recited *Kaddish* for the exaltation of souls before the community of Israel who prostrated themselves before the holiest of mountains, Mount Gerizim.

Turning to the literature of the Samaritan community, the earliest work was the Pentateuch, which is the centre of Samaritan life. The *Defter* constituted the oldest part of the liturgy and was probably written in the fourth century AD. There were also a number of Samaritan chronicles including the *Asatir*, a midrash work, and *Al-Tolidah* which contained various genealogical lists. The Samaritan *Book of Joshua* recounted the history of the Samaritan people from the initiation of Joshua to the days of Baba Rabbah. The *Annals* by Abu al-Fath were composed in the fourteenth century and were explained in the nineteenth to twentieth centuries by Jacob ben Harun. The *New Chronicle* was written in Samaritan Hebrew by Av-Sakhva ben Asad ha-Danfi and related events from Adam to AD 1900. The Samaritan corpus also included a variety of halakhic works, Pentateuch commentaries, and grammatical studies. In all cases Samaritan literature was centred around the Pentateuch and the religious life of the community. The purpose of these works was to guide the community in understanding the meaning of Scripture, insuring that the biblical precepts were fulfilled in the lives of the adherents. This traditional religious orientation illustrates the traditionalism of the Samaritan sect despite its deviation from mainstream Judaism. Holding fast to the religious tenets of the faith, the Samaritans strictly adhered to the Jewish way of life as they understood it. In this respect they should be viewed as an authentic form of Judaism despite their divergence from the rabbis. Throughout their history the Samaritan community was committed to observing the law and fulfilling their convenantal duties – in this respect they were an expression of diversity within a unified religious system.

Sadducees, Pharisees, Essenes and Rebels

According to the first-century AD historian Josephus, the three most important Jewish groups of the Hellenistic period were the Sadducees, Pharisees and Essenes. In his writings, Josephus asserted that the Sadducees and the Pharisees disagreed about the resurrection of the dead: the Sadducees maintained that the soul survives death whereas the Pharisees asserted that the soul of the righteous pass into another body. In addition, these two sects differed about free will and fate – the Sadducees denied that life was preordained whereas the Pharisees subscribed to a belief in both fate and freedom of choice. Finally, there was a fundamental difference of opinion between the Sadducees and the Pharisees concerning the interpretation of biblical law.

The term 'Sadducee' appears to have been derived from the Hebrew name of Zadok, the priest who lived during the time of David and Solomon. In the post-Maccabean period the Sadducees consisted largely of upper-class Judeans who supported the Temple priesthood as the highest religious authority and adhered to the literal meaning of the Pentateuch. The term 'Pharisee' on the other hand comes from the Hebrew *parash* meaning 'separated'. It may be that this term was applied to the Pharisees because they distanced themselves from the populace; alternatively they could have been given this name by their opponents who asserted that they had separated themselves from the Sadducean understanding of Scripture. In any event, the Pharisees were skilled in Scriptural exegesis and possessed a body of oral tradition. As Josephus explained:

> The Pharisees have passed down to the people certain regulations handed down by former generations and not recorded in the laws of Moses, for which reason they are rejected by the Sadducean group, who hold that only those regulations should be considered valid which were written down, and that those which had not been handed down by former generations need not be observed.
> (Antiquities, XIII, 297)

In rabbinic sources Pharisaic scholars were referred to initially as the 'men of the Great Assembly'. Later there was a chain of five generations of outstanding Pharisaic sages (*zugot*) – these individuals were the leaders of the Pharisaic supreme court until the first century AD. Josephus first mentioned the Pharisees as having been closely associated with the Hasmonean ruler John Hyrcanus. When they challenged his priestly legitimacy, he favoured the Sadducees. Subsequently during the civil war which took place during the reign of Alexander Janneus, the Pharisees joined the enemies of the king and a large number were executed. Under Salome Alexandra, however, the Pharisees were able to avenge the Sadducees. Josephus recorded that there were about six thousand Pharisees during the reign of King Herod. After his death a segment of the Pharisees which was opposed to Roman rule separated to become a distinct sect; the rest appear to have accepted the loss of Judean political independence.

By the second or third decade of the Common Era, the Pharisees divided into two groups: the school of Hillel and the school of Shammai. In rabbinic sources, Hillel was portrayed as responsible for introducing the use of hermeneutic rules of

interpretation which allowed Scriptural law to be applied to
new circumstances. Hillel's seven rules were subsequently
expanded in the second century AD by R. Ishamel ben Elisha
into thirteen (by sub-dividing some of them, omitting one, and
adding a new one of his own).

The first rule (the inference from minor and major) states
that if a certain restriction applies to a matter of minor
importance, we may infer that the same restriction is
applicable to a matter of major importance. Conversely, if a
certain allowance is applicable to a thing of major importance,
we may infer that the same allowance pertains to that which is
of comparatively minor importance. In the *Mishnah*, for
example, we read that the Sabbath is in some respects
regarded as being of more importance than a common
holiday. If, therefore, a certain kind of work is permitted on
the Sabbath, we may infer that such work is more permissible
on a common holiday; conversely, if a certain work is
forbidden on a common holiday, it must be all the more
forbidden on the Sabbath.

Another rule of exegesis (rule six) was intended to solve a
problem by means of a comparison with another passage in
Scripture. For example, in the *Talmud* the question why Moses
had to hold up his hands during the battle with Amalek
(Exod. 17.11) is answered by referrring to Numbers 21.8.
There the text states that in order to be cured from snakebite
the Israelites were to look at the fiery serpent raised up in the
wilderness. The hands of Moses could no more bring victory
than could the brass serpent cure those who had been bitten.
But the point is that, just as in the case of the fiery serpent, it
was necessary for the Israelites to lift up their hearts to God in
order to be saved.

These various methods of exegesis were based on the
conviction that the Bible is sacred, that it is susceptible to
interpretation and that, properly understood, it guides the life
of the worthy. By means of this process of explanation of God's
revelation, the rabbinic authorities were able to infuse the
tradition with new meaning and renewed relevance.

The dispute between the Sadducees and the Pharisees
revolved around their interpretation of the Pentateuch and

both these sects strove to win allegiance from the people. The Essenes, however, withdrew from society into small holy communities. Rejecting the priests who controlled the Temple cult as illegitimate, they believed in fate and the immortality of the soul. Initially this group existed as separatist associations in the towns of Judea and in communes. Living in a highly disciplined manner, they strove to achieve ritual purity and perfection. Admission to this group could only take place after a period of preparation. Initiates were obliged to swear obedience to the rules and leadership of the community and promise to keep secret its special doctrines. Property was jointly owned, and food, clothing and other goods were administered by guardians. Essene rituals included wearing white garments, frequent ritual baths, and communal meals accompanied by prayer and the recitation of the *Torah*. According to Josephus, the Essenes numbered about four thousand, and Essene holy men were venerated by the masses.

In the view of most scholars the Dead Sea Scrolls were produced by the Essene community and, therefore, provide a basis for understanding the beliefs and practices of this monastic sect. According to the Scrolls, the Qumran community was dominated by a priesthood who viewed the Temple as controlled by wicked individuals. It appears that Qumran was founded by a priestly 'Teacher of Righteousness' who was persecuted by a 'Wicked Priest'. The members of the sect considered themselves the true heirs of the covenant to whom the promises in the Bible would be fulfilled. Further, they believed they had been saved from evil powers in order to settle in the wilderness as a holy society under the leadership of their holy priests until they could return to a purified Temple cult. As members of a new covenant, the Qumran community constituted the elect (the Sons of Light) in opposition to the Sons of Darkness. Eventually, they believed, the Sons of Light would engage in ritual combat under their leaders to re-establish the remnant of Israel in the Holy Land and witness God's victory over all peoples.

A fourth group which flourished during this period were rebels who sought to overthrow Roman rule. In AD 6, Judas the Galilean and Zadok the Pharisee, encouraged other Jews to refuse to pay taxes to the empire. As Josephus related, they constituted a 'fourth philosophy' alongside the Sadducees, Pharisees and Essenes:

> This school agrees in all other respects with the opinions of the Pharisees except that they have a passion for liberty that is almost unconquerable, since they are convinced that God alone is their leader and master. They think little of submitting to death in unusual forms and permitting vengeance to fall on kinsmen and friends, if only they may avoid calling any man master. (Antiquities, XVIII, 23)

In about AD 46 two of Judas' sons were crucified by the Romans, and in 66 another son (or grandson) Menahem, seized the fortress of Masada. During the war against Rome, Menahem was assasinated in Jerusalem by hostile rebels. Under the leadership of Eleazar, those who inhabited Masada remained there until AD 74, when they martyred themselves before the Romans were able to capture their stronghold. After the war, some of those who belonged to this fourth sect escaped to Egypt and Crene when they refused to acknowledge Caesar's lordship. Those who belonged to this 'fourth philosophy' adopted a range of positions along the political spectrum. In the winter of 67–68 AD, a group known as the Zealots emerged in Jerusalem; this group attracted a following from among the priesthood. Another force consisting largely of free slaves became followers of the military leader, Simon bar Giora. During the first century AD these, and other groups, were continually at odds with one another except when they united in the face of the Roman onslaught.

The fragmentation of the Jewish people into these four distinct groups might suggest that in ancient times deep religious divisions existed in the Jewish community. Yet, despite the divergencies between Sadducees, Pharisees, Essenes and Rebels, the members of all these groups subscribed to the central principles of the Jewish faith and were united in their dedication to Jewish law. Each of these sects affirmed a belief in the one Lord of creation who sustains the universe and guides it to its completion. Like the Samaritans, the Sadducees dedicated themselves to the scriptural text which they believed provides the authoritative foundation for

Jewish life. As God's revelation to Moses on Mount Sinai the Five Books of Moses, they believed, should guide the life of the faithful. Although the Pharisees were anxious to make biblical law applicable to contemporary circumstances, they too, felt bound by scriptural teaching. In their view the Oral law had also been commanded to Moses when he received the written commandments; none the less, like the Sadducees they were bound by scriptural teaching no matter how interpreted. Similarly, the Essenes – despite their renunciation of the Jewish community – remained loyal to the covenant, believing themselves to be the true interpreters of God's will. Further, in line with these three groups, those who espoused rebellion against Rome were religiously pious – they too, accepted God's authority as recorded in Scripture. Thus, despite the differing orientations in these Jewish sects in the Greco-Roman world, they were based on a common heritage. Here too, was exhibited unity within diversity as Jews struggled to survive in a religiously and politically plural world.

Karaites

During the eighth century, messianic movements appeared in the Persian Jewish community which led to armed uprisings against Muslim authorities. Such revolts were quickly crushed, but an even more serious threat to traditional Jewish life was posed later in the century by the emergence of an anti-rabbinic sect, the Karaites. This group was founded in Babylonia in the 760s by Anan ben David, who had earlier been passed over as exilarch, and traced its origin to the time of Jeroboam in the eighth century BC. According to some scholars, Anan's movement absorbed elements of an extra-talmudic tradition and took over doctrines from Islam. The guiding interpretative principle formulated by Anan, 'Search thoroughly in Scripture and do not rely on my opinion', was intended to point to Scripture itself as the sole source of law. Jewish observances, the Karaites insisted, must conform to biblical legislation rather than rabbinic ordinances. Anan, however, was not lenient concerning legal matters. He did not, for example, recognize the minimum quantities of forbidden foods fixed by the rabbis; in addition, he introduced more complicated regulations for circumcision, added to the number of fast days, interpreted the prohibition of work on the Sabbath in stricter terms than the rabbis, and extended the prohibited degrees of marriage. In short, he made the yoke of the law more burdensome.

After Anan's death, the next important figure in the history of the movement was Benjamin of Nahawend in Persia who composed several law books. In his writing in the second quarter of the ninth century, he used the term 'Karaite' to designate followers of the Bible in contrast with 'Rabbinates' who adhered to the rabbinic tradition. According to Benjamin, individuals should be able to decide for themselves which practices are implied by legislation recorded in Scripture – personal freedom thereby became a central principle of the Karaite groups established in Palestine, Iraq and Persia. The adherents of Anan were referred to as 'Ananites' and remained few in number. In the first half of the century the Ukarite sect was established by Ishmael of Ukbara (near Baghdad); some years later another sect was formed in the same town by Mishawayh Al-Ukbari. Another group was formed by a contemporary of Mishawayh, Abu Imram Al-Tiflisi. In Israel, yet another sect was established by Malik Al-Ramli. By the end of the ninth century, Karaism had become a conglomerate of groups advocating different anti-rabbinic positions, but these sects were short-lived and in time the Karaites consolidated into a uniform movement. By the tenth century a number of Karaite communities were established in Israel, Iraq and Persia. These groups rejected rabbinic law and devised their own legislation which led eventually to the foundation of a Karaite rabbinical academy in Jerusalem; the Karaite community there produced some of the most distinguished scholars of the period who composed legal handbooks, wrote biblical commentaries, expounded on Hebrew philology and engaged in philosophical and theological reflection.

During this period the Karaites sought converts to their movement and attacked the Rabbinates. An impassioned letter by a Jerusalem Karaite who travelled throughout the

disapora to seek new members illustrates the religious fervour
and dedication of this new sect:

> This is the practice of Karaite Israelites who have sought God's
> pleasure and secluded themselves from the desires of this world.
> They have given up eating meat and drinking wine and have clung
> to the Lord's Law and have stood in assiduous watch before the
> doors of his Temple. Because of the greatness of their grief and the
> depth of their sighing, they have lost their strength to stand up
> against all stumbling blocks, and the skin of their bodies has
> become wrinkled with premature senility. Yet not withstanding all
> this, they forsook not their goal, nor did they relinquish their hope;
> rather they continued to read the Law and interpret it, acting as
> both teachers and pupils, turning people away from evildoing, and
> saying, 'O all ye who are thirsty, come ye who are thirsty, come ye
> to the water! . . . May God fulfil regarding them his promise to
> turn the ashes covering heads of Zion's mourners into an
> ornament of splendour . . . In God's mighty Name have I come to
> awaken the hearts of his people of Israel; to turn them back to the
> Law of the Lord; to arouse their conscience and their thoughts to
> the fear of their God; to make them dread the Day of Judgment,
> which is coming with terror and wrath, and the day of the Lord's
> vengeance upon those who forsake his law; and to warn them not
> to rely upon ordinances contributed by men and learned by rote
> . . . How can I fail to do so, when my bowels cry out within my
> belly and my kidneys are consumed within my bosom for pity for
> my brethren and for the children of my people? Many of them
> have been forced to put a great distance between themselves and
> the Lord and to walk in a way which is not good, because of their
> leaders (rabbis) who oppress them remorselessly . . . Whosoever
> does not give according to their demand? They wage holy war
> against him; they subjugate and tyrannize him by means of bans
> and excommunications and by recourse to the gentile officials.
> They punish the poor by forcing them to borrow at a high rate of
> interest and make payment to them. (Nemoy, 1952, 113–15)

For the Karaites the Bible served as the foundation of the
faith. All religious beliefs stem from this basis. Because of the
Karaites' adherence to Scripture, the principles of Karaism
were essentially the same as rabbinic Judaism. According to
the fifteenth-century scholar Elijah Bashyazi and his pupil
Caleb Afendopolo, the Karaite creed consists of ten central
tenets: (1) God created the universe out of nothing; (2) the

Creator was not created; (3) He is an absolute unity,
incorporeal, formless and incomparable to anything; (4) He
sent Moses as his prophet; (5) He revealed the *Torah* to
Moses which cannot be altered or complemented by other
laws; (6) every believer must know the *Torah* in the original
language as well as its proper meaning; (7) God revealed
himself to other prophets; (8) God will resurrect the dead on
the Day of Judgment; (9) God rewards each person according to his actions; (10) God does not despise those in exile;
rather he seeks to purify them through suffering, and they
should hope for his help daily and redemption through the
Messiah.

Just as these beliefs are grounded in the Bible, so are
Karaite practices based on Scripture. All prescriptions derive
from the biblical text based on the literal meaning of
the words. Tradition is accepted only in so far as it is
indispensable in applying the precepts, clarifying ambiguities
in the law, or making up for deficiencies in the details of
specific provisions. In this regard some rabbinic laws are
accepted as clarifying prescriptions – yet for the rest each
person must study Scripture for himself and be guided by his
knowledge and conscience. Initially the individualist trend
predominated in Karaite circles. Eventually, however,
Karaite doctrine underwent a process of systemization and a
number of principles were established as norms in interpreting the law: (1) the literal meaning of the text; (2) the
consensus of the community; (3) conclusions derived from
the Scripture by means of logical analogy; (4) knowledge
based on reason. Eventually the twelfth-century scholar
Judah Hadassi established approximately eighty hermen-
eutical rules; the most frequently used were; (1) analogous
interpretation of juxtaposed words and passages; (2) infer-
ences drawn *a fortiori*; (3) interpreting a general principle on
the basis of individual examples; (4) extensive interpretation
of a notion; (5) rules for the interpretation of special words
and grammatical forms.

Like rabbinic Judaism, Karaism did not contain a fixed
number of precepts; none the less Karaism was grounded in
biblical law. Regarding the Holy Days, the Karaites

stipulated that the New Year Festival may begin on any day of the week – as a consequence the Karaite Day of Atonement does not always coincide with the rabbinic celebration; Passover and *Sukkot* are observed for only seven days; *Shavuot* falls on the fiftieth day following the Sabbath of the Passover week; *Hanukkah* and the fast of Esther are not recognized although *Purim* is celebrated; the Fast of Gedaliah is observed on the twenty-fourth day of *Tishri*; other fast days are observed on different days from rabbinic fasts. Special rules also apply to the Sabbath and prohibitions of work extend beyond the thirty-nine actions prescribed by the rabbis. Concerning circumcision, the Karaites rejected various practices, and differed on certain aspects of ritual slaughter. In this connection the biblical prohibition of boiling a kid in its mother's milk was also understood by the Karaites as forbidding the consumption of meat with milk products, however they did not accept additional rabbinic restrictions. Further, Karaites permitted the eating of meat of only those animals mentioned in the Bible, and rejected the criteria for permitted mammals and birds as proposed by the *Talmud*.

Karaite laws regarding the prohibited degrees of consanguinity were especially severe. During the early period, even the most remote form of consanguinity was prohibited – this resulted in the near extinction of the community. Such a situation resulted from the acceptance of the *rikkuv* theory (based on the assumption that man and woman form a unity of flesh); on this basis it was assumed that persons related by marriage are also blood relations. Such a theory of incest, however, was rejected by Joseph ben Abraham ha-Kohen ha-Roeh al-Basir and his pupil Jeshua ben Judah and replaced by a less stringent law consisting of several regulations. The first states that according to the Bible and tradition 'blood relatives' for a man are father and mother, brother and sister, and their blood relatives (the father's or mother's sister, the son's daughter and the daughter's daughter and by analogy the brother's daughter). The corresponding relatives are regarded as prohibited for a woman. Another regulation forbids marriage between two blood relatives and two other blood relatives. The final regulation prohibits marriage between two blood relatives and two blood relatives once removed. Moreover, any prohibition which applies to one person also applies to all his blood relatives. Again, the Karaite regulations concerning the impurity of the menstruation period are more strict than those fixed by the rabbis.

The Karaite liturgy, which originally consisted solely of biblical psalmody, bears little relation with the rabbinic counterpart. In Karaite practice there were morning and evening prayer services each day. On the Sabbath and holy days the *musaf* prayer and other prayers were included. Initially the prayers relating to the Temple service served as the basis of the Karaite ritual. Prayers were either short or long, but they consisted of seven parts (*shevahim, hodaah, viddui, bakkashah, tehinnah, zeakah* and *keriah*) and the confession of faith. Karaite prayers consisted primarily of passages from the Bible as well as prayer poems. In the Karaite rite, the *Shema* is included; the *Amidah* is unknown; and the *haftarot* selection differs from the rabbinic order. During services Karaites wear *tzizit*, but the biblical prescriptions concerning *tefillin* were regarded as fugurative and the regulation concerning their use in rabbinic sources were therefore rejected.

Thus, although Karaites differed from the Rabbinates over the authority of post-biblical law, the Karaite community subscribed to the central teachings of the faith. For the Karaites as for the Samaritans and Sadducees the *Torah* was binding – in their view, God revealed the Written Law to Moses on Mount Sinai and as a consequence scriptural testimony about God's nature and activity as well as the legal code in the Bible function as the framework for Karaite life. Therefore, even though Karaites constituted a distinct sect separate from rabbinic Judaism, they stood within the tradition. For this reason a number of rabbinic authorities sought to stem rabbinic hostility directed towards members of this group. Maimonides, for example, wrote that the Karaites 'should be treated with respect, honour, kindness and humility, as long as they ... do not ... slander the authorities of the *Mishnah* and the *Talmud*. They may be associated with, and one may enter their homes, circumcise their children, bury their dead, and comfort their mourners' (*Encyclopaedia Judaica*, 1972, Vol. 10, 782).

The Shabbetean Movement

By the beginning of the seventeenth century, Lurianic mysticism had made a major impact on Sephardic Jewry, and messianic expectations had also become a central feature of Jewish life. In this milieu the arrival of a self-proclaimed messianic king, Shabbetai Tzevi, brought about a transformation of Jewish life and thought. Born in Smyrna into a wealthy family, Shabbetai had received a traditional Jewish education and later engaged in study of the *Zohar*. After leaving Smyrna in the 1650s he spent ten years in various cities in Greece as well as in Istanbul and Jerusalem. Eventually he became part of a kabbalistic group in Cairo and travelled to Gaza where he encountered Nathan Benjamin Levi who believed Shabbetai was the Messiah.

In 1665, Nathan proclaimed Shabbetai's Messiahship and sent letters to Jews in the diaspora asking them to repent and recognize Shabbetai Tzevi as their redeemer. In this correspondence he declared that the moment had arrived when there were no holy sparks left under the dominion of the *kelippot*, the powers of evil. According to Nathan, Shabbetai would take the crown from the Ottoman sultan, restore the lost tribes, and triumph in the final calamities that would accompany the birth pangs of the Messiah. As a consequence, special prayers were composed for the fasts proclaimed as preparations for these events. In Nathan's view, it was imperative that Jews throughout the world acknowledge this event otherwise they would be punished with divinely prescribed afflictions.

While Nathan was engaged in this activity, Shabbetai resided briefly in Jerusalem where he gained support from various quarters even though a number of prominent rabbis rejected his claims. He then travelled to Aleppo where a wave of prophesying seized the Jewish population. Just before *Rosh Hashanah* he arrived in Izmir and several months later entered the synagogue during *Hanukkah* wearing royal clothing. Not all were convinced by his claims, however, and the community divided into Shabbetai's followers and those whom the devout referred to as 'infidels' (*kofrim*). Subsequently Shabbetai broke into the Portuguese synagogue on the Sabbath and declared that he was the Anointed of the God of Jacob; he denounced the disbelievers among the congregation and distributed kingdoms to his disciples. This act evoked hysteria – the mass fell into trances and reported visions of him established on a royal throne crowned as King of Israel.

Following these events, Shabbetai travelled to Istanbul. On his arrival in February, 1666, he was arrested by the grand vizier and incarcerated in prison. During this time the sultan and the vizier were engaged in a war with Venice, and Shabbetai was later transferred to the fortress of Gallipoli on the European side of the Dardanelles. During the next few months, the prison became Shabbetai's court, and was visited by pilgrims from throughout the world who joined in messianic rituals and engaged in acts of penance and mortification. News of the arrival of the Messiah spread throughout the diaspora and hymns were composed in Shabbetai's honour. In addition, new festivals were proclaimed which were followed by the transformation of the Fast of *Av* into a celebration of Shabbetai's birth. During the summer of 1666, Nathan, who had remained in Gaza, explained that the alternation of Shabbetai's mood from excitation to withdrawal was symptomatic of an interior struggle with the demonic powers which at certain times overwhelmed him. At other times Shabbetai was able to conquer them.

The same year, Shabbetai spent three days with the Polish kabbalist, Nehemiah ha-Kohen, who later denounced him to the Turkish authorities. Shabbetai was brought to court and given the choice between death or conversion. Faced with this alternative, he converted to Islam and assumed the name Mehemet Effendi. Several of the believers who had accompanied him also converted as did his wife when she arrived in Gallipoli some time later. Such an act of apostasy scandalized most of his followers, but he defended himself by asserting that he had become a Muslim in obedience to God's commands. Many of his followers accepted this explanation and refused to give up their belief. Some thought it was not Shabbetai who had become a Muslim but rather a phantom who had taken on his appearance; the Messiah himself has ascended to heaven. Others cited biblical and rabbinic sources to justify Shabbetai's action.

Following Shabbetai's conversion to Islam, Nathan of Gaza attempted to defend his behaviour. According to Nathan, Shabbetai's apostasy should be understood as the fulfilment of a mission to lift up the holy sparks which were dispersed among the gentiles and had become concentrated in the Islamic faith. Although the task of the nation had been to restore the sparks of their own souls in the process of cosmic restoration (*tikkun*), there remained sparks which only the Messiah could redeem. To accomplish this task, Shabbetai was compelled to descend into the realm of the *kelippah* – in this process he had to submit to the domination of the evil realm but simultaneously struggled to vanquish the *kelippot*. The kabbalistic explanation of Shabbetai's conversion was linked to Nathan's earlier exposition of Shabbetai's struggle with evil. Thus the image of an apostate Messiah became the central theme of this new conception of messianic deliverance. To justify this interpretation, Nathan, as well as other followers of Shabbetai, searched the Bible as well as rabbinic sources for references to such a paradoxical role. As a result, the objectionable actions of biblical heroes came to be interpreted as a foretaste of Shabbetai's action, and passages in the *aggadah* and *Zohar* were interpreted as pointing to his scandalous behaviour.

From 1667 to 1668 messianic enthusiasm ebbed. When Nathan attempted to see Shabbetai in Adrianople, he was confronted by a group of rabbis who compelled him to abandon this quest. None the less Nathan succeeded in visiting Shabbetai and continued to declare him as the Messiah. At Shabbetai's request, Nathan travelled to Rome in order to perform magic rituals to bring about the fall of the papacy. Later, when Nathan arrived in Venice his presence created a sensation and the rabbis published a pamphlet depicting the interrogations in Ipsala and Venice when it was claimed Nathan admitted his errors. Such charges, however, were repudiated by Nathan and he continued to attract considerable support. Eventually he returned to the Balkans where he spent the rest of his life.

Meanwhile Shabbetai lived in Adrianople and Constantinople until 1672. Leading a double life, he performed the duties of Islam while observing Jewish law. Although the Turkish authorities expected him to act as a missionary, he admonished his followers to engage in combat against the *kelippah*. During this period Shabbetai alternated between periods of illumination and depression, yet he instituted new festivals, affirmed his messianic mission, and persuaded his followers to practise Islam which he referred to as the '*Torah* of grace'. In one report about his erratic behaviour, it was alleged that he divorced his wife but took her back even though he had made arrangements for another marriage.

Although the Shabbeteans continued to flourish in the Balkans and Asiatic Turkey, they were eventually driven underground. Shabbetai himself enjoyed the sultan's favour and established relationships with Muslim mystics. Letters between his group and believers in North Africa, Italy and elsewhere spread Shabbetean theological ideas. In August 1672, however, Shabbetai was arrested in Constantinople; the grand vizier considered executing him but instead exiled him to Dulcigno in Albania. Although he was allowed considerable freedom, he disappeared from public view though some supporters made pilgrimages to visit him. In 1674 his wife Sarah died and he married Esther, the daughter of Joseph Filosof, a rabbi of Salonika.

During the last years of his life Shabbetai revealed his understanding of the mystery of the Godhead. According to Shabbetai, the God of Israel was not the *Ayn Sof* but a second cause dwelling within the *sefirah* '*Tiferet*'. This distinction implied that the *Ayn Sof* has no providence over creation; this is exercised only by the God of Israel who came into being after the act of divine contraction (*tzimtzum*). Although the God of Israel was emanated from the *Ayn Sof*, he is the true

God of religion. The *Ayn Sof*, however, is irrelevant from a religious standpoint. Before his death Shabbetai formulated a more elaborate version of this doctrine. In the *Raza di-Meheimanuta*, he depicted a kabbalistic trinity referred to as the 'three bonds of the faith', consisting of the Ancient Holy One, the God of Israel, and the *Shekhinah*. In addition, during this period Shabbetai continued to believe in himself as the Messiah. On Shabbetai's death, Nathan declared that this event were merely an 'occultation' and that Shabbetai had actually ascended to the supernal lights.

In subsequent years a number of small Shabbetean groups flourished, especially in Salonika, Izmir and Istanbul. Although Nathan and others refrained from teaching that one should emulate the Messiah and abandon the laws of the *Torah*, a group in Salonika formed a sect known as the *Doenmeh*. This group professed Islam in public, but adhered to their own religious precepts in private. Marrying among themselves, they advanced antinomian ideals and deliberately flouted the sexual laws of Judaism as well as asserting that their leader Baruchiah Russo was divine in nature. In Italy there were also several secret Shabbetean circles which did not deviate from following the *halakhah*.

The most important Shabbetean group in Europe was formed by Jacob Frank in the eighteenth century. After living several years in Turkey where he had close relations with the *Doenmeh*, he returned to Poland and declared that he was the spiritual heir and reincarnation of Shabbetai Tzevi. According to Frank, the abandonment of the *Torah* was its true fulfilment. Persecuted by the rabbis for their orgiastic rites, Frank and his followers converted to Catholicism. This act of apostasy was encouraged by various Polish clerics until they discovered that Frank wished his sect to retain their separateness and remain loyal to him under a Christian guise. After an imprisonment of thirteen years, he established his sect in Moravia and later in Germany. In his teaching, Frank proclaimed that he was the representative of the second person of the Shabbetean trinity, teaching that true believers could pass through all religions and assume their outward appearance.

Despite these later Shabbetean developments which were a clear deviation from traditional Judaism, the earlier Shabbetean movement should be seen as an authentically Jewish development of the Jewish tradition. Isaac Luria's teaching in the sixteenth century intensified messianic expectations of the 1660s. For the Shabbeteans, Shabbetai Tzevi's arrival initiated the realization of Jewish longing through the ages. Shabbetai, they believed, was a fulfilment of ancient apocalyptic beliefs that had survived in talmudic and misrashic literature as well as in medieval apocalyptic tracts. In their view, God had initiated the long-awaited restoration of David's kingdom and the end of Israel's exile. Messianic hopes which were enshrined in daily prayers appeared at long last to have been achieved. Following Shabbetai's apostasy, the faithful continued to believe in his messiahship; in their explanation of this act, his disciples such as Nathan of Gaza used Lurianic motifs such as the ingathering of the sparks to explain his behaviour. Thus, Shabbeteanism, while provoking hostility from various quarters within the Jewish establishment should be seen as a manifestation of an ancient Jewish expectation radically interpreted in the light of kabbalistic notions.

Hasidism

During the second half of the eighteenth century, the authority of the Jewish communal structure was weakened by a series of developments. In 1764 the Council of the Four Lands and the Lithuanian Jewish Council were abolished; as a result the Polish government undertook to collect taxes from the Jewish population. Several years later, Russia, Austria and Prussia decreed that they would annex a large partition of Polish territory. In 1793 a second partition was carried out and after an outburst of Polish nationalism, a final partition occurred in 1795.

Although the Jewish *kehillah* system survived these partitions, its power was diminished and it was compelled to deal with the emergence of Hasidism, a popular spiritual movement which attracted thousands of followers. This new pietism was based on kabbalistic ideas and reinterpreted the role of the rabbi as a spiritual guide. It first appeared in the villages of the Polish Ukraine, especially Podolia where the Shabbetean Frankists had been active. According to tradition, Israel ben Eleazer, known as the Baal Shem Tov, was a folk-healer and wonder-maker. In his twenties he went with his wife to the Carpathian Mountains in Podolia where he cured the ill, practised exorcism, performed miracles and taught mystical doctrine. By the 1740s he attracted numerous followers. After his death in 1760 the leadership of this movement passed on to Dov Baer who resided in Mezhirech in Volhynia. Under his influence, followers of this sect settled in southern Poland, the Ukraine and Lithuania. By 1772 Hasidism came under attack and bitter feuds took place between the Hasidim and their opponents, the *Mitnagdim*. By the first quarter of the nineteenth century the movement had crystallized its pattern of organization into dynasties.

In the early stages of its evolution Hasidim reacted against current ascetic practices to achieve self-perfection. Such actions were witnessed by the eighteenth-century Jewish philosopher, Solomon Maimon:

Two or three instances, of which I was myself an eyewitness, will be sufficient to show what I mean. A Jewish scholar, well known on account of his piety, Simon of Lubtsch, had undergone the severest exercises of penance. He had already carried out the *teshuvat ha-kana* – the penance of *kana* – which consists in fasting daily and avoiding for supper anything that comes from a living being (flesh, milk, honey). He had also practised *glaut*, that is, a continuous wandering, in which the penitent is not allowed to remain two days in the same place; and, in addition, he had worn a hair shirt next to his skin. But he felt that he would not be doing enough for the satisfaction of his conscience unless he further observed the *teshuvat ha-mishkal* – the penance of weighing – which requires a particular form of penance proportionate to every sin. But as he found by calculation, that the number of his sins was too great to be atoned for in this way, he took it into his head to starve himself to death . . . Jossel of Klezk proposed nothing less than to hasten the advent of the Messiah. To this end he performed strict penance, fasted, rolled himself in the snow, undertook night-watches and similar severities. By all sorts of such operations he believed that he was able to accomplish the overthrow of a legion of evil spirits, who kept guard on the Messiah, and placed obstacles to his coming. (Maimon, 1954, 81–2)

In opposition to such ascetic practices, the Besht and his followers stressed that it was not necessary to be preoccupied with guilt and demonic forces. Further, they rejected excessive penance as well as melancholy. Embracing the Lurianic conception of the cosmos, they emphasized the omnipresence of God. As the divine sparks filled the world, they argued, there is no place where God is not present. According to some Hasidic teachers, the Lurianic conception of the *tzimtzum* should be understood as an apparent withdrawal of God from the Universe. In fact, however, divine light is everywhere – but it might be perceived as the spiritual reality behind the veil. Quoting the Besht, Jacob Joseph of Polonnoye stated: 'As I heard from my teacher: "In every one man's troubles, physical and spiritual, if he takes to heart that even in that trouble God himself is there, the garment is removed and the trouble is cancelled"' (Jacob Joseph of Polonnoye, 1954–5, 74a).

In the view of Hasidic sages, such as Dov Baer of Mezhirech, the highest aim of *devekut* (cleaving to God) in prayer is elimination of individual selfhood and the ascent of the soul to divine light. Again, Solomon Maimon gave an account of such religious intensity among the early Hasidim:

> Their worship consisted in a voluntary elevation above the body, that is, in abstracting their thoughts from all things except God, even from the individual self-denial arose among them which led them to ascribe, not to themselves, but to God alone, all the actions undertaken in this state. Their worship, therefore, consisted in speculative adoration, for which they held no special time or formula to be necessary, but they left each one to determine it according to the degree of his knowledge. Still they chose for it most commonly the hours set apart for the public worship of God. In their public worship they endeavoured to attain that elevation above the body which has been described; they became so absorbed in the idea of the divine perfection, they lost the idea of everything else, even of their own body, which became in this state wholly devoid of feeling. (Maimon, 1954, 171–2)

In attempting to achieve such a state of concentration, the Hasidim struggled to overcome distracting thoughts. This quest gave rise to the Hasidic doctrine of strange thoughts – these sinful impulses, they believed, do not have to be completely repressed since they contain a divine spark which can be released in order to thereby enable the faithful to come closer to God. As Jacob Joseph of Polonnoye stated:

> Behold I received from my teacher: When evil causes good, it becomes a footstool for the good and everything is completely good – which is almost the nullification of the *kelippot*, as in the future. Also there are deep matters here for the subject of strange thoughts ... I heard from my teacher: If some nullification of *Torah* or prayer happens to the complete man, he must understand that even here it is God's hand who thrusts him away in order to draw him closer, the secret meaning of 'His left hand is under my head and his right hand embraces me' (Song of Songs, 2.6). (Jacob Joseph of Polonnoye, 1954–5, 48b, 32a)

In the view of Beshtian Hasidim such *devekut* is attainable in secular affairs such as eating, drinking, business and even sexual relations. According to these pietists, material and bodily needs contain possibilities for making what is profane, holy. This conception gave rise to the Hasidic principle of 'worship through the physical'. A physcial act can be religious if one intends to cleave mentally to God in completing it. *Devekut* can, therefore, be attained in one's ordinary life and according to the person's capabilities.

The revitalization of Jewish life brought about by his new pietisic movement profoundly affected the Jewish masses. Unlike arid scholasticism practised by the rabbinical establishment, Hasidism offered a new outlet for religious fervour. The joy of carrying out the commandments and the intensity of worship involving singing and dancing appealed to many Jews who felt excluded from the scholarly circles that dominated the Jewish establishment. The main concern of these religiously active pietists was individual redemption. By denying the reality of evil and engendering devotion to God, Hasidism fostered widespread hope and optimism.

Connected with this Jewish revival was a reorientation of religious leadership. Critical of the religious establishment because it isolated scholars from the community, the Hasidim stated that all Jews are responsible for each other. Further, Hasidism offered a new conception of leadership based on the Lurianic notion of spiritually superior individuals who are able to attain a high level of *devekut*. This conception was institutionalized in the *zaddik*, a person of special spiritual gifts whose *devekut* is dependent on his followers. The task of the *zaddik* is to raise the souls of his followers towards the divine light – to do this he is compelled to descend from his own spiritual heights to the level of ordinary individuals. The *zaddik*'s duties involved pleading to God on behalf of his people, involving himself in the everyday affairs of his community, and counselling those who need help. The *zaddik* was the '*rebbe*' (an affectionate Yiddish term) rather than the more traditional image of the communal rabbi.

Despite such intimacy between the *rebbe* and his community, the *zaddik* was an authority figure invested with wide-ranging responsibility. Among the Hasidim faith in God entailed confidence in the miraculous powers of the *zaddik* who acted as his intercessor. For Hasidim, the biblical verse 'The righteous man is the foundation of the world' (Prov. 10.25) implied that the *zaddik* should be viewed as a channel through which divine grace flows downwards as well as the ladder by which individual souls are able to ascend to the higher realms. *Devekut* involves cleaving to the *zaddik* as well as God. Such reverence for the *rebbe* is enshrined in the Hasidic saying: 'I did not go to the Maggid of Mezhirech to learn *Torah* from him, but to watch him tie his bootlaces.' The *rebbe* was a saintly figure whose words of counsel, prayers and actions possessed spiritual and mystical significance.

In spite of such devotion to the *zaddik*, Hasidism encouraged individualism among the *zaddikim*. Thus Hasidic literature contains various tales about these spiritual leaders who espoused diverse doctrines and practices. Zsya of Hanipol, for example, was renowned for his innocence and humility; Shneur Zalman of Liady espoused an intellectual approach to Hasidic theology; Nahman of Bratzlav fostered a quasi-messianic conception of his role. As a result of this diversity, the *rebbes* developed traditions suited to their individual interests and attracted circles of disciples who made pilgrimages to their courts in the Ukraine and in Polish Galicia. In central Poland, *Habad* Hasidism emphasized the centrality of faith and talmudic study; Luvabich Hasidism in Lithuania, on the other hand, combined kabbalistic speculation and rabbinic scholarship.

Thus, regardless of the hostility generated by the emergence of this new spiritual movement among rabbinic authorities, the Hasidim were firmly within the boundaries of traditional Judaism. Like the *Mitnagdim*, they accepted the binding authority of the Written and Oral *Torah*. Loyal to the commandments, they rigorously observed the dictates of Jewish law. Further, the Hasidim were deeply influenced by Lurianic *kabbalah*, and formulated theories consonant with mystical teaching in midrashic and talmudic sources. Although they sought to distance themselves from what they perceived as the arid scholasticism of the rabbinic establishment, they remained faithful to the Jewish tradition.

Part II

NON-ORTHODOX JUDAISM

4

Reforming the Faith

The Enlightenment had a profound impact on Jewish life: no longer were Jews compelled to live an isolated existence in ghettos and shtetls. Instead they were increasingly accepted as free citizens in the countries where they lived. In this new milieu, advocates of Jewish Enlightenment such as Moses Mendelssohn encouraged fellow Jews to integrate into the mainstream of western European culture. Subsequently advocates of Jewish Enlightenment, the *maskilim*, attempted to reform Jewish education by widening the traditional curriculum in Jewish schools. In the wake of these cultural developments, reformers called for liturgical change in order to adapt Jewish worship to contemporary aesthetic standards. As a result of such reforming tendencies, a number of Jewish intellectuals founded the Society for the Culture and Academic Study of Judaism – the purpose of this approach to the past was to gain a true understanding of the evolution of the Jewish tradition. Despite Orthodox criticism of these developments, various reformers began to re-evaluate the Jewish faith and advocated major changes in Jewish belief and practice. To formulate a coherent policy, a series of Reform synods were held in various cities in Germany. In the United States reformers similarly promoted religious change, and in 1885 a formal list of Reform principles, the Pittsburgh Platform, was adopted by the movement. In the following years Reform Judaism underwent various changes which were reflected in a new declaration of principles, the Columbus Platform, endorsed by the movement in 1937. In contrast with the Pittsburgh Platform, this new declaration embraced

Zionist ideals and promoted the use of Hebrew as well as the retention of observances that had previously been rejected. After the Second World War, Reform Judaism continued to evolve as Reform belief and practice became increasingly diffuse. To bring a sense of order to the movement, the Central Conference of American Rabbis adopted a new platform, the San Francisco Platform, in 1971. Yet despite such a desire for unity, Reform Judaism through its history has distanced itself from traditional Orthodoxy, evolving a religious ideology far removed from the monolithic system of the past.

The Enlightenment

The roots of the Enlightenment go back to seventeenth-century Holland where a number of Jewish thinkers attempted to view the Jewish tradition in the light of the new scientific conception of the world. Uriel Acosta, for example, argued that the *Torah* was probably not of divine origin since it contains many features contrary to natural law. 'God, the creator of nature, cannot possibly have contradicted himself,' he wrote, 'which would have been the case had he given to men a rule of obedience contrary to that first law.'

The greatest of these Dutch Jewish thinkers was Baruch Spinoza, who published a treatise, *Tractatus Theologico-Politicus*, in which he rejected the medieval Jewish synthesis of faith and reason. In the first section of this work, Spinoza maintained that the prophets possessed moral insight rather than theoretical truth. Rejecting the Maimonidean belief that the Bible contains a hidden esoteric meaning, Spinoza argued that the Hebrew Scriptures were intended for the masses. God, he continued, was conceived as a lawgiver to appeal to the multitude; the function of biblical law was to ensure social stability. In addition, Spinoza asserted that God cannot be known through miraculous occurrences but only from the order of nature and from clear self-evident ideas. As far as the *Torah* is concerned, it was not composed in its entirety by Moses – the historical books were compilations assembled by many generations. Ezra, he believed, was responsible for harmonizing the discrepancies found in Scripture.

Such rational reflection about the foundations of the Jewish tradition provided the background to the philosophical enquiries of the greatest Jewish thinker of the Enlightenment, Moses Mendelssohn. Born in Dessau, Mendelssohn travelled to Berlin as a young student where he pursued secular as well as religious studies and befriended leading figures of the German Enlightenment, such as Gotthold Ephraim Lessing. Under Lessing's influence, Mendelssohn published a number of theological studies in which he argued for the existence of God and creation and propounded the view that human reason is able to discover the reality of God, divine providence and the immortality of the soul. When challenged by a Christian apologist to explain why he remained loyal to the Jewish faith, Mendelssohn published a defence of the Jewish religion, *Jerusalem*, or *On Religious Power and Judaism* in 1783. In this study Mendelssohn contended that no religious institution should use coercion. Addressing the question as to whether the Mosaic law sanctions such compulsion, Mendelssohn stressed that Judaism does not coerce the mind through dogma.

For Mendelssohn, Jewish law does not give power to the authorities to persecute individuals for holding false doctrines. Yet Jews, he argued, should not absolve themselves from following God's law: 'Adopt the mores and constitution of the country in which you find yourself,' he declared, 'but be steadfast in upholding the religion of your fathers, too . . . I cannot see how those who were born into the household of Jacob can in good conscience exempt themselves from the observance of the law' (Mendelssohn, 1969, 104–5). Thus despite Mendelssohn's recognition of the common links between Judaism and other faiths, he followed the traditions of his ancestors and advocated the retention of the distinctive features of the Jewish faith. By combining philosophical theism and Jewish traditionalism, Mendelssohn attempted to transcend the constrictions of ghetto life and enter the mainstream of western European culture as an observant Jew.

To bring about the modernization of Jewish life, Mendelssohn also translated the Pentateuch into German so that Jews would be able to learn the language of the countries in which they lived, and he spearheaded a commentary on

Scripture which combined Jewish scholarship with secular thought. Following Mendelssohn's example, a number of Prussian followers known as *maskilim* fostered the Jewish Enlightenment – the *Haskalah* – which encouraged Jews to abandon medieval patterns of life and thought. The *maskilim* also attempted to reform Jewish education by widening the curriculum to include several subjects; to further this end they wrote textbooks in Hebrew and established Jewish schools. The *maskilim* also produced the first Jewish literary magazine, *The Gatherer*, in 1783. Contributors to this publication wrote poems and fables in the classical style of biblical Hebrew and produced studies of biblical exegesis, Hebrew linguistics and Jewish history. By the second decade of the nineteenth century the *Haskalah* had spread to Bohemia, northern Italy and Galicia. During this period the journal, *First Fruits of the Times*, was published annually in Vienna between 1821 and 1832; this literary periodical included poetry, literature, philological studies, biography and satire. In 1830 the first Hebrew journal appeared which was devoted to modern Jewish scholarship.

From Germany and Galicia, the *Haskalah* spread to Russia. In Lithuania, European fiction and textbooks were translated into Hebrew; in addition, the first Hebrew novel was produced in 1854, and a number of Hebrew poets published lyrical poetry. Under Tsar Alexander II, several modern Hebrew weeklies appeared, and the Society for the Promotion of Culture among the Jews of Russia was founded in 1863. Later in the century a number of Hebrew writers, who had rejected the style of earlier *maskilim*, produced literary and social criticism. The nineteenth century thus witnessed an outpouring of Hebrew literature, promulgating the ideals of Jewish emancipation. These thinkers, however, were not typical of the Jewish masses. Many lived isolated lives because of their support of the Austrian and Russian governments' efforts to reform Jewish life. In addition, they were virulently critical of traditional rabbinic Judaism and so were regarded with suspicion and hostility by the religious establishment which endeavoured to perpetuate the faith of their fathers.

Political developments in central and eastern Europe during these decades of cultural ferment contributed to the emancipation of the Jewish community. After Napoleon's defeat and abdication, the map of Europe was redrawn by the Congress of Vienna between 1814 and 1815 and in addition the diplomats at the Congress issued a resolution that instructed the German confederation to ameliorate the status of the Jews. Yet despite this decree the German government disowned the rights of equality that had previously been granted to Jews by the French and instead imposed restrictions on residence and occupation. In place of the spirit unleashed by the French Revolution, Germany became increasingly patriotic and xenophobic. Various academics maintained that the Jews were Asiatic aliens and insisted that they could not enter into German–Christian culture without converting to Christianity – in 1819 Germany Jewry was attacked in cities and the countryside. After 1830, however, a more liberal attitude prevailed and various writers advocated a more tolerant approach. The most important Jewish exponent of emancipation, Gabriel Riesser, argued that the Jews were not a separate nation and were capable of loving Germany as their homeland. Jewish converts to Christianity such as Heinrich Heine and Ludwig Boerne, also defended the rights of Jews during this period.

The French Revolution of 1848 which led to outbreaks in Prussia, Austria, Hungary, Italy and Bohemia, forced rulers to grant constitutions which guaranteed freedom of speech, assembly and religion. In Germany, a National Assembly was convened to draft a constitution which included a bill of rights designating civil, political and religious liberty for all Germans. Although this constitution did not come into effect because the Revolution was suppressed, the 1850s and 1860s witnessed economic and industrial expansion in Germany in which liberal politicians advocated a policy of civil equality. In 1869 the parliament of the North German Federation proclaimed Jewish emancipation for all its constituents, and in 1871, when all of Germany excluding Austria became the German Reich under the Hohenzollern dynasty, Jewish emancipation was complete. All restrictions concerning professions, marriage, real estate and the right to vote were eliminated.

Compared with the west the social and political conditions of eastern European Jewry were less conducive to emancipation. After the partitions of Poland in the latter half of the eighteenth century and the decision of the Congress of Vienna to place the Duchy of Warsaw under Alexander I, most of Polish Jewry was under Russian rule. At the beginning of the nineteenth century, Russia preserved its previous social order: social classes were legally segregated; the aristocracy maintained its privileges; the peasantry lived as serfs; and the Church was under state control. In many towns and villages during this period Jews were in the majority and worked as leasers of estates, mills, forests, distilleries and inns, but increasingly many of these village Jews migrated to larger urban centres where they laboured as members of the working class. Despite this influx into the cities, the Jewish population retained its traditional religious and ethnic distinctiveness.

Initially, Catherine the Great exhibited tolerance towards her Jewish subjects, but in 1804 Alexander I specified territory in western Russia as an area in which Jews would be allowed to reside – the Pale of Settlement. After several attempts to expel Jews from the countryside, the Tsar in 1817 initiated a new policy of integrating the Jewish community in the population by founding a society of Israelite Christians which extended legal and financial concessions to baptized Jews. In 1824 the deportation of Jews from villages began; in the same year, Alexander I died and was succeeded by Nicholas I who adopted a severe attitude to the Jewish community. In 1827 he initiated a policy of induction of Jewish boys into the Russian army for a twenty-five year period in order to increase the number of converts to Christianity.

Nicholas I also deported Jews from villages in certain areas; in 1827 they were expelled from Kiev and three years later from the surrounding providence. In 1835 the Russian government propagated a revised code of laws to regulate Jewish settlement in the western border. In order to reduce Jewish isolation the government set out to reform education in 1841; a young Jewish educator, Max Lilienthal, was asked to establish a number of reformed Jewish schools in the Pale of Settlement which incorporated western educational methods and a secular curriculum. Initially Lilienthal attempted to persuade Jewish leaders that by supporting this project the Jewish community could improve their lot, but when he discovered that the intention of the Tsar was to undermine the *Talmud* he left the country. These new schools were established in 1844 but they attracted a small enrolment and the Russian government eventually abandoned its plans to eliminate traditional Jewish education.

In the same year, Nicholas I abolished the *kehillot* and put Jewry under the authority of the police as well as the municipal government. Despite this policy, it was impossible for the Russian administrator to carry out the functions of the *kehillot*, and it was recognized that a Jewish body was needed to recruit students for state military schools and to collect taxes. Between 1850 and 1851 the government attempted to forbid Jewish dress, men's sidecurls, and the ritual of shaving women's hair. In 1831 a plan was initiated to categorize all Jews in the country along economic lines. These who were considered useful subjects included craftsmen, farmers and wealthy merchants, whereas the vast majority of Jews were liable to further restrictions. After the Crimean War of 1853–6, Alexander II emancipated the serfs, modernized the judiciary and established a system of local self-government. In addition he allowed certain groups, including wealthy merchants, university graduates, certified artisans, discharged soldiers and all holders of diplomas, to reside outside the Pale of Settlement. As a result Jewish communities appeared in St Petersburg and Moscow. Furthermore, a limited number of Jews were allowed to enter the legal profession and participate in district councils. Government-sponsored Jewish schools also attracted more Jewish students, and in the 1860s and 1870s emancipated Jews began to take an active role in the professions and in Russian economic life.

The Beginnings of Reform Judaism

The Enlightenment brought about major changes in Jewish life. No longer were Jews insulated from non-Jewish currents of culture and thought, and this transformation of Jewish existence led many Jews to seek a modernization of Jewish worship. At the beginning of the nineteenth century the Jewish financier and communal leader, Israel Jacobson, initiated a programme of reform. He founded a boarding school for boys in Seesen, Westphalia in 1801, and subsequently established other schools throughout the kingdom. In these new foundations, general subjects were taught by Christian teachers while a Jewish instructor gave lessons about Judaism. The consistory under Jacobson's leadership also introduced external reforms to the Jewish worship service included choral singing, hymns and addresses, and prayers in German. In 1810 Jacobson built the first Reform temple next to the school, which was dedicated in the presence of Christian clergy and dignitaries. After Napoleon's defeat, Jacobson moved to Berlin where he attempted to put these principles into practice by founding the Berlin temple.

In Hamburg in 1817, the Reform temple was opened in which a number of innovations were made to the liturgy including prayers and sermons in German as well as choral singing and organ music. To defend these alterations, Hamburg reformers cited the *Talmud* in support of their actions. In 1819 the community issued its own prayerbook which omitted repetitions of prayers as well as medieval poems and changed some of the traditional prayers related to Jewish nationalism and messianic redemption. Israel Jacobson, to whom this prayerbook was dedicated, was instrumental in obtaining a number of rabbinic opinions in support of the temple. The Hungarian rabbi, Aaron Chorin, for example, declared that it was not only permissible but obligatory to free the liturgy from its adhesions, to hold the service in a language understandable to the worshipper, and to accompany it with organ and song. Not surprisingly such innovations provoked the Orthodox establishment to issue a proclamation condemning the Hamburg reformers.

The central aim of these early reformers was to adapt Jewish worship to contemporary aesthetic standards. For these innovators, the informality of the traditional service seemed foreign and undignified, and they therefore insisted on greater decorum, more unison in prayer, a choir, hymns and musical responses, as well as alterations in prayers and the length of the service. Under the impact of such reforming tendencies, a number of Jewish intellectuals founded the Society for the Culture and Academic Study of Judaism. This discipline encouraged the systematic study of history and a respect for historical fact. The purpose of this new approach to the past was to gain a true understanding of the origins of the Jewish tradition in the history of Western civilization, and in this quest the philosophy of Hegel had an important impact. In 1824, however, the society collapsed and several of its members, such as the poet Heinrich Heine and the historian of law Edward Gans, converted to Christianity to advance their careers.

In response to these developments, Orthodoxy asserted that any alterations to the tradition was a violation of the Jewish heritage. For these traditionalists the Written and Oral *Torah* constitute an infallible chain of divinely revealed truth. The most prominent of these scholars was Samson Raphael Hirsch who was educated at a German gymnasium and the University of Bonn. At the age of twenty-two, Hirsch was appointed as Chief Rabbi of the Duchy of Oldenburg. In 1836 he published *The Nineteen Letters on Judaism*, a defence of Orthodoxy in the form of essays by a young rabbi to a friend who questioned the importance of remaining a Jew. The work commenced with a typical critique of Judaism of this period: 'While the rest of mankind clinged to the summit of culture, prosperity and wealth, the Jewish people remained poor in every thing that makes human beings great and noble and that beautifies and dignifies our lives' (Hirsch, 1960, 24).

In response to such criticism, Hirsch replied that the purpose of human life is not to attain personal happiness and perfection; rather humans should strive to serve God by obeying his will. To serve as an example of such devotion, the Jewish people was formed so that through its way of life all people would come to know that true happiness lies in obeying God. Thus the people of Israel were given the Promised Land in order to be able to keep God's law. When the Jewish nation was exiled, they were able to fulfil this mission by remaining loyal to God and to the *Torah* despite constant persecution and suffering. According to Hirsch, the purpose of God's commands is not to repress physical gratification or material prosperity. Rather the aim of observing God's law is to lead to universal brotherhood. In this light Reform Judaism was castigated for abandoning this sacred duty. For Hirsch, citizenship rights are of minor importance since Jewry is united by a bond of obedience to God's laws until the time when the 'Almighty shall see fit in his inscrutable wisdom to unite again his scattered servants in one land, and the *Torah* shall be the guiding principle of a state, a model of the meaning of divine revelation and the mission of humanity' (Hirsch, 1960, 107).

Despite Hirsch's criticisms of reforming tendencies, a number of German rabbis who had been influenced by the Enlightenment began to re-evaluate the Jewish tradition. In this undertaking the achievements of Jewish scholars such as Leopold Zunz, who engaged in the scientific study of Judaism, had a profound impact. As this new movement began to grow, Orthodox authorities vigorously attacked its leadership and ideals. In 1838, for example, when Abraham Geiger was appointed as second rabbi of Breslau, the Chief Rabbi of the city, Solomon Tiktin, denounced him as a radical. According to Tiktin, anyone who did not subscribe to the inviolable and absolute truth of tradition could not serve with him.

Tiktin's allies joined in this protest and declared Geiger unfit for the position. In 1842 Tiktin published a tract in which he insisted on the validity of Jewish law and the authority of the rabbinic tradition. In response Geiger's supporters produced a defence of religious reform. The bitterness evoked by this controversy was reflected in the writing of one of Geiger's supporters, the Chief Rabbi of Treves, Joseph Kahn: 'We must publicly express our contempt for those who, like Tiktin and company', he wrote, 'blindly damn and ban, and in just indignation we must brand them as men who "some day will have to account for their deed"', so that 'they should bear and fear and not sin any more' (Plaut, 1963, 70).

During this period Reform Judaism spread to other countries. But it was in Frankfurt that the Society of the

Friends of Reform was founded, and published a proclamation justifying their innovative approach to tradition. In the declaration of their principles, the society stated that they recognized the possibility of unlimited progress in the Jewish faith and rejected the authority of the legal code as well as the belief in messianic redemption. Furthermore, members of the society considered circumcision a barbaric rite which should be elmininated from Judaism. Aware of the danger this group posed to the tradition, Solomon Rapoport, Rabbi of Prague, warned against associating with any members of this new movement: 'We must strictly insist and warn our co-religionists not to have any social contacts with members of this Reform association, and especially not to enter into matrimonial union with them' (Plaut, 1963, 52).

A similar group, the Association for the Reform of Judaism, was founded in Berlin in 1844 and under the leadership of Samuel Holdheim, called for major changes in the Jewish tradition. The Association produced a prayerbook in German which contained very little Hebrew and abolished customs such as praying with covered heads and blowing of the shofar. In their proclamation, the Berlin group decreed:

> We can no longer recognize a code as an unchangeable law-book which maintains with unbending insistence that Judaism's task is expressed by forms which originated in a time which is forever past and which will never return . . . we are stirred by the trumpet sound of our own time. It calls us to be of the last of a great inheritance in this old form, and at the same time, the first who, which unswerving courage are bound together as brothers in word and deed, shall lay the cornerstone of a new edifice. (Plaut, 1963, 57)

In 1844, a first Reform synod took place at Brunswick in which the participants advocated the formulation of a Jewish creed and the modifications of Sabbath and dietary laws as well as the traditional liturgy. This consultation was followed by another conference in 1845 in Frankfurt which recommended that petitions for the return to Israel and the restoration of the Jewish state be omitted from the prayerbook. At this meeting one of the more conservative rabbis, Zacharias Frankel of Dresden, expressed his dissatisfaction with the decision of the synod to regard the use of Hebrew in worship as advisable rather than necessary and resigned from the Assembly. Subsequently, Frankel became head of a Jewish theological seminary in Breslau which was based on free enquiry combined with a commitment to the Jewish tradition. In 1846 a third synod took place at Breslau and discussed Sabbath observance. Though these reformers upheld the rabbinic ordinances against work on the Sabbath, they stated that the talmudic injunctions regarding the boundary for working on the Sabbath were no longer binding. Further, they stipulated that the second day observance of festivals should be eliminated.

The Revolution of 1848 and its aftermath brought about the cessation of these conferences, and nearly a generation passed before reformers met again to formulate a common policy. In 1868, twenty-four rabbis led by Ludwig Phillipson and Abraham Geiger, assembled in Cassel to lay the foundations for a synodal conference of rabbis, scholars and communal leaders. In the following year over eighty congregations were represented when this gathering met in Leipzig under the leadership of Moritz Lazarus. Two years later another synod took place in Augsburg which dealt with pressing theological and practical problems. In a statement produced at this synod, the participants outlined the principles and tasks of Reform Judaism. First, they pointed out that in the past Judaism underwent different phases of development; Reform they believed, marks a new and important beginning. Though the essence and mission of Judaism remain constant, many ceremonies need to be regenerated and whatever is obsolete and antiquated must be set aside. To accomplish this task of renewal, the synod saw itself as a vehicle of change. Basing its reforming zeal on a quest for truth, the reformers declared: 'It (the synod) intends to labour with clear purpose so that the reform of Judaism for which we have striven for several decades should be secured in the spirit of harmony.'

In England, the West London Synagogue was established in the 1840s by members of the Spanish and Portuguese Synagogue and the Great Synagogue who sought to adopt a reform approach to Jewish life. In a sermon delivered at the opening of the synagogue, the Rev. D. W. Marks explained his departure from Orthodoxy:

> We must (as our conviction urges us) solemnly deny, that a belief in the divinity of the traditions contained in the Mishnah and the Jerusalem and Babylonian Talmuds, is of equal obligation to the Israelite with the faith in the divinity of the Law of Moses. We know that these books are human compositions; and though we are content to accept with reverence from our post-biblical ancestors advice and instruction, we cannot unconditionally accept their laws.

Subsequently, British Reform expanded outside London, and in the next century many new synagogues were established throughout the country. At the same time, the Union of Liberal and Progressive Synagogues was established as a more liberal interpretation of Judaism, and both movements were strengthened by the foundation of the Leo Baeck College in 1956 which trains rabbis for British and European Jewry.

The Development of Reform Judaism in the United States

In the seventeenth and eighteenth centuries a number of Sephardic Jews emigrated to the colonies of the New World. After 1815 the Jewish population of North America substantially increased as immigrants from Europe sought refuge from discrimination and persecution. The first signs of Reform appeared in 1824 when a small group of congregants in Charleston, South Carolina, attempted to introduce some of the reforms of Germany's Hamburg temple into synagogue worship. According to one of these early reformers, Isaac Harby, the desire of the Charleston Reform community was to take away everything that might excite the disgust of the well-informed Israelite. In the period preceding and following the Revolution of 1848, there was an outpouring of Jews, including some Reformers from Germany, to the United States; many of these immigrants settled in New York. By 1842 there were three German congregations in New York City, and three years later Congregation Emanuel was organized and introduced various reforms of worship. Among these German newcomers were several Reform rabbis who had taken part in the early European Reform synods and were anxious to initiate a policy of reform in this new setting.

Prominent among these early reformers were David Einhorn of Har Sinai congregation in Baltimore and Samuel Adler and Gustave Gottheil of Temple Emanuel in New York, but it was not until Isaac Mayer Wise exercised his leadership and organizing skills that Reform Judaism in America reached maturity. Born in Bohemia, Wise came to the United States in 1846 to accept a rabbinic post in Albany, New York, where his efforts at reform evoked a violent reaction. At a service on the New Year, he was physically assaulted by one of his opponents. 'At the conclusion of the song', he wrote:

> I stopped before the ark in order to take out the scrolls of the Law as usual, and to offer prayer. Spaniel (a member of the congregation) stepped in my way, and without saying a word, smote me with his fist so that my cap fell from my head. This was the signal for an uproar the like of which I have never experienced. (Cohn-Sherbok, 1988, 143)

Subsequently, Wise moved to Cincinnati, Ohio, where he published a new Reform prayerbook, *Minhag Amerika*, as well as several Jewish newspapers. Wise also directed his energies to convening an American synod; it was Wise's intention that American Jewry unite organizationally and spiritually to meet the challenges of life in the United States. After several abortive attempts at rabbinic union, the first Conference of American Reform Rabbis took place in Philadelphia in 1869; this was followed in 1873 by the founding of the Union of American Hebrew Congregations comprising lay and rabbinical representatives. Two years later Wise established the Hebrew Union College, the first Reform rabbinical seminary on American soil. But the principles of American Reform Judaism were not explicitly set out until 1885 when a gathering of Reform rabbis met in Pittsburgh. Their deliberations under the chairmanship of Kaufmann Kohler resulted in the adoption of a formal list of principles, the Pittsburgh Platform. In his address to the conference, Kohler declared that their purpose was to show that Judaism must be modernized in order to embrace the findings of scientific research as well as the fields of comparative religion and biblical criticism.

The Platform consisted of a number of basic principles:

First – We recognize in every religion an attempt to grasp the Infinite One and in every mode, source or book of revelation held sacred in any religious system the consciousness of the indwelling of God in man. We hold that Judaism presents the highest conception of the God-idea as taught in our holy Scriptures and developed and spiritualized by the Jewish teachers in accordance with the moral and philosophical progress of their respective ages. We maintain that Judaism preserved and defended amid continual struggles and trials and under enforced isolation this God-idea as the central religious truth for the human race.

Second – We recognize in the Bible the record of the consecration of the Jewish people to its mission as priest of the One God, and value it as the most potent instrument of religious and moral instruction. We hold that the modern discoveries of scientific researches in the domain of nature and history are not antagonistic to the doctrines of Judaism, the Bible reflecting the primitive ideas of its own age and at times clothing its conception of divine providence and justice dealing with men in miraculous narratives.

Third – We recognize in the Mosaic legislation a system of training the Jewish people for its mission during its national life in Palestine, and today we accept as binding only the moral laws and maintain only such ceremonies as elevate and sanctify our lives, but reject all such as are not adapted to the views and habits of modern civilization.

Fourth – We hold that all such Mosaic and Rabbinical laws as regulate diet, priestly purity and dress originated in ages and under the influence of ideas altogether foreign to our present mental and spiritual state. They fail to impress the modern Jew with a spirit of priestly holiness; their observance in our days is apt rather to obstruct than to further modern spiritual elevation.

Fifth – We recognize in the modern era of universal culture of heart and intellect the approach of the realization of Israel's great messianic hope for the establishment of the kingdom of truth, justice and peace among all men. We consider ourselves no longer a nation but a religious community, and therefore expect neither a return to Palestine, nor a sacrificial worship under the administration of the sons of Aaron, nor the restoration of any of the laws concerning the Jewish state.

Sixth – We recognize in Judaism a progressive religion, ever striving to be in accord with the postulates of reason. We are convinced of the utmost necessity of preserving the historical identity with our great past. Christianity and Islam being daughter-religions of Judaism, we appreciate their mission to aid in the spreading of monotheistic and moral truth. We acknowledge that the spirit of broad humanity of our age is our ally in the fulfilment of our mission, and therefore we extend the hand of fellowship to all who co-operate with us in the establishment of the reign of truth and righteousness among men.

Seventh – We reassert the doctrine of Judaism, that the soul of men is immortal, grounding this belief on the divine nature of the human spirit, which forever finds bliss in righteousness and misery in wickedness. We reject as ideas rooted in Judaism the belief both in bodily resurrection and in *Gehenna* and *Eden* (hell and paradise), as abodes for everlasting punishment or reward.

Eighth – In full accordance with the spirit of Mosaic legislation which strives to regulate the relation between rich and poor, we deem it our duty to participate in the great task of modern times, to solve on the basis of justice and righteousness the problems presented by the contrasts and evils of the present organization of society. (Plaut, 1965, 33–4)

This statement of religious beliefs – radically different from Maimonides' Thirteen Principles of the Jewish Faith – together with the rabbinical and congregational organizations of Reform Judaism founded in the late nineteenth century – provided a framework for the growth and development of Reform Judaism in the next century.

Fifty years after the Pittsburgh meeting of 1885, the Jewish world had undergone major changes: America was the centre of the diaspora; Zionism had become a vital force in Jewish life; Hitler was in power. The Columbus Platform of the Reform movement adopted in 1937 reflected a new approach to liberal Judaism. Divided into three sections, the Platform began by defining the essential elements of the Jewish faith.

1. *Nature of Judaism.* Judaism is the historical religious experience of the Jewish people. Though growing out of Jewish life, its message is universal, aiming at the union and perfection of mankind under the sovereignty of God. Reform Judaism recognizes the principle of progressive development in religion and consciously applies this principle to spiritual as well as to cultural and social life. Judaism welcomes all truth, whether

written in the pages of Scripture or deciphered from the records of nature. The new discoveries of science, while replacing the older scientific views underlying our sacred literature, do not conflict with the essential sprit of religion as manifested in the consecration of man's will, heart and mind to the service of God and of humanity.

2. *God*. The heart of Judaism and its chief contribution to religion is the doctrine of the One, living God, who rules the world through law and love. In him all existence has its creative source and mankind its ideal of conduct. Though transcending time and space, he is the indwelling Presence of the world. We worship him as the Lord of the universe and as our merciful father.

3. *Man*. Judaism affirms that man is created in the divine image. His spirit is immortal. He is an active co-worker with God. As a child of God, he is endowed with moral freedom and is charged with the responsibility of overcoming evil and striving after ideal ends.

4. *Torah*. God reveals himself not only in the majesty, beauty and orderliness of nature, but also in the vision and moral striving of the human spirit. Revelation is a continuous process, confined to no one group and to no one age. Yet the people of Israel, through its prophets and sages, achieved unique insight in the realm of religious truth. The *Torah*, both written and oral, enshrines Israel's ever-growing consciousness of God and of the moral law. It preserves the historical precedents, sanctions and norms of Jewish life, and seeks to mould it in the patterns of goodness and of holiness. Being products of historical processes, certain of its laws have lost their binding force with the passing of the conditions that called them fourth. But as a depository of permanent spiritual ideals, the *Torah* remains the dynamic source of the life of Israel. Each age has the obligation to adapt the teachings of the *Torah* to its basic needs in consonance with the genius of Judaism.

5. *Israel*. Judaism is the soul of which Israel is the body. Living in all parts of the world, Israel has been held together by the ties of a common history, and above all, by the heritage of faith. Though we recognize in the group the loyalty of Jews who have become estranged from our religious tradition, a bond which still unites them with us, we maintain that it is by its religion and for its religion that the Jewish people have lived.

The non-Jews who accept our faith are welcomed as full members of the Jewish community. In all lands where our people live, they assume and seek to share loyally the full duties and responsibilities of citizenship and to create seats of Jewish knowledge and religion. In the rehabilitation of Palestine, the land hallowed by memories and hopes, we behold the promise of renewed life for many of our brethren. We affirm the obligation of all Jewry to aid in its upbuilding as a Jewish homeland by endeavouring to make it not only a haven of refuge for the oppressed but also a centre of Jewish culture and spiritual life. Throughout the ages it has been Israel's mission to witness to the Divine in the face of every form of paganism and materialism. We regard it as our historic task to co-operate with all men in the establishment of the kingdom of God, of universal brotherhood, justice, truth and peace on earth. This is our messianic goal.

6. *Ethics and Religion.* In Judaism religion and morality blend into an insoluble unity. Seeking God means to strive after holiness, righteousness and goodness. The love of God is incomplete without the love of one's fellow men. Judaism emphasizes the kinship of the human race, the sanctity and worth of human life and personality and the right of the individual to freedom and to the pursuit of his chosen vocation. Justice to all, irrespective of race, sect or class is the inalienable right and the inescapable obligation of all. The state and organized government exist in order to further these ends.

7. *Social Justice.* Judaism seeks the attainment of a just society by the application of its teachings to the economic order, to industry and commerce, and to national and international affairs. It aims at the elimination of man-made misery and suffering, of poverty and degradation, of tyranny and slavery, of social inequality and prejudice, of ill-will and strife. It advocates the promotion of harmonious relations between warring classes on the basis of equity and justice, and the creation of conditions under which human personality may flourish. It pleads for the safeguarding of childhood against exploitation. It champions the cause of all who work and of their right to an adequate standard of living, as prior to the rights of property. Judaism emphasizes the duty of charity, and strives for a social order which will protect men against the material disabilities of old age, sickness and unemployment.

8. *Peace.* Judaism, from the days of the prophets, has proclaimed to mankind the ideal of universal peace. The spiritual and physical disarmament of all nations has been one of its essential teachings. It abhors all violence and relies upon moral education, love and sympathy to secure human progress. It regards justice as the foundation of the well-being of nations and the condition of enduring peace. It urges organized international action for disarmament, collective security and world peace.

9. *The Religious Life.* Jewish life is marked by consecration to these ideals of Judaism. It calls for faithful participation in the life of the Jewish community as it finds expression in home, synagogue and school, and in all other agencies that enrich Jewish life and promote its welfare. The home has been, and must continue to be, a stronghold of Jewish life, hallowed by the spirit of love and reverence, by moral discipline and religious observance and worship. The synagogue is the oldest and most democratic institution in Jewish life. It is the prime communal agency by which Judaism is fostered and preserved. It links the Jews of each community and unites them with all Israel. The perpetuation of Judaism as a living force depends upon religious knowledge and upon the education of each new generation in our rich cultural and spiritual heritage. Prayer is the voice of religion, the language of faith and aspiration. It directs man's heart and mind Godward, voices the needs and hopes of the community, and reaches out to goals which invest life with supreme value. To deepen the spiritual life of our people, we must cultivate the traditional habit of communion with God through prayer in both home and synagogue. Judaism as a way of life requires in addition to its moral and spiritual demands, the preservation of the Sabbath, festivals and Holy Days, the retention and development of such customs, symbols and ceremonies as possess inspirational value, the cultivation of distinctive forms of religious art and music and the use of Hebrew, together with the vernacular, in our worship and instruction. These timeless aims and ideals of our faith we present anew to a confused and troubled world. We call upon our fellow Jews to rededicate themselves to them, and, in harmony with all men, hopefully and courageously to continue Israel's eternal quest after God and his kingdom. (Plaut, 1965, 96–9)

Reform Judaism in a Post-Holocaust World

The 1937 Columbus Platform reflected the gradual changes that had been occurring in the Reform movement. In contrast with the Pittsburgh Platform, this new declaration embraced Zionist ideals, endorsed the use of Heberew as well as the retention of ceremonies and observances that had previously been rejected by reformers. After the Second World War the movement continued to evolve, and Reform theology became increasingly diverse. On the right of the religious spectrum a number of rabbis advocated a personalist basis for religious faith. Bernard Martin, Professor at Case Western Reserve University, for example maintained that God 'is personal . . . in the sense that he lives, acts, is conscious, and enters into personal relationships with man, addressing him and demanding his personal response'. For Emil Fackenheim, Professor of Philosophy at the University of Toronto, 'God surely resembles a human person far more closely than he does an impersonal force . . . the most exalted picture we can make of God is as a person'. Again, Eugene Borowitz, Professor of Religious Thought at the Hebrew Union College, emphasized a personal God whom we meet and confront: 'He hears us . . . (he) is always ready for a prayer.' In the view of Jacob Petuchowski, Professor at the Hebrew Union College, 'Tradition does speak of God's will, and of God's love, and of God's concern. And to have a will, love and concern means that one is so constituted as to have them; and, in our human language, that kind of constitution is called "personality"' (Raphael, 1984, 56–7).

Other Reform thinkers, however, had more radical interpretations of Divine reality. Roland Gittelsohn, rabbi of Temple Israel in Boston, for example, stressed that increasing numbers of modern religious Jews no longer think of God as a Person. 'I did not conceive God as a Person', he wrote, 'but as a process of Power or Thrust within the universe . . . (God) is the creative, spiritual Seed of the universe – the Energy, the Power, the Force, the Direction, the Thrust . . . in which the universe and mind find their meaning.' For Gittelsohn, prayer is thus not directed to a God who hears, but inward to oneself.

'It is', he wrote, 'a reminder of who I am, of what I can become, and of my proper relationship to the rest of the universe' (Raphael, 1984, 58). Other Reform thinkers have similarly rejected the traditional depiction of God. Henry Slonimsky, Professor of Theology at the Jewish Institution of Religion, for example, denied God's perfection and unlimited power – in his view God struggles against evil and is dependent on human beings for help.

Although similar divisions exist within the movement regarding the status of the *Torah*, there has in recent years been an increased use of the *Torah* in worship: *bar mitzvah* and *bar mitzvah* ceremonies are currently commonplace in which boys and girls read from the *Torah*, and the traditional blessing over the *Torah* (Blessed art Thou O Lord our God who has given us the *Torah*) is universally used in Reform synagogues. Even such radical thinkers as Roland Gittelsohn, who has produced naturalist creative liturgies, employed the following blessing over the *Torah*: 'Praised be the Eternal our God, Ruling Spirit of the universe, who has chosen us from among all peoples to give us the *Torah*.' Yet despite such reverence, Reform rabbis in line with the Pittsburgh and Columbus Platforms continued to reject the traditional doctrine of *Torah MiSinai*. Instead, they subscribed to a belief in progressive revelation, affirming that men and women throughout history have been recipients of God's disclosure. As Maurice Eisendrath, President of the Union of American Hebrew Congregations explained: 'God is a living God – not a God who revealed himself and his word once and for all times at Sinai and speaks no more' (Raphael, 1984, 59).

In line with renewal of interest in the *Torah*, a number of Reform rabbis have also become increasingly preoccupied with *halakhah* in order to attain orderliness and authority in Jewish life. Since the Second World War, Solomon Freehof, rabbi of Rodef Shalom in Pittsburgh, formulated Reform responses based on traditional rabbinic sources. In various books Freehof sought to uncover the halakhic background to current Reform Jewish practice – these collections of halakhic precedents have provided rabbis and laity with a basis for

reconstructing ceremonies and observances within a Reform
context. In addition, in 1957 David Polish and Frederick A.
Doppelt produced a guide which attempted to regulate
Reform Jewish conduct; this was followed in 1972 by a
comprehensive code for Sabbath observance. This work
contained specific recommendations for individual Jews: It is
proper to 'prepare for *Shabbat* . . . to light *Shabbat* candles . . .
to recite or chant the *kiddush* . . . to maintain and enjoy the
special quality of *Shabbat* throughout the afternoon . . . (it is
best not to) engage in gainful work on *Shabbat* . . . perform
housework on *Shabbat* . . . (shop) on *Shabbat* . . . participate in
a social event during *Shabbat* . . . (or engage in) public
activity which violates (the *Shabbat*)'. More recently a new
body has been founded within the movement to encourage
the formulation of a Reform code of Jewish law.

Despite this revival of interest in *halakhah*, however, the
Reform movement has recently departed from traditional
Judaism in a number of important areas. In 1973 the Central
Conference of American Rabbis (CCAR) debated the issue of
rabbinic participation in interfaith marriages which are
forbidden by Jewish law. Although a resolution was passed in
1909 discouraging such participation, an increasing number
of Reform rabbis officiated at such ceremonies. After a
lengthy debate a resolution opposing such activity was
passed by the majority of the CCAR, yet despite this stance
many Reform rabbi continued to play a role in such marriage
services. An issue of even greater consequence was the
decision taken in 1983 by the CCAR that a child of either a
Jewish mother or a Jewish father should be regarded as
Jewish. By expanding the determination of Jewishness to
include children of both matrilineal and patrilineal descent,
the Reform movement defined as Jews, individuals whom the
other branches of Judaism regard as gentiles; this means that
neither these persons nor their descendants can be accepted
as Jews by the non-Reform religious establishment.

The Reform attitude towards Israel has also undergone
significant change since the time of the Columbus Platform.
Following the Second World War, the Jewish state was
enthusiastically welcomed by the Reform movement despite

its earlier hestiation. As a result, the study of Israeli culture
and civilization was included in the curriculum of religion
schools, and the Ashkenazic pronunciation of Hebrew previously used in worship was replaced by the Sephardic
pronunciation currently in use in Israel. The movement also
encouraged the growth of Reform Judaism in Israel: congregations were founded in the Jewish state, and since 1970 Reform
rabbinic students have been required to spend the first year of
their training at the Jerusalem campus of the Hebrew Union
College. Further, for many Reform Jews, Israel has become
pivotal in their understanding of Jewish history and the future
survival of the Jewish people. Such attitudes are reflected in
the writings of a number of Reform Jewish theologians such as
Emil Fackenheim who has argued that the establishment of a
Jewish state after two thousand years of statelessness is of
fundamental importance. In Fackenheim's view diaspora
Judaism is now a spiritual impossibility; Jews today must
make Israel their home. In the past the *Torah* was the
fatherland of all Jews, but in contemporary society the *Oleh*
(immigrant to Israel) occupies the place once occupied by
the *Torah* student: 'What the Jew by birth can do in our time',
he wrote, 'is to recognize that just as one kind of Jew –
the *Torah* student – set the unifying standard for all Jews, so
the standard is set today by another kind – the *Oleh*'.
Though thoroughly at home in his country of birth, the *Oleh*
makes *aliyah* because of love. The Zionist enterprise thus
serves as the paramount act of Jewish loyalty in a post-
Holocaust world.

In post-war decades synagogues also underwent major
changes, becoming increasingly democratic: women moved
into positions of leadership, serving as presidents, members of
the board of directors, and youth group leaders; in addition,
men, women and students sat on rabbinic search committees
and the entire membership normally voted on the search
committee's selection. During these years, the synagogue
served as the centre of Jewish communal life and added
recreational, cultural and social activities into a full programme of religious worship. Simultaneously, Reform Jewish
commitment was fostered by Reform Jewish summer camps

staffed by rabbis, rabbinic students and others. Later in the 1970s, Reform Jewish day schools, sponsored or housed in synagogues, also fostered Jewish identity and loyalty. Alongside such activity, small independent groups of Reform congregants (*havurot*) emerged and held worship services and study groups independent of the synagogue's structure.

The nature of the synagogue service also underwent important modifications. Frequently cantors replaced or supplemented choirs; contemporary Israeli melodies and songs were introduced; and rabbis adopted a more informal approach to preaching. In the 1960s, creative liturgies were used, and in the 1970s a new Reform prayerbook was published which changed the content as well as the format of worship. The *New Union Prayer Book* (*Gates of Prayer*) removed sexist language, included special services for Israel Independence Day, and adopted a positive attitude towards Zion.

Unlike the previous Reform prayerbook, this volume lacked formal instructions to the leader or worshipper and presented ten different Sabbath services reflecting a variety of different religious attitudes. In this way *Gates of Prayer* gave expression to a range of religious positions within the movement (traditionalist, existentialist, classicist, naturalist and nontheist).

Like the synagogue, the role of the rabbi underwent considerable modification in the post-war years. During this period between the Pittsburgh and Columbus Platform, a number of rabbis gained prominence as Jewish scholars. Yet by the 1960s and 1970s, Jewish academics in universities had usurped this role. In addition, a large number of rabbis were engaged in normal congregational positions. Further, the male-dominated nature of the rabbinate had profoundly altered: in 1972 the first woman rabbi was ordained and by the early 1980s more than seventy-five women had entered the rabbinate. In the 1960s and 1970s those graduating from the Hebrew Union College were more likely to have come from Reform backgrounds and the majority of rabbinic students were married. Paradoxically many of those ordained were agnostic – a situation which provoked considerable dilemmas for those who entered the active rabbinate.

A Centenary Perspective

Nearly a century after the Pittsburgh Platform, the Central Conference of American Rabbis sponsored a study of the beliefs and practices of Reform Jews. This study, *Rabbi and Synagogue in Reform Judaism*, published in 1971, provided a panoramic overview of the state of Reform Judaism in the latter half of the twentieth century. According to this survey, Jewish consciousness was identified by most Reform Jewish congregants in terms of being an ethical person. Although Jewish identification was a significant factor in the lives of most Reform Jews, many stated that they remained Jews 'because it is simply the most convenient thing to do'. Even the most traditional among those questioned were not very observant. More had a family Thanksgiving dinner, for example, than observed the High Holy Days at home; nearly as many exchanged Christmas gifts as attended Friday night services. Regarding religious conviction, 17 per cent stated that they believed in God 'in the more or less traditional sense of the term'; 49 per cent qualified their belief in terms of their own views of what God is, and what he stands for; 8 per cent declared they were non-religious believers; 21 per cent, however, maintained they were agnostics; and 4 per cent atheists. A religiosity index constructed on the basis of response patterns to 'belief in God' and 'being an ethical person' revealed the following distribution: Reform congregants who are religious, 48 per cent; marginally religious, 24 per cent; non-religious, 28 per cent. Turning to the Reform rabbinate, 10 per cent stated that they believed in God 'in the more or less traditional Jewish sense'; 62 per cent believed in God 'in the more or less traditional Jewish sense' but qualified such conviction in terms of their own views of what God is and what he stands for; 14 per cent identified themselves as non-traditionalists; 13 per cent were agnostics; and 1 per cent atheists. In terms of belief in God and other aspects of religiosity, Reform rabbis were categorized as: traditionalists, 10 per cent; moderates, 62 per cent; and radicals, 28 per cent.

In 1976, the Reform movement produced the San Francisco Platform under the guidance of Eugene Borowitz, Professor at the Hebrew Union College. The purpose of this statement was to provide a unifying document which would bring a sense of order into the movement. It was adopted in 1976 by the Central Conference of American Rabbis. Although it avoided taking a theological position, it affirmed 'God's reality' without specifying the details of such religious commitment. *Torah*, it explained, resulted from 'the relationship between God and the Jewish people', and Israel was conceived as an 'uncommon union of faith and peoplehood'. *Mitzvot* were interpreted as 'claims made upon us'. Although vague and equivocal, the San Francisco Platform did provide a sense of unity despite the deep divisions within the movement.

The Platform itself commenced with a declaration explaining that the centenaries of the founding of the Union of American Hebrew Congregations and the Hebrew Union College–Jewish Institute of Religion provided an appropriate opportunity to describe the spiritual state of Reform Judaism. This was followed by an historical account of the evolution of Reform Judaism in North America, the lessons learned during this period, and the importance of diversity within Reform. It explained:

> Reform Judaism does more than tolerate diversity, it engenders it . . . We stand open to any position thoughtfully and conscientiously advocated in the spirit of Reform Jewish beliefs. While we may differ in our interpretations and application of the ideas enunciated here, we accept such differences as precious and see in them Judaism's best hope for confronting whatever the future holds for us.

Following this introduction, the text was divided into seven sections:

1. *God.* The affirmation of God has always been essential to our people's will to survive. In our struggle through the centuries to preserve our faith we have experienced and conceived of God in many ways. The trials of our own time and the challenges of modern culture have made steady belief and clear understanding difficult for some. Nevertheless, we ground our lives, personally and communally, on God's reality and remain open to new experiences and conceptions of the Divine. Amid the mystery we call life, we affirm that

human beings, created in God's image, share in God's eternality despite the mystery we call death.

2. *The People Israel.* The Jewish people and Judaism defy precise definition because both are in the process of becoming Jews by birth or conversion and so constitute an uncommon union of faith and peoplehood. Born as Hebrews in the ancient Near East, we are bound together like all ethnic groups by language, land, history, culture and institutions. But the people of Israel are unique because of its involvement with God and its resulting perception of the human condition. Throughout our long history our people has been inseparable from its religion with its messianic hope that humanity will be redeemed.

3. *Torah.* Torah results from the relationship between God and the Jewish people. The records of our earliest confrontations are uniquely important to us. Lawgivers and prophets, historians and poets gave us a heritage where study is a religious imperative and whose practice is our chief means to holiness. Rabbis and teachers, philosophers and mystics, gifted Jews in every age amplified the *Torah* tradition. For millennia, the creation of *Torah* has not ceased and Jewish creativity in our time is adding to the chain of tradition.

4. *Our Obligations: Religious Practice.* Judaism emphasizes action rather than creed as the primary expression of a religious life, the means by which we strive to achieve universal justice and peace. Reform Judaism shares this emphasis on duty and obligation. Our founders stressed that the Jews' ethical responsibilities, personal and social, are enjoined by God. The past century has taught us that the claims made upon us may begin with our ethical obligations but they extend to many other aspects of Jewish living, including: creating a Jewish home centred on family devotion; life-long study; private prayer and public worship; daily religious observance; keeping the Sabbath and holy days; celebrating the major events of life; involvement with the synagogue and community; and other activities which promote the survival of the Jewish people and enhance its existence. Within each area of Jewish observance, Reform Jews are called upon to confront the claims of Jewish tradition, however differently perceived, and to exercise their individual autonomy, choosing and creating on the bases of commitment and knowledge.

5. *Our Obligations: The State of Israel and the Diaspora.* We are privileged to live in an extraordinary time, one in which a third Jewish commonwealth has been established in our people's ancient homeland. We are bound to that land and to the newly reborn State of Israel by innumerable religious and ethnic ties. We have been enriched by its culture and ennobled by its indomitable spirit. We see it providing unique opportunities for Jewish self-expression. We have both a stake and a responsibility in building the State of Israel, assuring its security and defining its Jewish character. We encourage *aliyah* for those who wish to find maximum personal fulfilment in the cause of Zion. We demand that Reform Judaism be unconditionally legitimized in the State of Israel.

At the same time we consider the State of Israel vital to the welfare of Judaism everywhere, we reaffirm the mandate of our tradition to create strong Jewish communities wherever we live. A genuine Jewish life is possible in any land, each community developing its own particular character and determining its Jewish responsibilities. The foundation of Jewish community life is the synagogue. It leads us beyond itself to co-operate with other Jews, to share their concerns, and to assume leadership in communal affairs. We are, therefore, committed to the full democratization of the Jewish community and to its hallowing in terms of Jewish values.

The State of Israel and the diaspora, in fruitful dialogue, can show how a people transcends nationalism even as it affirms it, thereby setting an example for humanity which remains largely concerned with dangerously parochial goals.

6. *Our Obligations: Survival and Service.* Early Reform Jews, newly admitted to general society and seeing in this the evidence of a growing universalism, regularly spoke of Jewish purpose in terms of Jewry's service to humanity. In recent years we have become freshly conscious of the virtues of pluralism and the values of particularism. The Jewish people in its unique way of life validates its own worthwhile working toward the fulfilment of its messianic expectations.

Until the recent past, our obligations to the Jewish people and to all humanity seemed congruent. At times now these two imperatives appear to conflict. We know of no simple way to resolve such tensions. We must, however, confront them without abandoning either of our commitments. A universal concern for humanity unaccompanied by a devotion to our particular people is self-destructive: a passion for our people without involvement in humankind contradicts what the prophets have meant to us. Judaism calls us simultaneously to universal and particular obligations.

7. *Hope: Our Jewish Obligations.* Previous generations of Reform Jews had unbounded confidence in humanity's potential for good. We have lived through terrible tragedy and been compelled to reappropriate our tradition's realism about the human capacity for evil. Yet our people have always refused to despair. The survivors of the Holocaust, on being granted life, siezed it, nurtured it, and, rising above catastrophe, showed humankind that the human spirit is indomitable. The State of Israel, established and maintained by the Jewish will to live, demonstrates what a united people can accomplish in history. The existence of the Jew is an argument against despair; Jewish survival is warrant for human hope. We remain God's witness that history is not meaningless. We affirm that with God's help, people are not powerless to affect their destiny. We dedicate ourselves, as did the generations of Jews who went before us, to work and wait for that day when 'They shall not hurt or destroy in all my holy mountain for the earth shall be full of the knowledge of the Lord as the waters cover the sea'. (Meyer, 1988).

5

Non-Orthodox Alternatives

The development of Reform Judaism gave rise to several other non-Orthodox movements. In 1845, Zacharias Frankel walked out of the rabbinical conference in Frankfurt, intent on formulating a conservative approach to the tradition (later known as Conservative Judaism). Subsequently, a number of American rabbis advanced a similar stance, and at the end of the century, the Jewish Theological Seminary was founded in New York to foster positive historical Judaism. Headed by Solomon Schechter, this new institution was dedicated to Jewish traditionalism combined with the scientific study of Judaism. Later under the influence of Mordecai Kaplan, the Reconstructionist movement emerged from the ranks of Conservative Judaism. This new philosophy rejected supernaturalism while retaining many of the traditional features of the Jewish way of life. According to Kaplan, Judaism is a religious and secular civilization; thus all aspects of Judaism should be viewed as integral parts of the tradition. In modern society, he argued, the Jewish faith must undergo adaptation and change. More recently, another form of non-supernatural Judaism – Humanistic Judaism – appeared which espouses a humanistic ideology rooted in the Jewish heritage. Largely inspired by Rabbi Sherwin Wine of Detroit, Michican, this new movement now has branches throughout the world. The final form of Judaism, Polydoxy, is a religious ideology propounded by the American Jewish philosopher, Alvin Reines. For Reines, Polydox Judaism champions an approach to Jewish belief and practice based on personal autonomy. These various non-Orthodox systems coupled with Reform

Judaism range across the religious spectrum. Detached from Orthodoxy, they provide a variety of interpretations of the Jewish faith, offering widely divergent responses to Jewish theology and observance.

The Rise of Conservative Judaism

The founder of what came to be known as Conservative Judaism was Zacharias Frankel. Born in Prague, he was ordained and received a doctorate in Classical Philology at the University of Pesth in 1831. Subsequently he held rabbinical positions in Teplitz, Bohemia and Dresden, before becoming president of the Jüdisch-Theologischen Seminar in Breslau. An advocate of moderate reform, he was committed to an historically evolving dynamic Judaism. The aim of such an approach (positive historical Judaism), he believed, would be to uncover the origins of the Jewish people's national spirit and the collective will. Both the past as enshrined in tradition and the present as embodied in the religious consciousness of the people, he argued, should determine the nature of Jewish life.

In 1845, Frankel left the Reform rabbinical conference in Frankfurt because a majority of the participants had voted that there was no need to use Hebrew in the Jewish worship service. At this synod one of the Reform leaders, Abraham Geiger, maintained that since Hebrew was simply a national element in the service which Reform Judaism sought to replace with universal symbols, it could be eliminated. In response, Frankel stated that Hebrew is a vital historical feature of the Jewish tradition – it is the sacred tongue in which Jews have expressed their beliefs and ideas through the ages. Following the conference, Frankel wrote a letter to a Frankfurt newspaper, stressing his commitment to positive historical Judaism. Although he agreed with other reformers that Judaism needed to be revised, he disputed with them over the legitimate criteria for religious change. None the less, he broke with Orthodoxy in asserting that the Oral law was rabbinic in origin, that the *halakhah* had evolved over time, and that the source of religious observance was not divine but rather the role that rituals and observances had for the Jewish people throughout history.

In the United States a similar approach to the tradition was adopted by a number of leading figures. The German-born *hazzan* of Mikveh Israel, Isaac Leeser, for example, pioneered the introduction of the sermon in English and advocated liturgical change. Although a staunch traditionalist in other respects, he co-operated with Isaac Mayer Wise in attempting to organize rabbinic and congregational unions. Such efforts were unsuccessful, however he did succeed in creating a rabbinical school, Maimonides College in 1867. Even though it ceased to function in 1873, it graduated four men trained for the American rabbinate. Benjamin Szold, another moderate reformer, came to Baltimore where he founded the first Zionist group in the United States. Two other scholars, Marcus Jastrow and Alexander Kohut, also advocated change to the Orthodox worship service. When the Reform rabbinate published the Pittsburgh Platform in 1885, Kohut took issue with Kaufmann Kohler (the principal author of this document) and together with another conservative reformer of this period, Sabato Morais, encouraged the creation of a rabbinical school dedicated to the knowledge and practice of historical Judaism. In 1887 this institution was founded by Morais, Mendes and Kohut, as well as a number of prominent laymen. In its Articles of Incorporation the Jewish Theological Seminary of American Assocation declared its dedication to 'the preservation in America of the knowledge and practice of historical Judaism as ordained in the law of Moses expounded by the prophets and sages in Israel in biblical and talmudic writings'.

In 1902 the Cambridge scholar Solomon Schechter became president of the Seminary; his Rumanian background, traditional Jewish education and strict adherence to Jewish law made him an ideal head of this new institution. According to Schechter, 'the observance of the Sabbath, the keeping of the dietary laws, the laying of *tefillin*, the devotion to Hebrew literature, and the hope for Zion in Jerusalem are all things as absolutely necessary for maintaining Judaism in America as elsewhere' (Raphael, 1984, 88).

It was Schechter's desire to combine Jewish traditionalism with a commitment to the scientific study of Judaism so as to build 'a school of Jewish learning, which should embrace all the departments of Jewish thought . . . which alone deserves the name of research' (Schechter, 1959, 232). Yet despite his adherence to traditional practices, the Union of Orthodox Rabbis issued a writ of excommunication against the Seminary in June 1904. In response, Schechter began to delineate the nature of what came to be regarded as Conservative Judaism. In a letter written in 1907 he stated what he believed to be the task of this movement: 'Conservative Judaism can only be saved in this country by giving to the world trained men on scientific lines, and proving to the world that *Wissenchaft* and history are on our side' (Raphael, 1984, 89). Several years later, he emphasized that Conservative Judaism should combine elements of both traditional and non-traditional Judaism: 'Conservative Judaism unites what is desirable in modern life with the previous heritage of our faith . . . that has come down to us from ancient times' (Raphael, 1984, 89).

Disdainfully, Schechter rejected both Reform ('Lord, forgive them, for they know nothing'), and Orthodoxy ('A return to Mosaism would be illegal, pernicious and indeed impossible'). Instead Schechter emphasized the importance of traditional rituals, customs, observances, as well as belief while simultaneously stressing the need for a historical perspective. In contrast with the Orthodox, Schechter admired modern scientific biblical scholarship. In line with contemporary biblical criticism, he maintained that the Pentateuch was not of divine origin – what is required, he stated, is the continual reinterpretation of the tradition. 'The *Torah*', he wrote, 'is not in heaven; its interpretation is left to the conscience of catholic Israel' (Raphael, 1984, 90). As a champion of such an evolutionary understanding of Jewish civilization, he pressed for the establishment of a union of congregations sympathetic to conservatism. In February 1913, a union of twenty-two congregations was founded, committed to maintaining the Jewish tradition in its historical continuity. In the preamble to its constitution the United Synagogue stated its intention to separate from Reform Judaism – it was committed to a heterogenous, traditional mode of belief and practice through the observance of ritual in the home and the synagogue.

The distinctiveness of this new movement was reflected in Schechter's rejection of a European form of tradition; rather he insisted that Conservative Jews should be thoroughly American in habits of life and mode of thinking and imbued with the best culture of the day. In this light, Conservative Jewry was obliged to demonstrate to east European immigrants that secular education and the traditional mode of Jewish life are fully compatible. To accomplish this goal, ordinands were trained in scientific research at the Jewish Theological Seminary, encouraged to preach in English rather than Yiddish, and urged to publish modern textbooks about Judaism. Convinced that the survival of the tradition depended on fostering such an approach, the congregations that joined this new movement endorsed the fusion of ancient practice and modern life. Typical among these congregations was Birmingham's K'nesseth Israel that consisted of 'gentlemen whose devotion to Judaism has never permitted them to diverge from its most orthodox aspects'; Chicago's Anshe Emeth where there prevailed a 'mode of worship that would reflect somewhat the modern tendencies and still retain the essential features of the old orthodoxy'; and St Paul's Temple of Aaron in which 'conservatism was absolutely necessary to promote modern American Judaism (and where) the old traditional form of the Jewish ritual should be followed, omitting such portions of it that would not interest the younger folks and the coming generation' (Raphael, 1984, 92).

As Conservative Judaism expanded in the 1920s and 1930s a degree of uniformity developed in congregational worship: services usually began late Friday evening and early Saturday morning; head coverings were required; prayer shawls were usually worn on Sabbath morning; rabbis conducted the service and preached English sermons; prayerbooks other than the *Union Prayer Book* of the Reform movement were used; and many congregants participated in afternoon study with the rabbi. In addition, many synagogues had organs, mixed choirs, family pews, and *minyans* that met three times a day for prayer. Others had a junior congregation where younger members elected their own officers as well as a board of trustees and conducted their own High Holy Days and Sabbath services.

Such departures from tradition at times caused dissension; occasionally those of a more orthodox inclination attempted to restore traditional practices to communal life. Such diversity of practice led some figures in the movement to seek a clearer definition of the nature of Conservative Judaism. Thus, in 1919 a group of six rabbis and professors from the Jewish Theological Seminary urged colleagues to formulate a statement of principles. Opposed to such an action, the president of the Jewish Theological Seminary, Louis Ginzberg, refused to let these men meet at the Seminary. In the 1940s the Conservative scholar, Robert Gordis complained that 'many of our most distinguished scholars and thinkers have declined to formulate a specific programme' or to 'enunciate the philosophy of Conservative Judaism' (Raphael, 1984, 95). Similarly, Morris Adler, rabbi of Shaarey Zedek in Detroit, lamented that 'our members sense that they are not orthodox, they are not moved by reform, but they have yet to learn that they are conservative' (Adler, 1964, 25).

In the 1970s, Hillel Silverman, rabbi of Sinai Temple in Los Angeles, continued to criticize Conservative Judaism as 'a "catch-all" for the dissatisfied, a conglomeration of many needs, pluralistic in approach to the extreme, boasting a left, a centre and a right, a tepid orthodoxy at the same time a timid reform'. In his view, Conservative Judaism '*is nisht a hin and nisht a her*, a synthesis that avoids extremes and yet stands for little that is novel and authentic' (Raphael, 1984, 95). Later in the 1970s, Benjamin Z. Kreitman of Brooklyn's Shaare Torah in Brooklyn, called for a definition of principles, and David Lieber, President of the University of Judaism in Los Angeles, urged the Conservative movement to 'articulate a definition of Conservative Judaism which is intelligible and unambiguous, a clear and persuasive definition' (Raphael, 1984, 95). Yet despite these pleas, Conservative Judaism never produced an offical declaration of its principles like the Pittsburgh,

Columbus, and San Francisco Platforms issued by the Reform movement. As a result, Conservative Judaism has remained amorphous in character.

None the less, the Conservative movement embraced a general policy regarding the tradition. From its beginnings in the nineteenth century, Conservatism stressed that east European immigrants should adjust to the social, economic and cultural conditions of American life while retaining their Jewish identity. For this reason, there was a desire to conserve essential customs, beliefs, traditions and rituals of the faith. In the words of Max Arzt of Temple Israel in Scranton and later Vice-Chancellor of the Jewish Theological Seminary:

> We are anxious to conserve those tangible and visible and time-honoured elements of Jewish life which make for continuity with our past and which have intrinsic value and content. (Arzt, 1955, 63)

In subscribing to this approach, Conservative Jews viewed Judaism as an evolving organism that remained spiritually vibrant by adjusting to environmental and cultural conditions. In consequence, Conservative Jewish thinkers attempted to preserve those elements of the tradition which they believed to be spiritually meaningful while simultaneously setting aside those observances which actually hindered the continued growth of Judaism. Such obsolete practices were not abrogated, but simply ignored. In a similar spirit, Conservative Jews in contrast with the Orthodox, felt no compulsion to accept theological doctrines which they believed were out-moded – thus Conservative Judaism broke with Orthodoxy regarding the belief that the *Torah* was revealed in its entirety to Moses on Mount Sinai. In its quest to modernize the faith, Conservative scholars sought to establish an authoritative body to adapt Judaism to contemporary circumstances; as early as 1918 there was a considerable desire to establish 'a body of men learned in the law who will be able to advise us concerning the great questions that arise in our present day religious life' (Raphael, 1984, 97). Thus, even though the Conservative movement refused to formulate a detailed platform or series of creedal statements, these features of

Conservative Judaism provided a coherent and imaginative approach to the tradition.

Conservative Beliefs

Although the Conservative movement has not issued a specific statement of its underlying beliefs, it is possible to isolate a number of its ideological principles. Regarding belief in God, Conservative thinkers have generally subscribed to the traditional understanding of the Deity as omnipotent, omniscient, and all-good. For example, Seymour Siegel, Professor of Theology at the Seminary, depicted God as a transcendent person who gave the *Torah* to Israel and who 'is addressed and . . . addressed us . . . reveals himself . . . and tells man what he wishes and what he expects of mankind' (Siegel, 1980, 398–402). Throughout its history such a conception of the Divine dominated Conservative thought. Conservative thinkers have also largely endorsed the traditional doctrine of divine revelation. In the words of Louis Finkelstein, Professor of Talmud and Chancellor at the Seminary, 'The codes of law in Exodus, Leviticus and Deuteronomy, though expressed in prosaic form . . . can only be recognized as prophetic and divine, in the same sense that the fiery words of Isaiah and Jeremiah are prophetic and divine (Finkelstein, 1948, 45).

Yet in contrast with Orthodoxy, there remains considerable ambiguity about the nature of this divine communication. Unlike Orthodox thinkers who view revelation as verbal in nature and Reform theologians who conceive of the *Torah* as a human product, the Conservative movement has generally attempted to bridge these two extremes. Within Conservative Judaism revelation is understood as a divinely initiated process involving human composition. As to what constitutes the nature of such a divine–human encounter, Conservative writers vary: some argue that human beings correctly recorded the divine will as revealed on Sinai; others that those who wrote the Scriptures were simply divinely inspired. Yet despite such differences of interpretation, most Conservative thinkers acknowledge greater divine involvement in the *Torah* as opposed to the other books of the Hebrew Scriptures even though they reject the Orthodox conviction that God had literally revealed the entire *Torah* to Moses.

The theological extremes with the movement are represented by a number of leading thinkers who wrestled with this issue. Abraham Heschel, Professor of Ethics and Mysticism at the Seminary, for example, viewed God as an overwhelming presence; in his view, 'the speech of God is not less, but more than literally real . . . If God is alive, then the Bible is his voice' (Heschel, 1955, 244–5). For Heschel, revelation is not simply inspiration, although those who heard God recorded more what they understood than what they actually heard. Revelation, he believed, is the transmission of thought and will from heaven to earth; however, since heaven remains heaven and what is earthly remains earthly, such divine disclosure must be translated into human thought-forms. Along similar lines, Gilbert S. Rosenthal, rabbi of Temple Beth El in Cedarhurst New York, affirmed that the 'biblical kernel of Jewish law . . . is divine – the revealed will of God' (Rosenthal, 1980, 376). Again, Ernst Simon, Visiting Professor at the Seminary, depicted the Bible as a 'human echo of the divine voice . . . a human translation of God's word' (Simon, 1958, 3–4). In contrast with this conception, Ben Zion Bokser, rabbi of the Forest Hills Jewish Centre in Long Island, New York, maintained that revelation should be understood essentially as inspirational in character. According to Bokser, since revelation is the power behind oneself that brought new visions of truth and beauty to the world, it is the breathing in by humans of the message they felt compelled to record. In the opinion of other Conservative writers, however, the Hebrew Scriptures are devoid of divine inspiration. The Bible, they insist, is solely the product of human creativity.

Regarding *halakhah*, Conservative writers emphasized the importance of conserving the laws of traditional Judaism, including dietary observances; Sabbath, festival and liturgical prescriptions; and ethical precepts. None the less, Conservative thinkers advocated change and renewal. On the whole they stressed the historical importance of the Jewish heritage. As Ben Zion Bokser explained:

Conservatism admits the propriety of change. It admits the divine origin of the *Torah*; but it asserts that, as we encounter it, every divine element is encumbered with a human admixture, that the divine element . . . rests in specific forms which are historically conditioned. These historically conditioned forms are . . . subject to adjustment. (Bokser, 1964, 12–13)

Guided by such an approach to law, the Conservative movement resorted to what Schechter called the 'conscience of catholic Israel' in reaching decisions about the status of biblical and rabbinic law. In the early years of the United Synagogue, such figures as Louis Ginzberg urged Conservative Jews to strive for consensual agreement. As a result 'catholic Israel' came to signify the vast majority of the membership of Conservative congregations. In addition, a body of representative rabbis chosen by the Rabbinic Assembly of America (the rabbinical body of the movement) formed the Committee on Jewish Law; later this body was expanded into a Committee on Jewish Law and Standards. The Committee ruled on issues of Jewish law in the light of past needs and present circumstances. In the words of Alexander Kohut, 'the teaching of the ancients is the starting point', yet the Committee was anxious not to lose sight of what is needed in every generation. Initially the Committee was criticized for its reactionary conservatism, however, when the committee was enlarged the new chairman, Morris Adler, vowed no longer to halt between 'fear of the orthodox and danger to reform', but instead to articulate 'positive and unambiguous affirmations' and to 'introduce into our thinking this revolutionary fact – the impact of an entirely changed world both outer and inner' (Raphael, 1984, 102).

Unless the Committee made unanimous recommendations, congregational rabbis were free to use their own authority to decide which course of action to follow. Although this resulted in charges of inconsistency, this approach allowed freedom of decision-making for individual rabbis. In formulating its attitude to *halakhah*, Conservative Judaism maintained that halakhic change does not emanate from God's revelation on Mount Sinai, but from catholic Israel – the Conservative movement thus based its decisions on human reasoning rather than the divine will. In the words of the rabbi and writer, Harold Kushner, the authority of the law is grounded in *Torah Mitoldot Ameninu* rather than *Torah MiSinai*. By this he meant that 'generations of our people have found holiness in performing them (laws) and continue to do so today' (Raphael, 1984, 104). In expanding this approach the Conservative movement has in general considered the main outlines of the halakhic system as binding but have allowed individuals to fill in the amount of detail they wish to select – this is the area where personal choice is paramount.

Concerning Jewish peoplehood, the Conservative movement consistently affirmed the pre-eminence of *Klal Yisrael* (the body of Israel). Yet despite this insistence, there has not been the same unanimity about the notion of God's chosen people. Although the Sabbath and High Holy Day prayerbooks have retained the traditional formula ('You have chosen us from all the nations'), there has been a wide diversity of interpretation of the concept of chosenness among Conservative thinkers. According to Robert Gordis, for example, 'no other people has produced a group of men comparable in spiritual insight and moral character to the Hebrew prophets'. In light of this view he defined chosenness as 'service': 'Israel is "the chosen people", chosen . . . for the service of humanity' (Gordis, 1970, 27–8). For Simon Greenberg, Professor of Theology at the Seminary, chosenness is not 'innate biological superiority', nor is it 'privileges denied to any other human being'. Instead it consists of 'a greater obligation to study and obey the *Torah*' (Greenberg, 1955, 123). In Ben Zion Bokser's view, chosenness is not unique to the Jews. 'All groups', he argued, 'are equally God's chosen, the unique vehicles of his revelation and the instruments of his purposes in history' (Bokser, 1941, 252). Similarly, Louis Finkelstein was anxious to avoid attributing special excellence to any particular group; the Jewish nation, he stated, had done great things, but it also had its share of weaknesses. Thus, even though the formal language of the prayerbook stated that the Jewish people had been elected by God, Conservative thinkers have radically modified this concept.

As a consequence of its dedication to the peoplehood of Israel, the Conservative movement has from its inception been dedicated to the founding of a Jewish state. Religion and nationality, Conservative thinkers argued, are inseparably related. For Louis Ginzberg, Jewish nationalism without religion would be a tree without fruit; Jewish religion without Jewish nationalism would be a tree without roots. In the late nineteenth and early twentieth century, leading figures in Conservative Judaism were thus ardent Zionists, and as early as 1927, Israel Goldstein, rabbi of New York's Bnai Jeshurun, reported that the Zionist Organization of America regarded the Conservative rabbinate as a bulwark of American Zionism. Nearly twenty years later, Solomon Freehof, a leading Reform rabbi, noted that nearly the entire Conservative rabbinate as well as membership of Conservative congregations were pro-Zionist. By 1983 more than a hundred rabbis ordained at the Seminary had left America for Israel.

Related to its espousal of Jewish peoplehood, the Conservative movement under the influence of Mordecai Kaplan, Professor at the Seminary, embraced the concept of Judaism as both a religious and secular civilization. As early as the First World War, he wrote that Judaism is 'the *tout ensemble* of all the elements of what is usually termed the cultural life of a people, such as language, folkways, patterns of social organization, social habits and standards, creative arts, religion' (Kaplan, 1916, 170). According to Kaplan, the totality of Jewish activities at all levels – not simply the ostensibly religious acts – should be considered aspects of Judaism. During this period Kaplan's writing began to have an impact on Seminary ordinands, and there was an increase in the creation of synagogue-centres which combined religious and secular functions. In 1916, Kaplan created the first synagogue-centre in New York City; in 1920, Israel Levinthal established the Brooklyn Jewish Centre, the most famous of these institutions. Such centres were developed to serve as the focus of Jewish life. As Levinthal wrote: 'in our community all the Zionist, all the work for Hebrew culture, for philanthropy, for every phase of Jewish life, is being done through the centre' (Levinthal, 1928, 65). Similar synagogue-centres were later established in Cleveland, Philadelphia, Newark, Chicago, Manhattan, Jacksonville and several Long Island communities. These new Jewish centres not only conducted religious services but also showed films, housed orchestras, organized athletic teams, fostered drama clubs, and held adult education classes. Some hired rabbis to direct the social and educational activities; others employed full-time recreational leaders. This new Jewish establishment was organized to encompass all dimensions of Jewish life. As Israel Goldstein explained, these synagogue-centres were 'built on the theory that there should be no cleavage between the religious and secular activities of man (and) to give full expression to all interests, physical, social, intellectual, within the province of the synagogue' (Goldstein, 1928, 32). In the 1930s and 1940s fewer of these intitutions were created, but after the Second World War a number of Conservative leaders called on the movement to remake the synagogue into a synagogue-centre.

A final aspect of Conservative ideology relates to the status of women. In 1947, Mordecai Kaplan distinguished between three distinct attitudes in the movement towards *halakhah*. On the right, traditionalists were most reluctant to make changes in ritual law. Centrists on the other hand no longer believed in the revelation at Sinai as a historical event but viewed it as a historical process continuing into the twentieth century. As a consequence, they permitted change in ritual and law if it was sanctioned by legal precedent. Finally, leftists, including Kaplan, did not hesitate to advocate modification to the code of Jewish law if it was necessary in the light of contemporary circumstances. In 1948 the Rabbinical Assembly Law Committee attempted to represent these three tendencies in its ruling about the status of women, but in later years the leftists along with centrists issued rulings which attempted to remove the traditional legal distinctions based on gender.

In 1955, the Committee on Jewish Law and Standards voted in favour of women being called to the reading of the *Torah* and added to the *ketubah* (the Jewish marriage document) a clause which equalized men and women, and women counted equally with men in a quorum necessary for communal prayer. In addition, the United Synagogue recommended that married women have a vote equal to their husbands, single women be entitled to membership, and women be eligible for any congregational office. Although there was initially considerable reluctance to ordain women as rabbis, in 1978 a commission of lay and professional Conservative Jews ruled that there is no direct halakhic objection to acts of training and ordaining a woman to be a rabbi, preacher and teacher. The Seminary at first rejected this proposal, but in 1983 the Faculty approved the admission and ordination of women.

The Origins of Reconstructionist Judaism

Unlike Reform and Conservative Judaism, Reconstructionist Judaism developed out of the thinking of an individual scholar. Born in Lithuania in 1881, Mordecai Kaplan had a traditional education in Vilna and came to New York City as a child in 1889. After graduating from the City College of New York and the Jewish Theological Seminary, he received a master's degree from Columbia University in 1902. He then became an associate minister of Rabbi Moses S. Margolis at New York's Orthodox Kehilath Jeshurun. Although officially Orthodox, Kaplan increasingly became disenchanted with traditional Jewish doctrine. In 1909 he was invited by Solomon Schechter to direct the Teachers' Institute of the Seminary. The following year he became Professor of Homiletics at the Seminary's rabbinical school where he taught philosophy of religion.

During the 1910s and 1920s, Kaplan enaged in wide-ranging congregational work. In 1915, together with several former Kehilath Jeshurun members who had moved to the Upper West Side, Kaplan organized the New York Jewish Centre where he experimented with the concept of Judaism as a civilization. Two years later the first stage of a million-dollar synagogue-centre was completed on West 86th Street where Kaplan officiated as rabbi. In addition to overseeing religious worship he implemented a programme of activities including study, drama, dance, song, basketball and callisthenics. During these years Kaplan supported controversial political issues and challenged traditional Jewish belief. When the Board of Directors demanded strict Orthodoxy in 1921, Kaplan resigned and founded the Society for the Advancement of Judaism which he led for the next two decades.

According to some scholars, Reconstructionism as a movement began in 1922 when Kaplan initiated a policy of reconstructing Judaism to meet the demands of modern life; others trace its origin to the publication of *Judaism as a Civilization* in 1934. Kaplan himself contended that the movement emerged in 1935 when as a result of publishing *Judaism as a Civilization*, he and others launched the Reconstructionist magazine. In any event, his book provided the foundation for Reconstructionist ideology. In this work Kaplan began by evaluating the main religious groupings of American Jewry. In his view, Reform had correctly recognized the evolving character of Judaism, yet it ignored the social basis of Jewish identity as well as the organic character of Jewish peoplehood. Neo-Orthodoxy, on the other hand, acknowledged Judaism as a way of life and provided an intensive programme of Jewish education. None the less, it mistakenly regarded the Jewish religion as unchanging. In contrast, Conservative Judaism was committed to the scientific study of the history of the Jewish faith while recognizing the unity of the Jewish people. Conservative Judaism, however, was too closely bound to the *halakah* and thus unable to respond to new circumstances. All of these movements failed to adjust adequately to the modern age; what was needed, Kaplan argued, was a definition of Judaism as an evolving religious civilization.

In the light of this vision of a reconstructed Judaism, Kaplan called for the re-establishment of a network of organic Jewish communities that would insure the self-perpetuation of the Jewish heritage. Membership of this new movement would be voluntary; leadership should be elected democratically; and private religious opinions would be respected. In addition, Kaplan proposed a worldwide Jewish assembly which would adopt a covenant defining the Jews as a transnational people. This formulation was based on the Jewish historian Simon Dubnow's concept of an autonomous global Jewry with the

Jewish essayist Ahad ha-Am's stress on the land of Israel as the spiritual centre of the Jewish nation. According to Kaplan, religion is the concretization of the collective self-consiousness of the group which is manifest in *sancta* (spiritual symbols such as persons, places, events and writings). Such *sancta* inspire feelings of reverence, commemorate what the group believes to be most valuable, provide historical continuity, and strengthen the collective consciousness of the people. In order for the Jewish community to survive, Kaplan believed it must eliminate its authoritarian, dogmatic features. In particular Judaism must divest itself of supernatural belief. The spiritual dimension of the faith must be reformulated in humanistic and naturalistic terms:

> When religion speaks of salvation it means in essence the experience of the worthwhileness of life. When we analyse our personal experience of life's worthwhileness we find that it is invariably based on specific ethical experiences – moral responsibility, honesty, loyalty, love, service. If carefully pursued, this analysis reveals that the source of our ethical experience is found in our willingness and ability to achieve self-fulfilment through reciprocity with others. This reciprocity in turn is an expression of a larger principle that operates in the cosmos in response to the demands of a cosmic force, the force that makes for creativity and interdependence in all things. (Kaplan, 1970, 70)

According to Kaplan, God is not a supernatural being but the power that makes for salvation. 'God', he wrote, 'is the sum of all the animating, organizing forces and relationships which are forever making a cosmos out of chaos' (Kaplan, 1962, 76). In his view, the idea of God must be understood fundamentally in terms of its effect:

> We learn more about God when we say that love is divine than when we say God is love. A veritable transformation takes place ... Divinity becomes relevant to authentic experience and therefore takes on a definiteness which is accompanied by an awareness of authenticity'. (Kaplan, 1970, 73)

In Kaplan's view, God is a 'trans-natural', 'super-factual' and 'super-experiential' transcendence which does not infringe on the law of nature. Such a notion is far-removed from the biblical and rabbinic concept of God as the creator and sustainer of the universe who chose the Jewish people and guides human humanity to its final destiny.

Many of the ideas found in *Judaism as a Civilization* were reflected in religious literature that appeared during this period. The *New Haggadah*, edited by Kaplan, Eugene Kohn and Ira Eisenstein, for example, applied Kaplan's theology to liturgical texts, subordinating miracles and plagues in the traditional *Haggadah* to the narrative of Israel's redemption from Egypt and its contemporary significance. Again, the *Sabbath Prayer Book* was designed for those who were dissatisfied with synagogue worship – its aim was to arouse emotion by eliminating theologically untenable passages and adding inspirational meterial drawn from the tradition. This new prayerbook deleted all references to the revelation of the *Torah* on Mount Sinai, the chosenness of Israel, and the doctrine of a personal Messiah. In response, a number of Kaplan's colleagues denounced him and the Union of Orthodox Rabbis excommunicated him for expressing atheism, heresy, and disbelief in the basic tenets of Judaism.

In the 1940s and 1950s the leaders of Reconstructionism insisted that they were not attempting to form a new branch of Judaism. As Jacob Agus, rabbi of Chicago's North Shore Agudas Achim, stated: 'Reconstructionism is "not a sect but a movement to concentrate and give organizational form to the elements of strength within all sections of American Judaism"' (Raphael, 1984, 185). Throughout this period Reconstructionists hoped to be able to infuse the three major groups within North American Judaism (Orthodoxy, Conservative Judaism and Reform Judaism) with its ideas. However, by the end of the 1960s the Reconstructionist movement had become a denomination – it had established a seminary to train Reconstructionist rabbis and had instituted a congregational structure. Regarding *halakhah*, the Reconstructionist Rabbinical Association issued a statement of its 1980 convention that placed authority in the Jewish people (as opposed to the rabbis) and created a process whereby each congregation would be free to evolve its own *minhag* (customs). Three years later the Association produced guidelines on intermarriage, encouraging rabbis to welcome mixed couples (a Jew and non-Jew), permit them to participate in Jewish synagogue life, and recognize their children as Jewish if raised as Jews. In addition, the Association decreed that rabbis could sanctify an intermarriage as long as it was accompanied by a civil, rather than a religious, ceremony.

Humanistic Judaism

Humanistic Judaism originated in 1965 when the Birmingham Temple in Detroit, Michigan, began to publicize its philosophy of Judaism. In 1966 a special committee for Humanistic Judaism was organized at the Temple to share service and educational material with rabbis and laity throughout the country. The following year a meeting of several leaders of the movement met in Detroit, issuing a statement which affirmed that Judaism should be governed by empirical reason and human needs; in addition, a new magazine, *Humanistic Judaism*, was founded. Two years later, two new Humanistic congregations were established: Temple Beth Or in Deerfield, Illinois, and a Congregation for Humanistic Judaism in Fairfield County, Connecticut. In 1969 the Society for Humanistic Judaism was founded in Detroit to provide a basis for co-operation among Humanistic Jews; the next year the first annual conference of the Society met in Detroit. During the next ten years new congregations were established in Boston, Toronto, Los Angeles, Washington, Miami, Long Beach and Huntington, New York. In subsequent years, Secular Humanistic Judaism became an international movement with supporters on five continents. The National Federation, consisting of thirty thousand members, currently comprises nine national organizations in the United States, Canada, Britain, France, Belgium, Israel, Australia, Argentina and Uruguay.

In 1986 the Federation issued a proclamation stating its ideology and aims:

> We believe in the value of human reason and in the reality of the world which reason discloses. The natural universe stands on its own, requiring no supernatural intervention. We believe in the

value of human existence and in the power of human beings to solve their problems both individually and collectively. Life should be directed to the satisfaction of human needs. Every person is entitled to life, dignity and freedom. We believe in the value of Jewish identity and in the survival of the Jewish people. Jewish history is a human story. Judaism, as the civilization of the Jews, is a human creation. Jewish identity is an ethnic reality. The civilization of the Jewish people embraces all manifestations of Jewish life, including Jewish languages, ethical traditions, historic memories, cultural heritage, and especially the emergence of the state of Israel in modern times. Judaism also embraces many belief systems and lifestyles. As the creation of the Jewish people in all ages, it is always changing. We believe in the value of a secular humanistic democracy for Israel and for all the nations of the world. Religion and state must be separate. The individual right to privacy and moral autonomy must be guaranteed. Equal rights must be granted to all, regardless of race, sex, creed or ethnic origin.

In accordance with this philosophy of Judaism, the Federation advocated a new conception of Jewish identity. In answer to the question 'Who is a Jew?', the movement declared:

We, the members of the International Federation of Secular Humanistic Jews, believe that the survival of the Jewish people depends on a broad view of Jewish identity. We welcome into the Jewish people all men and women who sincerely desire to share the Jewish experience regardless of their ancestry. We challenge the assumption that the Jews are primarily or exclusively a religious community and that religious convictions or behaviour are essential to full membership in the Jewish people.

The Jewish people is a world people with a pluralistic culture and civilization all its own. Judaism, as the culture of the Jews, is more than theological commitment. It encompasses many languages, a vast body of literature, historical memories and ethical values. In our times the shadow of the Holocaust and the rebirth of the State of Israel are a central part of Jewish consciousness.

We Jews have a moral responsibility to welcome all people who seek to identify with our culture and destiny. The children and spouses of inter-marriage who desire to be part of the Jewish people must not be cast aside because they do not have Jewish mothers and do not wish to undergo religious conversion. The authority to define 'who is a Jew' belongs to all the Jewish people and cannot be usurped by any part of it.

In response to the destructive definition of a Jew now proclaimed by some orthodox authorities, and in the name of the historic experience of the Jewish people, we therefore, affirm that a Jew is a person of Jewish descent or any person who declares himself or herself to be a Jew and who identifies with the history, ethical values, culture, civilization, community and fate of the Jewish people.

Such an ideology of Judaism is based on a radical reinterpretation of the tradition. According to the major exponent of Humanistic Judaism, Sherwin Wine, the traditional conception of Jewish history is mistaken. In his view, Abraham, Isaac and Jacob never existed. Further, the Exodus account is a myth:

> There is no historical evidence to substantiate a massive Hebrew departure from the land of the Pharaohs. As far as we can surmise, the Hebrew occupation of the hill country on both sides of the Jordan was continuous. The twelve tribes never left their ancestral land, never endured 400 years of slavery, and never wandered the Sinai desert. (Wine, 1986, 35–6)

Moreover, Moses was not the leader of the Hebrews, nor did he compose the *Torah*. In this light, it is an error to regard the biblical account as authoritative; rather it is a human account of the history of the Israelite nation whose purpose is to reinforce the faith of the Jewish nation. Humanistic Judaism, however, rejects this presupposition of traditional Judaism and insists that each Jew should be free to exercise his own personal autonomy concerning questions of religious belief and practice.

Dedicated to Jewish survival, Humanistic Judaism emphasized the importance of Jewish festivals in fostering Jewish identity. Yet for Humanistic Jews, they must be detached from their supernatural origins and be reinterpreted in the light of modern circumstances. As Wine explained:

> The Jewish holidays have no intrinsic divine connection. They derive from the evolution of the human species and human culture . . . For Humanistic Jews the holidays need to be rescued from rabbinic tyranny and given a secular language and a secular story. (Wine, 1985, 150)

Shabbat, for example, can serve as a testimony to the human bonds which make survival possible; it should be a time when Humanistic Jews celebrate the human support system: 'Our Shabbat dinner is a tribute to the family that sits around the table. Our Shabbat service is a tribute to the Jewish extended family that shares our history and social fate' (Wine, 1982, 154). Similarly, the High Holy Days can serve as a time in which to reflect on human needs: '*Rosh Hashanah* and *Yom Kippur* open our Jewish year with the most important message of Jewish history. Human dignity is not the gift of destiny. It is a human achievement, requiring courage and human self-reliance' (Wine, 1982, 157).

Parallel humanistic themes are featured in the seasonal holidays: *Sukkot, Hannukah* and Passover. A humanistic *Sukkot* should be a tribute to human culture, agricultural, pastoral and urban. *Hannukah,* too, celebrates human potential:

> If *Rosh Hashanah* and *Yom Kippur* are testimonies to the assumption of human responsibility for human life in the face of an absurd and indifferent universe, if *Sukkot* is the witness to the power of human ingenuity and creativity, then *Hanukkah* is the celebration of human power, the increasing power of people to use the world to enhance the quality of human life. (Wine, 1985, 164)

Passover also glorifies human achievement – it celebrates the rediscovery of human dignity.

Such an interpretation of these traditional holidays as well as others in the Jewish calendar provides a basis for extolling human potential. So, too, does Humanistic Judaism's understanding of life-cycle events. The ceremonies connected with these events emphasize the importance of group survival. However, humanistic philosophy – grounded in the conviction that all persons are equal – rejects the practice of male circumcision:

> A humanistic morality that defends female quality would have a hard time justifying a birth ritual that excludes women . . . The *brit* (the covenant ceremony) is by its very nature, inconsistent with a humanistic Jewish value system. (Wine, 1985, 181)

In its place Humanistic Jews have substituted an occasion that provides equal status to boys and girls and dramatizes the connection of the child with the future of the family, the Jewish people and humanity.

Likewise, Humanistic Judaism fosters a humanistic maturity ceremony which reflects the ethical commitments of Humanistic Jews. Insuring the equality of both sexes, such ceremonies are designed to express the beliefs of the individual celebrants as well as the ideals of the community. Within a humanistic framework, there are a variety of alternatives available:

> Presenting a lecture to an adult audience is only one of many options. Music, dance, humour, science and business are as much a part of Jewish culture as worship. (Wine, 1985, 186)

As an important transitional event, the marrage ceremony should also embody humanistic values. According to Wine, the wedding should embrace the conception of a bride and groom publicly declaring their commitment of support and loyalty to one another. The most important feature of this ritual is the pledge made by both partners in the presence of family and friends. Such a statement should not be simply a ritualistic formula – rather it should be a personal declaration, accompanied with the exchange of rings or other gifts symbolic of their commitment. Humanistic marrage ceremonies also include songs and poetry about love and loyalty, a marriage contract expressive of the couple's personal relationship, and a philosophic statement about the humanistic meaning of marriage.

Rituals connected with death should similarly be expressive of humanistic principles. For Humanistic Jews, mortality is an unavoidable and final event. Accepting this truth, it is possible to live courageously and generously in the face of tragedy. 'A humanistic Jewish memorial service is an opportunity to teach a humanistic philosophy of life. Both the meditations and the eulogies must serve to remind people that the value of personal life lies in its quality, not in its quantity' (Wine, 1982, 182).

Humanistic Judaism then offers an option for those who wish to identify with the Jewish community despite their rejection of the traditional understanding of God's nature and activity. Unlike Reconstructionist Judaism, with its emphasis on the observances of the past, Humanistic Judaism fosters a radically new approach. The Jewish heritage is relevant only in so far as it advances humanistic ideals. In addition, traditional definitions and principles are set aside in the quest to create a Judaism consonant with a scientific and pluralistic age. Secular in orientation, Humanistic Jews seek to create a world in which the Jewish people are dedicated to the betterment of all humankind.

Polydoxy

A final form of non-Orthodox Judaism is Polydoxy, a new religious ideology propounded by Alvin Reines, Professor of Philosophy at the Hebrew Union College. Although this new approach has not led to the establishment of religious institutions or associations of synagogues, it has had an important impact on a number of Reform rabbis. As Reines explained in *Polydoxy*, this new movement arose from an analysis of the form of authority that is proper for liberal Jews. According to Reines, it is no longer possible for contemporary Jews to accept the authority of the biblical and rabbinic tradition since the belief in verbal revelation is no longer viable. In the past, traditional Jews felt bound to accept the theological tenets of Judaism as well as both biblical and rabbinic ordinances because of their belief in *Torah MiSinai*. However, given that most Jews have rejected this cardinal tenet of the faith, there is no reason for Jews to feel compelled to accept the authority of the *Torah* or the rabbinic tradition. 'Having, therefore, rejected the concept of verbal revelation,' he wrote, 'any documents put forth in the Reform Jewish community as revelation must be regarded as constituting either ambiguous or natural revelation and, as such, are fallible' (Reines, 1987, 22).

Given this rejection of authority, Reines asked whether any person or group of persons within the Reform Jewish community can claim to possess absolute authority – can they morally choose to lay down prescriptions that others must obey? The answer, he stated, is that they cannot. Instead, he argued that each person must be allowed to exercise personal autonomy:

The principle has been laid down that every person is religiously free, possessing an ultimate right to religious self-authority. Now, if this principle is to be rebutted by any members of a religious community, they must demonstrate that they possess absolute authority, namely, a right to authority over the other members superior to the latter's own right to authority over themselves. The only way in which members who wish to exercise authority in a religious community can demonstrate possession of this superior right is to show that they have received the right from a theistic God. Members of the Reform Jewish community . . . however, owing to their rejection of verbal revelation, cannot demonstrate that they possess such a right. (Reines, 1987, 22–3)

The principle of freedom – the Freedom Covenant – Reines insisted, is paramount. It states that:

every member of a religious community possesses an ultimate right to religious self-authority, and that every member of the religious community pledges to affirm the ultimate religious self-authority of all other members in return for their pledge to affirm her or his own. The corollary of the Freedom Covenant is that the freedom of each member of the community ends where the other members' freedom begins. (Reines, 1987, 25)

Another name for a Freedom Covenant religion, he explained, is Polydoxy, which literally means 'many beliefs'. Those who subscribe to such a system may hold differing beliefs regarding such subjects as revelation, immortality, and the meaning of the word 'God'. Hence Polydoxy contrasts with Orthodoxy in that its adherents are under no compulsion to accept any particular theological doctrine. Similarly, within Polydoxy, practices cannot be determined by any small group or through a majority vote. Here as well, individuals are free to embrace those commandments which they find religiously significant. As far as authority is concerned, each member of the Polydox community is free to exercise his own judgment.

Comparing Polydoxy with Orthodoxy, Reines outlines a number of central differences:

1. A polydox community is created by a free act. When a group of individuals enter into a Freedom Covenant, Polydoxy is created. Orthodox communities, on the other hand, view themselves as established through a supernatural action. Thus

Orthodox Jews contend that the Jewish people were formed through the covenant established by God with the Hebrews on Mount Sinai.

2. The simple dogma of a polydox community is the Freedom Covenant which is entered into through free choice. Orthodox Judaism, however, maintains that its central tenets were revealed by God, and is therefore true and binding on all members of the community. No alteration to this revealed system is permitted, and those who reject its authority should be regarded as heretics.

3. Every member of a polydox community is invested with self-autonomy – there is, therefore, no person in the community who has the power to prescribe rules for others. In Orthodox Judaism, by contrast, the community is governed by religious leaders who possess the authority to legislate what members of the community should believe and how they should behave. As a result, individuals are compelled to surrender their own decision-making to those who claim to act through divine right.

4. In Polydoxy there are no services, rituals or ceremonies which are obligatory on all – rather each person is free to determine his own religious lifestyle. Orthodox Judaism, however, obliges members to follow the ritual prescriptions of the faith.

5. Within Polydoxy there should be no attempt to indoctrine adherents; instead each person is free to exercise his own freedom in assessing the truth or falsity of religious doctrines and the relevance of traditional practices. The aim of Orthodox education, however, is to impart and reinforce the teachings of the Jewish faith.

In presenting this new interpretation of Judaism, Reines offered a theology of Jewish Polydoxy. Emphasizing that throughout history theological concepts have undergone radical revision, Reines argued that religious terms have no fixed meaning. As a consequence, in a Polydox community all religious views are valid. None the less, Reines proposed a theoretical framework for determining what he believes to be the most appropriate interpretation of God's nature. In his view religious belief should be based on objective evidence since this is the underlying principle of Polydoxy as a theological system:

Polydoxy came into existence as a result of the conclusion that
Scripture is fallible, the work at least in part, of humans. This
conclusion was arrived at through critical and objective study,
scientific inquiry applied to Scripture. It it not natural to apply
this same method to the theology of Polydox Judaism as well?
(Reines, 1987, 174)

The basic requirement for determining the objective validity
of religious language is the theory of empirical verification.

On the basis of this theory, 'a proposition or series of
propositions concerning the external world will be true if there
are predictable or observable consequences of such a proposition or propositions' (Reines, 1987, 175). Thus, if there are
empirical consequences of a definition of God, then the
proposition 'God exists' will be true; alternatively if no
consequences are present, it must either be meaningless or
false. In conformity with this principle, Reines stated that
'God is the enduring possibility of being'. As he explained:

> By being is meant *selfa* (of self-data) and *sensa* (or sense-data).
> Inasmuch as being is analysable without remainder into *selfa* and
> *sensa*, the existence of God is verified whenever *selfa* and *sensa* can
> both be experienced, and the existence of God is disproved when,
> under equivalent conditions of personal normalcy, *selfa* are
> experienced and *sensa* no longer are. God is disproved as the
> enduring possibility of being, rather than as the enduring
> possibility of sense experience alone because the person (that is,
> the continuing self-consciousness that is constructed out of *selfa*) is
> evidently dependent upon the external world (*sensa* and the
> unobservables reducible to *sensa*) and with the annihilation of the
> external world, the inexorable annihilation of the person may be
> inferred. (Reines, 1987, 175–6)

The definition of God as the enduring possibility of being is
what Reines calls hylotheism, and should be subsumed under
the category of finite God concepts. Like similar theories,
hylotheism does not envisage the Divine as a perfect being –
instead the imperfection attributed to God refers to his
inability to overcome the force of evil. As a result of this view,
Reines argued that God cannot exist without the world:

> God has no meaning without being; being has no endurance
> without God. God's existence is not absolute; the enduring

possibility of being exists as a correlative of being. The world was not created by an absolute God who arbitrarily willed it so; rather the world exists because the divine existence is unconditionally dependent upon it. (Reines, 1987, 177)

Further Reines insisted that such a conception of God undermines the traditional understanding of divine activity:

> The perfect providence of theistic absolutism, its Messiahs and supernatural eschatologies, have no place in a world where the enduring exists only as a possibility and the actual world is always finite. (Reines, 1987, 178)

Instead, human beings are partners with God in the process of actualization. This he contended, is the ethics of hylotheistic necessity: if a person acts, then God reacts. Such a theology, Reines pointed out, is most consistent with Polydoxy. Yet no member of a Polydox community is under an obligation to accept this view; rather every person is free to formulate his own personal religious convictions. Here then, is a radical approach to contemporary Jewish existence. Grounded in the ideology of liberalism and directed primarily to members of the Reform community, Polydoxy provides an alternative theological approach to the dilemmas posed by the post-Enlightenment world.

Part III
OPEN JUDAISM

6

Disassembling Traditional Judaism

Through the centuries the Jewish people were sustained by a belief in an all-good and all-powerful God who revealed his will on Mount Sinai and exercised providence over all creation. On the basis of such a commitment, the nation was united by a dedication to a shared religious tradition. Yet as we have seen, in a post-Enlightenment world the Jewish community has fragmented into a number of sub-groups with conflicting orientations and ideologies. This shattering of the monolithic system of Judaism has resulted from a variety of causes. First, it has become increasingly difficult to sustain the biblical and rabbinic picture of God in the light of scientific discovery; in addition, the events of the Holocaust have posed fundamental questions about the notion of a benevolent Deity who cares for his children as a loving father. Further, the findings of biblical scholarship have called into question the doctrine of *Torah MiSinai*. Under the impact of these developments, Jewish belief has undergone a process of disintegration: no longer is it possible for most Jews to believe in such doctrines as the coming of the Messiah, the resurrection of the dead, messianic redemption, and final judgment, and there has been a growing disenchantment with religious observances. Jewry has ceased to be one people with a common heritage; rather the Jewish community has disintegrated into antagonistic factions which lack a shared religious vocabulary.

The Challenge to Theism

As we have seen, throughout history Jews have subscribed to a belief in an all-good, all-powerful, and all-knowing God who created the universe, sustains it, and guides humanity to its ultimate fulfilment in a world-to-come. Such belief sustained the Jewish people through suffering and tragedy and provided the nation with a sense of ultimate purpose. Since the Enlightenment, however, this religious conviction has been challenged in various ways, leading to the fragmentation of the monolithic religious system of the Jewish past. Arguably the most serious challenge to traditional Jewish belief has been due to the expansion of scientific investigation. Since the Renaissance scientific knowledge has increased in such fields as astronomy, geology, zoology, chemistry and physics. Discoveries in these areas have called into question biblical claims about the origin and nature of the universe.

Increasingly it has become clear that in giving an account of the history of the Jewish nation, the biblical writers relied on a pre-scientific understanding of the world. In the last few centuries, scholarly investigations into the culture of the ancient Near East have provided a basis for reconstructing the primitive world-view that provided the framework for the thinking of the ancient Israelites. As a result of the expansion of scientific knowledge and an increased awareness of the thought-world of biblical writers, most modern Jews are no longer able to accept the scriptural account of the origin and nature of the world as well as God's activity. The vast majority of Jews, for example, no longer find credible the biblical cosmology of a three-storied universe with heaven in the sky, hell beneath, and the sun circling around the earth. Further, most Jews have abandoned the belief that the world was created some six thousand years ago, and that human beings and animals came into being in their present forms at the same time. Again, the notion that at a future date the decomposed corpses of humanity will be resurrected no longer seems plausible in the light of a scientific understanding of the laws of nature. In essence, the modern age has witnessed scientific advance on the one hand and the retreat of traditional belief on the other.

The climate of thought in the twentieth century is thus one in which scientific explanation has taken over the role of theological interpretation. Even though the sciences have not disproved the claims of religion, they have provided a rational explanation of events that previously would have been understood as the result of God's will. In this light faith has come to be regarded as a personal preoccupation that is destined to be ousted from the central areas of human knowledge until at last it will have the same status as such fields as astrology. In the future, religion is likely to be perceived as an antiquated relic of previous ages when scientific knowledge was less extensive. The sciences have thus effectively established the autonomy of the natural world. As the philosopher of religion, John Hick, explained:

> From the galaxies whose vastness numbs the mind to the unimaginably small events and entities of the subatomic universe, and throughout the endless complexities of our own world, which lies between these virtual infinities, nature can be studied without any reference to God. The universe investigated by the sciences proceeds exactly as though no God exists. (Hick, 1973, 45)

A second objection to belief in God is the fact of evil. For many Jews it is the existence of human suffering that makes the idea of a perfectly loving God utterly implausible. As a challenge to religious belief the problem of evil has traditionally been formulated as a dilemma: If God is perfectly loving, he must wish to abolish evil; and if he is all-powerful, he must be able to abolish evil. But evil exists; therefore, God cannot be both omnipotent and perfectly loving.

In a post-Holocaust world this religious perplexity has been highlighted by the terrors of the Nazi era. An illustration of the potency of this problem is elucidated by the Jewish writer, Elie Wiesel. In his autobiographical memoir *Night* he depicted his transition from youthful belief to disillusionment. At the beginning of the novel the author described himself as a young boy fascinated with God's mystery, studying *Talmud* and *Kabbalah* in the Transylvanian town of Sighet. Later, he was transported to Auschwitz where the erosion of his faith began. Shortly after his arrival, he questioned God: 'Some talked of God, of his mysterious ways, of the sins of the Jewish people and of their future deliverance. But I had ceased to pray. How

I sympathized with Job. I did not deny God's existence but I doubted his absolute justice' (Cohn-Sherbok, 1989, 92).

In a short time his religious rebellion deepened. In particular he was shocked by the incongruity of the Jewish liturgy that praised God and the events of the camps that indicted him. Dismayed by the new arrivals who recited the *Kaddish* when they recognized the nature of their plight, he felt revolt rise within him. 'Why should I bless his name?' he asked. 'The Eternal, Lord of the Universe, the all-powerful and terrible was silent. What had I to thank Him for?' As the novel continues, Wiesel's anger increased. At the New Year service, he refused to bless God and praise the universe in which there was mass murder: 'This day I had ceased to plead. I was no longer capable of lamentation. On the contrary, I felt very strong. I was the accuser, God the accused' (Cohn-Sherbok, 1989, 92). On Yom Kippur, he decided not to fast, 'There was no longer any reason why I should fast. I no longer accepted God's silence. As I swallowed my bowl of soup, I saw in the gesture an act. In the depths of my heart, I felt a great void' (Cohn-Sherbok, 1989, 93). Many Jews have shared Wiesel's despair; no longer are they are able to subscribe to a belief in an all-good, providential Deity who lovingly watches over his chosen people. Although a number of Jewish theologians have suggested solutions to this problem of suffering, none has provided an adequate answer. The Orthodox theologian, Bernard Maza, for example, argued in *With Fury Poured Out* that God brought about the Holocaust so as to ensure that *Torah* Judaism would flourish in the modern world. In formulating this thesis Maza presupposed that God is an all-powerful, benevolent Lord of history who is concerned with the destiny of his people. However, if God was ultimately responsible for the horrors of the death camps, it seems impossible to reconcile such mass murder with the traditional concept of God's nature. Surely if God is all-good, he would have wished to rescue innocent Jewish victims from the hands of the Nazis; if he is omnipotent he would have had the power to do so. Yet Maza contended that the Holocaust was an outpouring of divine fury. Surely, if God was concerned with the future of *Torah* Judaism, he could have accomplished his purposes without slaughtering a vast segment of the Jewish population.

Like Maza, the Reform theologian Ignaz Maybaum believed that the Holocaust was the result of divine providence. But in contrast to Maza, Maybaum argued in *The Face of God after Auschwitz* that God did not pour out his fury to revitalize *Torah* Judaism. Rather Maybaum believed that six million Jews who died in the concentration camps were chosen by God to become sacrificial victims in order to bring about God's purposes for the modern world. Again, there are serious difficulties with such a view. First, it makes no sense to think that God entered into a covenantal relationship with the Jewish people only to crucify them. Maybaum contended that like Nebuchadnezzar, Hitler was an instrument of God's, yet if God is omnipotent there would have been no need to murder six million Jews to inaugurate a new epoch in human history. While Maybaum appeared to follow the doctrine of omnipotence to its seemingly logical conclusion (God must be the cause of the Holocaust), he did not defend his attributes of love and justice. For most Jews it is impossible to believe in a God who would be the source of the terrors of the death camps.

Like both Maza and Maybaum, the Jewish philosopher Emil Fackenheim offered a positive theological response to the Holocaust in a wide range of writings. In his view God issued a further commandment to his chosen people out of Auschwitz. This 614th commandment decrees that Jews are forbidden to hand Hitler posthumous victories – they are commanded to survive as Jews, lest the Jewish people perish. The central difficulty with this position is that Fackenhein failed to give a justification for this claim; for those individuals who find it difficult to believe in God after the Holocaust, he did not provide an explanation for his conviction that God was present at Auschwitz and is providentially concerned with the destiny of his chosen people.

Such attempts to provide an explanation for God's ways have not persuaded most Jews whose faith has been shaken by the events of the Nazi era. In contemporary society traditional religious belief in God has been eclipsed by an overwhelming

sense that the universe is devoid of a divine presence. For many
the views of the radical Jewish theologian, Richard Rubenstein,
reflect their predicamant. In *After Auschwitz* Rubenstein
declared that he was no longer able to accept the traditional
biblical and rabbinic conception of God. 'When I say we live in
the time of the death of God,' he wrote, 'I mean that the thread
uniting God and man, Heaven and earth, has been broken. We
stand in a cold, silent, unfeeling cosmos, unaided by any
powerful power beyond our own resources. After Auschwitz,
what else can a Jew say about God' (Cohn-Sherbok, 1989, 82).

A third major challenge to Jewish theism stems from
naturalistic interpretations of the origin of religion – sceptics
assert that supernatural experience can be adequately accounted
for without postulating the existence of God. Preeminent
among these views in the sociological theory of religion
postulated by such thinkers as Emile Durkheim. According to
this theory, the gods whom human beings worship are
imaginary – they are unconsciously fabricated by society as
instruments whereby the thoughts and behaviour of individuals
can be controlled. Even though the devout believe they are in
the presence of a higher power that transcends their lives, they
are in fact, under an illusion. The reality they acknowledge,
however, is not in fact a supernatural being; rather it is a symbol
of society itself. God is thus simply a reflection of society's
absolute claim upon the loyalty of its members. On this
account, the religious practices of a particular group are rooted
in the needs of the community. As social beings, men and
women have conceived of society as an external reality invested
with holiness. Here then, is an interpretation of religion that
involves no reference to God as an external Deity who created
and oversees human destiny.

For many Jews such an understanding of religion has had
considerable appeal. Mordecai Kaplan, the founder of Reconstructionist Judaism, for example, based his explanation of
Judaism as a civilization on such an interpretation. Explaining
the evolution of religious belief, he wrote:

> Long before the human being was able to formulate the idea 'God',
> he was aware that there were elements in his environment, certain
> animate and inanimate objects, definite places, particular

persons upon whose help he depended for the fulfilment of his needs. He ascribed to them power, which he believed he could direct to his advantage by resorting to actions and formulas which we term magic . . . As man developed further, he extended the domain of holiness to include not only visible or picturable objects, events and persons, but also customs, laws, social relationships, truths and ideals. (Kaplan, 1967, 317–18)

Within the Jewish world such a naturalistic interpretation of religious belief has gained a considerable following.

Another naturalistic explanation of religion that has had a similar impact is psychological in character. Writers such as Sigmund Freud have contended that religious beliefs are nothing more than psychic defences against the threats of human existence. As Freud explained, 'nature rises up against us, majestic, cruel and inexorable' (Freud, 1961, 16). Yet human beings can employ methods to subdue such dangers:

We can apply the same methods against these violent supermen outside that we employ in our own society; we can try to adjure them, to appease them, to bribe them and, by so influencing them, we may rob them of part of their power. (Freud, 1961, 16–17)

In contemporary society there has been a growing acceptance of such a psychological explanation of religious belief. So these challenges to theism – stemming from the growth of science, the existence of human misery and suffering, and the emergence of naturalistic explanations of religious commitment – constitute major obstacles to traditional religious belief in the modern world.

Divine Revelation and Biblical Scholarship

According to traditional Judaism, the Five Books of Moses were dictated by God to Moses on Mount Sinai. This doctrine implies that the entire text – including precepts, theology and history – is of divine origin: all of its contents are inerrant. Such a belief guarantees the validity of the legal system, the Jewish view of God, and the concept of Israel's pre-eminence among the nations. In the modern period, however, it has become increasingly difficult to sustain this concept of

Scripture in the light of scholarly investigation and discovery. As early as the sixteenth century, scholars pointed out that the Five Books of Moses appear to be composed of different sources. In the sixteenth century, Thomas Hobbes in his *Leviathan*, accepted the Mosaic authorship of the Pentateuch but not of the anachronisms in the biblical text. In the same century, Baruch Spinoza in his *Tractatus Theologico-Politicus* asserted that the Pentateuch is a composite work compiled during the time of Ezra. Again, Richard Simon published a work at this time in which he argued that the Pentateuch is a compilation of different documents of different dates. In his view, the commandments were inspired by God, but the biblical narrative is of human origin.

These studies were followed by the work of Jean Astruc in the next century, generally considered to be the founder of modern biblical criticism. In a work published in 1753, he noted that entire portions of Genesis use the divine name *Elohim* whereas other portions use the Tetragrammaton, YHWH. This observation led Astruc to conjecture that one of the documents used by Moses was the Elohist (the document describing the origins of the universe). In Astruc's view there were thirteen documents that Moses used in compiling the *Torah*. Later other scholars, basing their interpretations on Astruc's work, maintained that various fragments of documents could be detected in the *Torah*, or that an original work of Moses had been expanded at different times. Eventually, scholars concluded that two major documents were used in the compilation of the Pentateuch: one using the divine name *Elohim*, and the other the Tetragrammaton. At the beginning of the nineteenth century, De Wette published a work in which he claimed that Deuteronomy was compiled shortly before it was discovered in the time of Josiah.

In the middle of the nineteenth century, sustained investigation by Karl Heinrich Graf and Julius Wellhausen concluded that the Five Books of Moses were composed of four main documents which once existed separately but were later combined by a series of editors or redactors. The first document, J, dating from the ninth century BC, attributes the most anthropomorphic character to God, referred to by the four Hebrew Letters YHWH. The second source, E, stemming from the eighth century BC, is less anthropomorphic and utilizes the divine name *Elohim*. In the seventh century BC the D source was written, concentrating on religious purity and the priesthood. Finally the P source from the fifth century BC, which has a more transcendental view of God, emphasizes the importance of the sacrificial cult.

By utilizing this framework, Graf and Wellhausen maintained that it is possible to account for the manifold problems and discrepancies in the biblical text: for example, there are two creation accounts in Genesis; the appointment of a king is sanctioned in Deuteronomy but opposed in 1 Samuel; Isaac appears to have spent eighty years on his death bed; camels bearing loads are mentioned in the narratives even though they were not domesticated until much later; the centralization of worship in Deuteronomy was unknown in prophetic times. These are only a few illustrations of textual difficulties which can be resolved by seeing the Five Books as the result of the weaving together of source material from different periods in the history of ancient Israel. The Graf–Wellhausen hypothesis was, however, modified by subsequent writers. Some scholars have preferred not to speak of separate sources, but of circles of tradition. On this view, J, E, P and D represent oral traditions rather than written documents. Further, these scholars stressed that the separate traditions themselves contain early material; thus it is a mistake to think they originated in their entirety at particular periods. Other scholars rejected the theory of separate sources altogether; they argued that oral traditions were modified throughout the history of ancient Israel and only eventually were compiled into a single narrative. Yet despite these different theories, there is a general recognition among biblical critics that the Pentateuch was not written by Moses; rather, it is seen as a collection of traditions originating at different times in ancient Israel.

Another major challenge to the traditional belief that God revealed the *Torah* to Moses on Mount Sinai stems from the field of biblical archaeology. From what is now known of Mesopotamian civilization, we can see that the Bible reflects various aspects of this cultural milieu. The physical structure of the universe as outlined in Genesis, parallels what is found in Near Eastern literature: the earth is conceived as a thin disk floating in the surrounding waters; under the earth is the abode of the dead. Like the gods of ancient literatures, the God of Israel is understood anthropomorphically. As with other peoples, the Israelites accepted magical procedures (Exod. 7.11–12), recognized the power of blessings and curses (Num. 22–4), and believed that God's will can be known through dreams, dice and oracles. Furthermore, as in other cultures, holy men, kings and priests were revered, and there was a preoccupation with ritual uncleanliness and purity as well as priestly rites.

In addition to these similarities, there are strong parallels between the Bible and literature of the ancient Near East: Genesis appears to borrow details from the Mesopotamian Epic of Gilgamesh in connection with the legend of the flood; biblical law bears a striking resemblance to ancient legal codes, such as the Assyrian treaties between a king and his vassals which are very like the covenantal relationship between God and Israel. Yet despite these parallels, Israelite monotheism radically transformed these mythological features: themes retained in the Bible are only briefly mentioned; biblical heroes are not worshipped; nor is the underworld a subject for speculation. The cult is free of rites to placate ghosts and demons; there is no ancestor worship; divination (such as investigating the livers of sacrificial animals) is forbidden. In essence, the biblical narratives are simplified and demythologized. There are no myths of the birth of gods, their rivalries, sexual relations or accounts of death and resurrection. Moreover, there is no mention of fate to which both men and gods are subject. Instead, the Bible concentrates on the moral condition of humanity within the context of divine providence.

Such demythologization is a particular feature of the biblical narratives. According to modern scholarship, the priestly editors composed a creation account (Gen. 1.2–4) markedly different from the Babylonian narrative. In the 'Enuma Elish', which is a reworking of old Sumerian themes, the primordial power Tiamat (salt water) and Apsu (sweet water) gave birth to a pair of forces which engendered other gods such as Anu (the god of heaven) and Ea (the god of running waters). Apsu plotted the destruction of the gods but was prevented by Ea. Later Tiamat with a second husband and an army of gods and monsters attacked the younger gods. Marduk (the god of Babylonia), however, slaughtered Tiamat and from her corpse fashioned the cosmos and from the blood of her consort Ea made man. Though there are echoes of this mythology in the Bible, Genesis decreed that God formed the universe without any struggle against other gods. The enemies created by God's fiat have no divine aspect. Further, the abyss simply refers to the original state of the universe after a primary substance – an unformed and watery chaos – came into existence. Turning to the flood story – a central element of Mesopotamian myth – the Bible ignores such detail as the god's terror at the cataclysms accompanying the flood. In the Gilgamesh Epic, the flood is seen as the god Enil's remedy to reduce the level of human noise in the world. The Bible, however, proclaims that man's wickedness is its cause; and when the flood came, God gave no laws to restrain future human evil and promised that this devastation will never happen again. A comparison of texts from the Babylonian flood-story and the Bible forcefully illustrates the demythologizing intention of the biblical authors:

Gilgamesh Epic (eleventh canto)
I sent forth a dove and let her go,
But there was no resting place,
and she returned.
Then I sent forth a raven and let
her go,
The raven flew away, she beheld
the abatement of waters,
And she came near, wading and
croaking, but did not return.
Then I sent everything forth to
the four quarters of heaven, I
offered sacrifice,
I made a libation on the peak of
the mountain.

By sevens I sent out the vessels,
Under them I heaped up reed and cedarwood and myrtle,
The gods smelt the savour,
The gods gathered like flies about
him that offered up the sacrifice.

Genesis 8

Then he sent forth a dove from
him, to see if the waters had
subsided from the face of the
ground; but the dove found no
place to set her foot, and she
returned to him . . .
He waited another seven days,
and sent forth the dove; and she
did not return to him any
more . . .
So Noah went forth, and his sons
and his wife and his sons' wives
with him. And every beast,
every creeping thing, and every
bird, everything that moves upon
the earth, went forth by families
out of the ark.
Then Noah built an altar to
the Lord, and took of every clean
animal and every clean bird,
and offered burnt offerings on the altar,
And when the Lord smelled the
pleasing odour, the Lord said in
his heart, 'I will never again curse
the ground because of man, for
the imagination of man's heart is
evil from his youth; neither will I
ever again destroy every living
creature as I have done'.

In these passages the Hebrew writer reshaped this story to emphasize God's dominion over the cosmos as well as his concern for human morality. By refashioning the myths of the Near East, the ancient Israelites proclaimed the God of Israel as the creator and ruler of all things.

A final challenge to the traditional belief of *Torah MiSinai* is derived from textural criticism. The assumption of Orthodoxy is that the text of the *Torah* is the same as that revealed on Mount Sinai. This view suffers from a number of difficulties. First, the *Torah* Scrolls used in the synagogue are written in square script, yet in ancient times the Hebrew script was in a different form as exhibited in the Gezer calendar (tenth century BC), the Moabite Stone (ninth century BC), the Siloam inscription (eighth century BC), and the Lacish Letters (sixth century BC). Thus, the evidence of archaeology suggests that the original Hebrew script of the *Torah* was earlier than the square script that appears to have been adopted at a later date. This means that the older form of the Five Books of Moses was in old Hebrew characters rather than in what appears in later Hebrew manuscripts.

A more serious issue concerns the actual text of the *Torah*. The standard text was produced by the Masoretes who flourished from the sixth to the ninth centuries. These textual scholars strove to produce an authoritative reading of the Bible. Consequently they divided the biblical text into words and sentences as well as into segments of verse length, added vowel signs to the Hebrew words as well as cantillation marks indicating the articulation and inflections of the text for chanting, and indicated those cases where pronunciation or even the actual word used varied when the text is read aloud. Subsequently the Masoretic Text was viewed as standard by Jewry. However, other texts suggests that the Masoretic Text does not conform to the original *Torah*.

The Dead Sea Scrolls from the second and first century BC, for example, contain an early manuscript of the Book of Isaiah, the first two chapters of Habbakuk, and various other fragments. Even though these texts have a close affinity unlike the Masoretic Text, they contain a number of variants. Again, the Samaritan Pentateuch, contains a number of alternative readings. Some of these variants appear to be a reworking of the original text in accordance with Samaritan doctrine, however, the Samaritan Pentateuch does contain nearly two thousand variant readings which are in accord with the Greek translation, the Septuagint, of the third century BC. Thus these two early texts of the Bible may well more accurately mirror the original Hebrew of the *Torah* than that produced by the Masoretes. In addition to the Septuagint, there are other versions of the Pentateuch in Aramic, Syriac and Latin which similarly contain variants – they, too, may be closer to the original Hebrew. Hence it appears improbable that the Masoretic Text is, as traditionalists claim, the same text as revealed to Moses.

The Dissolution of Traditional Belief and Practice

Under the impact of modern science and contemporary secular trends, the monolithic system of Jewish belief and practice has undergone a process of dissolution. As we have seen, many non-Orthodox Jews have abandoned various aspects of traditional Judaism. Regarding the concept of God, a number of Jewish thinkers have found it increasingly difficult to accept the fundamental tenets of the Jewish faith: some wish to modify various elements of Jewish theism, imposing limits to God's omnipotence or omniscience; others have sought a more radical solution, wishing to substitute the concept of a supernatural deity in naturalistic terms. Mordecai Kaplan, for example, asserted that the idea of God must be redefined – the belief in a supernatural deity must be superseded by a concept of God as 'man's will to live'. At the far end of the religious spectrum, an even more radical approach has been advanced by Humanistic Jews who wish to dispense with God altogether. For these Jews, it is possible to live a Jewishly religious life without any acknowledgement of a divine reality. Thus, across the various groupings in contemporary Judaism there exists a wide range of different and conflicting beliefs about the nature of the Divine – no longer is the Jewish community committed to the view that God created and sustains the universe, guiding it to its ultimate fulfilment.

Similarly, for many Jews, the traditional belief in *Torah MiSinai* no longer seems plausible. The rabbinic understanding of *Torah* as revealed to Moses and infallibly transmitted through the sages has been undermined by the findings of modern scholarship. Thus, from the earliest period, reformers continued to believe in divine revelation, but they were anxious to point out that God's disclosure is mediated by human understanding. According to Reform Judaism, the Bible is a spiritual record of the history of ancient Israel, reflecting the primitive ideas of its own age. Similarly, the Conservative movement views Scripture as historically conditioned and mediated through human apprehension. As Solomon Schechter explained, the *Torah* is not in heaven – it is on earth and must be interpreted to be understood. For Reconstructionist Jews, the *Torah* is prominently a human document, shaped by those who composed this epic account of Israel's origins and development. In this light, the Reconstructionist movement seeks to incorporate the Bible into the life of its members without ascribing to it a supernatural origin. Humanistic Jews as well share a similar veneration of the *Torah* even though they do not believe it was divinely revealed. Hence, as in the case of belief about God, there are fundamental differences of opinion regarding the status of Scripture among the various branches of contemporary Judaism.

The doctrine of messianic redemption has likewise been radically modified within the various branches of non-Orthodox Judaism. In the earliest stage of development, reformers rejected the notion of a personal Messiah; instead they believed that the Messianic Age was beginning to dawn in their own time. In their view, history was evolving progressively towards an era of liberty, equality and justice for all people. Even though the events of the twentieth century have eclipsed these earlier messianic expectations, Reform Judaism still embraces the conviction that human progress is possible in the modern world. Similarly, many Zionists saw the founding of a Jewish homeland as the fulfilment of messianic hope. Rejecting the belief in a personal Messiah, they advocated a naturalistic interpretation of historical progress in which the Jewish people would be restored to the land of their ancestors. Such reinterpretations of traditional belief are indicative of the general shift away from supernaturalism in the modern world. As the Jewish theologian, Louis Jacobs, has noted:

> Most modern Jews prefer to interpret the messianic hope in naturalistic terms, abandoning the belief in a personal Messiah, the restoration of a sacrificial system, and to a greater or lesser degree, the idea of direct divine intervention. (Jacobs, 1964, 388–9)

The doctrine of the resurrection of the dead has likewise been largely rejected in both the Orthodox and non-Orthodox camps. The original belief in resurrection was an eschatological hope bound up with the rebirth of the nation in the Days of the Messiah, but as this messianic concept faded into the background so did this doctrine. For most Jews, physical resurrection is simply inconceivable in the light of the scientific understanding of the world. Thus, the Orthodox writer Joseph Seliger criticized the doctrine of resurrection as unduly materialistic. According to Seliger, in the ancient world the Afterlife was depicted in terms of earthly existence. The Egyptians, for example, believed so strongly in the bodily aspect of the Afterlife that they mummified the body and erected pyramids to protect it. In Seliger's view, such a notion is a mistaken folk-belief and has little in common with the Law of Moses. Judaism, he maintained, does not in fact, adhere to the belief in physical resurrection but, belief in the immortality of souls. In a similar vein, the former Chief Rabbi of the British Empire J. H. Hertz argued that what really matters is the doctrine of immortality. In his commentary on the Pentateuch, he wrote:

> Many and various are folk beliefs and poetical fancies in the rabbinical writings concerning Heaven, *Gan Eden* and Hell, *Gehinnom*. Our most authoritative religious guides, however, proclaim that no eye hath seen, nor can mortal fathom, what awaiteth us in the Hereafter; but that even the tarnished soul will not forever be denied spiritual bliss. (Jacobs, 1964, 415)

In the Reform community a similar attitude prevails. As noted previously, the Pittsburgh Platform categorically rejected the doctrine of the soul and such a conviction has been a dominant feature of the movement in subsequent years. Reform Jews, the Platform stated:

> reassert the doctrine of Judaism that the soul is immortal, grounding this belief on the divine nature of the human spirit, which

forever finds bliss in righteousness and misery in wickedness. We reject as ideas not rooted in Judaism the belief in bodily resurrection and in *Gehenna* and *Eden* (Hell and Paradise) as abodes for eternal punishment or reward.

The point to note about the concept of the immortal soul in both Orthodox and non-Orthodox Judaism is that it is disassociated from traditional notions of messianic redemption and divine judgment.

The belief in eternal punishment has also been discarded by a large number of Jews partly because of the interest in penal reform during the past century. Punishment as retaliation in a vindictive sense has been generally rejected. As Louis Jacobs has remarked: 'the value of punishment as a deterrent and for the protection of society is widely recognized. But all the stress today is on the reformatory aspects of punishment. Against such a background the whole question of reward and punishment in the theological sphere is approached in a more questioning spirit' (Jacobs, 1964, 364). Further, the rabbinic view of Hell is seen by many as morally repugnant. Jewish theologians have stressed that it is a delusion to believe that a God of love could have created a place of eternal punishment. In his commentary on the prayerbook, Chief Rabbi Hertz categorically declared, 'Judaism rejects the doctrine of eternal damnation' (Jacobs, 1964, 415). And in *Jewish Theology*, the Reform theologian, Kaufman Kohler, argued that the question whether the tortures of Hell are reconcilable with divine mercy, 'is for us superfluous and superseded. Our modern conception of time and space admits neither a place or a world-period for the reward and punishment of souls, nor the intolerable conception of eternal joy without useful action and eternal agony without any moral purpose' (Kohler, 1968, 309).

Traditional theological belief has thus lost its force for a large number of Jews in the modern period – no longer is it possible to discover a common core of religious belief underpinning Jewish life. The community instead is deeply divided on the most fundamental features of the Jewish tradition. Likewise, there is a parallel disunity within Jewry concerning Jewish observance. As far as Orthodoxy is concerned, it is in theory a system of law, going back consistently and without interruption for thousands of years to the beginning of Jewish history; all the elaborations of *halakhah* in the later Orthodox Codes are held to be rediscoveries rather than novelties. Yet, this picture of an eternal developing legal system breaks down when we face its astonishing shrinkages in contemporary society – great areas of Jewish law have disappeared for a wide variety of reasons. Frequently, individuals who consider themselves Orthodox have simply ceased to resort to rabbinical courts in a wide variety of areas of life. There is thus a large gap between the Orthodox system of practice and the limited observance of Jewish life within a large segment of the Orthodox Jewish community.

The rapidly contracting area of observance within Orthodoxy is in part the reason for the existence of Conservative Judaism. Since its inception, Conservative rabbis have been anxious to make Jewish law more flexible so as to provide for change legally. This approach to the tradition has provided a framework for the reinterpretation of Jewish law in the light of changed circumstances and modern needs. While acknowledging the historical importance of the Jewish heritage, the movement has sought to discover new ways to adjust the legal system where necessary. As a result, many traditional observances have been abandoned and other features altered to suit contemporary circumstances. In this way Conservative Judaism has provided a means of legitimizing deviations from tradition, thereby contributing to the further shrinkage of the Jewish legal code.

Similarly, within Reform Judaism, there has been an attempt to reinterpret Jewish law in the light of contemporary conditions. As the Reform Jewish scholar, Solomon Freehof, explained:

> Some of its provisions have passed from our lives. We do not regret that fact. But as to those laws that we do follow, we wish them to be in harmony with tradition . . . Our concern is more with people than with the legal system. Wherever possible, such interpretations are developed which are feasible and conforming to the needs of life. Sometimes, indeed, a request must be answered in the

negative when there is no way in the law for a permissive answer to be given. Generally the law is searched for such opinion as can conform with the realities of life. (Freehof, 1960, 22–3)

Due to such a liberal approach to the tradition, even greater areas of the legal system have been rejected within the ranks of Reform Judaism. For many Reform Jews, traditional Jewish Law has no bearing on their everyday lives.

Across the religious spectrum then, there is a wide divergency concerning Jewish observances and ceremonies. At the far right, traditional Orthodox Jews scrupulously adhere to the tradition, yet within the Orthodox camp there are many who have ignored the dictates of Jewish law. Within Conservative Judaism deviation from the *halakhah* is legitimized resulting in the abandonment of large areas of the tradition. And on the left, within Reform Judaism, there is a virtual abandonment of the traditional *Code of Jewish Law*. Surveying such variations of practice, it is none the less possible to isolate a number of criteria which have been loosely used to determine whether Orthodox laws should be retained within the various branches of Judaism. In some cases particular laws are retained simply because they have been followed for centuries. In other cases, an appeal is made to the spirit as opposed to the letter of the law. Alternatively, particular observances are adopted if they are grounded in biblical Judaism even if they run counter to present-day Orthodoxy. On other occasions traditional law is abandoned because it is not well adapted to modern life, or because it undermines the status of women. Unseemly rituals are also neglected as are practices which appear to be based on superstition. Choices about Jewish practice are thus ultimately motivated by personal considerations, resulting in a lack of consistency and coherence. Hence, within modern Judaism there is no agreement about either practice or religious belief: the monolithic character of traditional Judaism as it existed from ancient times to the Enlightenment has been replaced by chaos and confusion.

Jewish Peoplehood under Threat

The fragmentation of Judaism into a variety of sub-groups has brought about a major revolution in Jewish life. No longer is it possible to speak of one people with a common heritage. Rather the various segments of Jewry subscribe to radically different ideologies and religious orientations – in the history of the Jewish faith there has been no precedent for the co-existence of so many rival systems. Such a proliferation of interpretations of Judaism has given rise to a widespread concern about the nature of Jewish identity in the modern world. Pre-eminent among issues facing Jewry are the problems of divorce and conversion which have brought about irresolvable fissures in the Jewish community.

According to Jewish law, if a Jewish woman is divorced she must obtain a valid religious bill of divorce (*get*) from her previous husband. Otherwise, any children of a subsequent marriage are deemed illegitimate (*mamzerim*) since they are considered to have been born adulterously (because the woman is viewed as still married to her former husband). In Jewish law such children are only allowed to marry other *mamzerim* or proselytes. As early as the 1840s, however, German reformers were beginning to abandon this religious procedure in favour of a civil divorce. Thus, the nineteenth-century reformer Samuel Holdheim argued that as a result of emancipation, whatever has reference to interhuman relationships of a political, legal and civil character should no longer come under the province of biblical and rabbinic law. Rather the rabbinic principle that 'the law of the land is the law' should apply to such cases.

Such a rejection of the *halakhah* has widespread implications given the high incidence of divorce in contemporary society. In recent years the Jewish divorce rate in Western countries has increased enormously – by 1971, for example, the National Jewish Population Survey revealed that among the 25–29-year-old group, 15 per cent of all households were separated or divorced. Such a statistic combined with the fact that non-Orthodox groups constitute the majority of American Jews has led the Orthodox scholar Irving Greenberg to conclude that there will be 100,000 to 200,000 *mamzerim* in America by the year 2000 (Sacks, 1993, 184). Even though such predictions have been challenged by other writers, there is no doubt that the growing number of *mamzerim* will be acute in the future, thereby deepening the schism between Orthodoxy and Reform.

A second related dilemma concerns conversion to Judaism. According to Jewish law, an individual is Jewish if he or she is born of a Jewish mother – otherwise a formal process of conversion is required. Such a procedure involves immersion in a *mikveh*, circumcision for males, and the acceptance of the divine commandments (*kabalat hamitzvot*). Yet within the various branches of non-Orthodox Judaism various features of the traditional process of conversion have been altered. In Reform Judaism, for example, immersion and circumcision have generally been abandoned; there is no obligation to accept the *Code of Jewish Law*; the requirement that conversion procedures should take place in the presence of a court of law has in most cases, been set aside; and the traditional ruling that one must not convert for the sake of marriage has been ignored. As a result, all conversions undertaken outside the auspices of Orthodoxy have been rejected by the Orthodox establishment. This lack of recognition of non-Orthodox conversion has resulted in widespread confusion about Jewish identity. Today there are a large number of persons who are deemed to be Jewish by the various branches of non-Orthodox Judaism who are regarded as gentiles by the Orthodox.

Linked with this intractable difficulty about conversion is a recent ruling by American Reform Judaism concerning Jewish descent. In 1983 the Reform movement decreed that a child is presumed to be Jewish if either of his or her parents is Jewish, assuming that this presumption is confirmed by timely and appropriate acts of identification with the Jewish faith and people. By expanding the determination of Jewishness to include children of both matrilineal and patrilineal descent the Reform movement thus defined, as Jews, individuals whom the other branches of Judaism regard as gentiles. This means that neither these persons nor their descendants can be accepted as Jews by the non-Reform religious community.

The rift between Orthodoxy and the various denominations of non-Orthodox Judaism concerning personal status has important consequences for the State of Israel. From its inception, Israel has been determined to provide a homeland for Jewry; this principle is enshrined in the Law of Return. According to this law, any Jew who wishes to live in Israel can become a citizen without undergoing a naturalization procedure. As amended in 1970, the Law of Return states that a Jew is one born to a Jewish mother or who has been converted to Judaism. In subsequent years there have been innumerable attempts by the religious parties to amend the Law of Return so that only those who have been converted according to *halakhah* are deemed Jewish and thereby eligible to settle in the State of Israel. If accepted, such an alteration would render invalid all conversions undertaken by the Conservative and Reform rabbinate.

In recent years Jewish thinkers have proposed a number of solutions to such challenges to Jewish peoplehood. For example, in 1956 the Orthodox halakhic authority, Moses Feinstein, delivered a ruling which was aimed to dissolve the problem of the status of children of Reform second marriages. According to Feinstein, a marriage ceremony itself is invalid if it is not observed by two witnesses. Since those present at Reform marriages are most likely to be Reform Jews, it is probable that they transgress Jewish law in ways that disqualify them as witnesses. Thus Reform marriages are not halakhically valid, and therefore need no valid divorce. As a consequence, children from remarriages should not be considered *mamzerim*. Although previous authorities held that regardless of the validity of the ceremony the marriage was established by cohabitation, Feinstein maintained that this could not be so since this was not the intent of the couple as everyone assumed that the marriage was established by the synagogue ceremony. By annulling all Reform marriages, Feinstein's aim was to remove the status of illegitimacy from the children of remarriages where the first marriage had been conducted under Reform auspices. Not surprisingly, however, many Reform rabbis were scandalized by this ruling. By rendering Reform marriages as halakhically non-existent, Feinstein implicitly denied Reform's authenticity – thus instead of healing rifts that divide modern Jewry, this proposal exacerbated the tensions that exist between the different movements.

Another solution to the fragmentation of Jewish peoplehood has recently been proposed by Jonathan Sacks in *One People?*. In his view the divisions in the Jewish world must be overcome by an attitude of inclusivism which acknowledges that God's covenant is with all Jews. A philosophy of Jewish inclusivism, he believes, calls for a number of positive steps. First, inclusivists must be sensitive to the ways in which non-Orthodox Jews are described: 'We may not speak of other Jews except in the language of love and respect' (Sacks, 1993, 219). Further, inclusivists should not seek to use coercive means to bring these individuals back to tradition; rather they should seek to draw Jews to *Torah*-observant Judaism by 'words of peace' and 'cords of love' (Sacks, 1993, 2).

Within such an inclusivist perspective, education must be regarded as supremely important:

> The inclusivist recognizes that education must speak to the cultural situation. For it is through constant study that *Torah* is transformed from external law to internalized command . . . The inclusivist recognizes that education must speak to the cultural situation of the student . . . He knows that 'learning leads to doing', that education is Judaism's classic alternative to coercion, and that secular culture can only be confronted . . . by an intensification of Jewish learning. (Sacks, 1993, 219)

Moreover, the inclusivist should seek to apply *halakhah* to its widest possible constituency. In this regard, he should aim to attain a nuanced understanding of both secular and liberal Jews. 'In so doing', Sacks argued, 'he relies on the general inclusivist argument that secular and liberal Jews are not to be judged as deliberate rebels but as unwitting (*shogeg*) or coerced (*anus*) products of their environment' (Sacks, 1993, 221). Even though Sacks cannot countenance the religious interpretation of non-Orthodox Judaism, he stressed that the various branches of non-Orthodoxy played a role in keeping alive the value of Jewish identity, faith and practice for many Jews. Regarding Israelis, Sacks insisted that whatever their religious attitudes, they should be seen as fulfilling the command of 'settling in the land' which has traditionally been regarded by some scholars as equivalent to all other commandments combined.

The inclusivist should also acknowledge that Jewish liberalism and secularism has given new life to some aspects of tradition. Secular Zionism, for example, has reminded Jews that political activity is part of Judaism; secularists and liberals revived the Hebrew language, the Jewish national ideal, prophetic commitment to social action, and renewed interest in rabbinic sources and medieval literature. None the less, the inclusivist has the duty to call on liberal and secular Jewish leaders to act responsibly in the context of the totality of Judaism and the Jewish people. In particular, he should warn against the laxity of non-Orthodox conversions and the Reform ruling about patrilineal descent as well as its endorsements of homosexuality, premarital sex, and abortion on demand.

Here then, is a plea for all Jews – whether Orthodox or non-Orthodox – to recognize their common ancestry and shared peoplehood. From the Orthodox side, Sacks entreated his co-religionists to refrain from hurling abuse at those who have rejected *halakhah*. Such a stance of tolerance and understanding should help ameliorate the conflict between the various branches of contemporary Judaism, yet Sacks' recommendations do not provide a basis for the unity he seeks. No doubt many Reform Jews would simply view his position as patronizing and imperialistic – Conservative, Reform, Reconstructionist, Humanistic and Polydox Jews wish to be respected for their own interpretations of Judaism, but this is precisely what Sacks refuses to do.

Orthodoxy, Sacks maintained, is the true Jewish path and he is anxious to bring all Jews to a recognition of this truth. Thus he wrote:

> The inclusivist faith is that Jews, divided by where they stand, are united by what they are travelling towards, the destination which alone gives meaning to Jewish history: the promised union of *Torah*, the Jewish people, the land of Israel, and God. (Sacks, 1993, 228)

For most Jews, however, there is no possibility of such a return. Inclusivist Orthodoxy thus fails to provide a unifying theology which would hold together the scattered fragments of the Jewish community.

The Lack of a Common Religious Language

In the past Jewry was united by a common tradition in which there was a universal acknowledgement of the meaning of religious terminology. Thus, despite the different theological views of Jewish thinkers through the ages, religious language was univocal in its implication. Through the centuries Jews acknowledged the existence of a supernatural deity who created and sustains the universe, chose the Jewish people, and guides them to their ultimate destiny. In the Bible and rabbinic literature, as well as in the liturgy, the Jewish nation expressed their commitment to the Lord of history who is their redeemer and saviour. Although Jewish philosophers, theologians and mystics formulated different conceptions of the nature and activity of God, there was constant recognition of a shared religious inheritance. For this reason such writers as Maimonides had no hesitation in propounding what he believed to be the fundamental tenets of the faith.

With the emergence of Reform Judaism in the nineteenth century, however, the religious vocabulary of the Jewish tradition began to take on a new and altered meaning: no longer was there a fixed reference to the language of religious faith. Hence, in the earliest formulation of the principles of the movement, central religious concepts were detached from their previous moorings. As we have seen, the Pittsburgh Platform declared that in the history of the Jewish people the God-idea had undergone an evolution in the light of the philosophical progress of the nation. Such a belief implied that the conception of God in the Bible and the rabbinic tradition is not fixed – instead it has undergone a gradual process of transformation. Similarly, the Pittsburgh Platform affirmed that the Bible is a record of the spiritual history of the nation reflecting the primitive ideas of its own time. Such interpretations are far removed from the traditional understanding of God's word divinely revealed to Moses on Mount Sinai.

The Pittsburgh Platform's reference to 'Messianic hope' is also at variance with the traditional understanding of the Messianic Age. As we have seen, the rabbis believed that with the advent of the Messiah, the dead would be resurrected, there would be an ingathering of the exiles to Zion, and a period of messianic redemption would take place in which earthly life would be utterly transformed. Finally, at the end of the Days of the Messiah, all human beings would be judged and either rewarded in heaven or condemned to eternal punishment. The Reform movement, however, rejected this chain of eschatological fulfilment, substituting a this-worldly vision of peace and harmony on earth. Thus messianic terminology was uprooted from its original significance.

Later, in the Columbus Platform of 1937, the same shift in the meaning of religious terms was evident. Here revelation was viewed as a continual process; the Written and Oral *Torah* were described as the product of historical evolution; the religious life was hallowed even though Reform Jews were urged to discard those features of the tradition which they regarded as lacking spiritual significance. Such a transformation of religious meaning was evident as well in the San Francisco Platform of 1976 where God's reality was affirmed without specifying its nature; *Torah* was viewed as resulting from the relationship between God and the Jewish people; Israel was depicted as a union of faith and peoplehood; and *mitzvot* were understood as claims made upon the Jewish people without indicating their origin. Such ambiguity about the content of traditional terminology was similarly evident among Reform thinkers who expressed widely divergent views of God, *Torah*, revelation and *halakhah*.

Within Conservative Judaism there has been a similar shift away from a traditional understanding of religious terminology. The scientific study of Judaism was based on the assumption that the Jewish faith has undergone a historical development: in contrast with the Orthodox, Conservative Jews have been anxious to trace the evolution of Jewish beliefs and practices through the ages. Like the reformers, Conservative Jews have thus envisaged the *Torah* as a product of human reflection. As we have seen, some Conservative thinkers maintained that human beings accurately recorded God's word as revealed on Mount Sinai; others insisted that those who wrote Scripture were divinely inspired. More radical theologians on the other hand argued that Scripture is solely a human product. Regarding *halakhah*, Conservative thinkers have continually debated about which precepts are binding. Such uncertainty is reflected in the debates which took place concerning the rulings of the Committee on Jewish Law and Statutes. Concerning Jewish peoplehood, the Conservative movement affirmed its commitment to *Klal Yisrael*, yet there has been no unanimity about the notion of God's chosen people.

Within Reconstructionist Judaism the meaning of conventional theological language is even more attenuated. Mordecai Kaplan's rejection of a belief in a supernatural God utterly altered the significance of such terms as 'God', '*Torah*', 'revelation' and 'salvation'. For Kaplan, the religious terminology of the past should be divested of any form of supernaturalism. As we have seen, he advanced a reconstructionist interpretation of divine reality construed in naturalistic terms. As a result, Reconstuctionist Jews, while using the religious terminology of the past, have infused such language with new meaning. In a similar vein, Polydox Judaism has fostered a radical revision of Judaism in which the religious vocabulary of mainstream Judaism has been completely revised. According to Alvin Reines, this approach is completely justified. Thus he wrote:

> In the course of the present exposition, new meanings for old terms will be introduced . . . The question will then be raised whether it is proper to employ a term in a novel manner, so that no direct historical justification for the usage can be given. The immediate and fundamental answer to this question is that words belong to those who use them. This principle has been applied on countless occasions in intellectual and religious history, whenever a generation has given names to its new perceptions and insights in the language bequeathed to it by its predecessors. Words . . . have no one legitimate or authoritative meaning, and their use with new meanings is a process apparently destined to continue so long as humans, knowledge and society continue to advance and evolve. (Reines, 1987, 156–7)

Within Humanistic Judaism, there is a similar radical shift away from the traditional understanding of Jewish terminology.

Among secular Jews, there has been the same vagueness and uncertainty about traditional religious language. Such confusion was dramatically illustrated at the founding of the State of Israel. From a traditional perspective, this event could be perceived as a development guided by divine providence: the ingathering of the nation appeared to be a fulfilment of biblical prophecy:

> Even if you have been banished to the most distant land under the heavens, for there the Lord will gather you and bring you back. He will bring you to the land that belonged to your fathers, and you will take possession of it. (Deut. 30.4–5)

Yet for secularists the return of the Jewish people to their ancestral homeland was conceived as solely due to human initiative. Thus, the nineteenth-century Zionist thinker, Leon Pinsker, stressed that the time had come for the Jewish nation to establish a national home:

> We must not sit even one moment longer with folded hands; we must not admit we are doomed to play on in the future the hopeless role of the wandering Jew . . . it is our bounden duty to devote all our remaining moral force to re-establishing ourselves as a living nation, so that we may finally assume a more fitting and dignified role. (Hertzberg, 1959, 191)

Again, Theodor Herzl wrote that the Jewish question could only be solved if the Jews struggled to constitute themselves as one people: 'The Maccabees will rise again,' he wrote. 'The Jews who will it, shall achieve their state. We shall live at last as free men on our own soil, and in our own homes peacefully die (Hertzberg, 1959, 225–6).

These conflicting perceptions of the establishment of a Jewish state were glossed over in Israel's Declaration of Independence. Religious groups were adamant that this document should contain a reference to divine activity. As a consequence, the final draft included a reference to divine purposes in the creation of a Jewish homeland: 'Placing our trust in the Rock of Israel, we set our hand at testifying to this Declaration, here on the soil of the Homeland, in the city of Tel Aviv, on this day, the eve of the Sabbath, 5 Iyar 5708, 14 May 1948.' For the religious, the terms 'Rock of Israel',

'Homeland' and 'Sabbath' possessed religious connotations, whereas for secularists such terms were devoid of any theological significance. As a result, the Declaration of Independence contained language with multiple associations dependent on the interpretation given. As Jonathan Sacks explained:

> The sentence, a triumph of diplomatic ambiguity, is a paradigm of the fate of the contemporary vocabulary of Judaism. Jews are, to use Bernard Shaw's phrase, 'divided by a common language'. Our condition is an ironic inversion of Babel. 'Behold there is one people speaking the same language.' Yet despite this, they cannot understand one another's speech. (Sacks, 1993, 6)

Hence, within the Jewish world, there is widespread confusion about the meaning of the religious terms of the past. The various sub-groups of Jewry – Hasidim, Orthodox Jews, Reform Jews, Conservative Jews, Reconstructionist Jews, Polydox Jews, Humanistic Jews, as well as Jewish secularists – utilize the same words while giving them utterly different interpretations. The fragmentation of the Jewish people in the post-Enlightenment age has thus led to the disintegration of a shared religious vocabulary.

7

Open Judaism

Throughout the centuries the Jewish people were united by a common religious heritage. However, from the time of the Enlightenment, Jewry fragmented into a variety of sub-groups with their own religious identities. What is now required is a new philosophy of Judaism which will serve as a basis for the Jewish way of life in contemporary society. Arguably such a revised Jewish theology should be based on the Kantian distinction between the world-as-it-is and the world-as-perceived. From a Jewish standpoint this distinction should lead to a radical reconsideration of Jewish claims about Divine Reality. Within this framework, the Jewish understanding of the nature and activity of God cannot be viewed as definitive and final – rather it should be viewed as only one way among many of making sense of Ultimate Reality. The implications of this new perspective are fundamental in the shaping of Judaism for the future. A theology of religious pluralism in which Judaism is perceived as simply one religion among many, calls for an attitude of openness. Aware of the inevitable subjectivity of religious belief, all Jews should feel free to draw from the past those elements of the tradition which they find spiritually meaningful. Unlike all the main branches of Judaism, this new interpretation of Judaism is grounded in an ideology of individual freedom, granting each person independence of thought and action. This approach – which I have called Open Judaism – thus provides a non-dogmatic foundation for integrating Jewish belief and practice into modern life and serves as a basis for interfaith encounter in a post-Holocaust world.

Religious Pluralism and a New Jewish Theology

As we have seen, until the time of the Enlightenment the Jewish people were unified by a common religious inheritance which they believed to be the one true path to God. According to Scripture, God had created the universe, chose the Jewish people from among all nations, delivered them from exile, revealed himself to Moses on Mount Sinai, and exercised providential care over his children throughout their history. For centuries, Jews were sustained by such a conviction through persecution, suffering and death. In the post-Enlightenment world, however, such a theological framework has disintegrated for a variety of reasons: no longer are most Jews able to accept such a depiction of God's nature and activity. Thus, among the varying religious sub-groups within the Jewish community there has been a loss of faith in the theological framework of the past.

As a result of this disintegration of belief, a new Jewish theology – which for convenience sake is referred to as 'Open Judaism' – is required for the modern age which will provide a basis for both religious belief and practice. Today, what is needed is a theological structure consonant with a contemporary understanding of Divine Reality as conceived by the world's faiths. Arguably such a revised theology of Judaism should be based on the Kantian distinction between the world-as-it-is (the noumenal world) and the world-as-perceived (the phenomenal world). Following this differentiation, the Real *an sich* (in itself) should be distinguished from the Real as conceived in human thought and experience. Such a contrast is a central feature of many of the world's faiths: thus in Judaism God the transcendental Infinite is conceived as *Ayn Sof* as distinct from the *Shekinah* (God's Presence) which is manifest in the terrestrial plane; in Hindu thought the nirguna Brahman, the Ultimate in itself, beyond all human categories, is distinguished from the saguna Brahman, the Ultimate as known to finite consciousness as a personal deity, Isvara; in Taoist thought 'the Tao that can be expressed is not the eternal Tao'; in Mahayana Buddhism there is a contrast between the eternal cosmic Buddha-nature, which is also the infinite void and on the other hand the realm of the heavenly Buddha figures in their incarnations in the earthly Buddhas.

In attempting to represent Ultimate Reality, the different religions have conceptualized the Divine in two distinct modes: the Real personalized and the Real as absolute. In Judaism, God is understood as Lord; in the Christian faith as Father; in Islam as Allah; in the Indian traditions as Shiva or Vishnu, or Parameter. In each case these personal deities are conceived as acting within the history of the various faith communities. Thus, as John Hick explained with regard to Yahweh in the Jewish tradition and Shiva in Hinduism:

> The Yahweh *persona* exists and has developed in interaction with the Jewish people. He is a part of their history, and they are a part of his; and he cannot be extracted from this historical context. Shiva, on the other hand, is a quite different divine *persona* existing in the experience of hundreds of millions of people in the Shivite stream of Indian religious life. These two *personae*, Yahweh and Shiva, live within different worlds of faith, partly creating and partly created by the features of different human cultures . . . From a pluralistic point of view Yahweh and Shiva are not rival gods, or rival claimants to be the one and only God, but rather two different concrete historical *personae* in terms of which the ultimate divine Reality is present and responded to by different large historical communities within different strands of the human story. (Hick, 1985, 42)

The concept of the Absolute is alternatively schematized to form a range of divine conceptualizations in the world's religions such as Brahman, the Dharma, the Tao, Nirvana and Sunyata in Eastern traditions. Unlike divine *personae* which are concrete and often visualized, divine *impersonae* constitute a variety of concepts such as the infinite being–consciousness–bliss of Brahman, the beginningless and endless of cosmic change of Buddhist teachings, the ineffable further shore of Nirvana, the eternal Buddha-nature or the ultimate Emptiness which is also the fullness of the world, and the eternal principle of the Tao. These non-personal representations of the Divine inform modes of consciousness ranging from the experience of becoming one with the Infinite to the finding of total reality in a concrete historical moment of existence.

Given the diversity of images of the Real among the various religious systems that have emerged throughout history, it is not surprising that there are innumerable conflicts between the teachings of the world's faiths – in all cases believers have maintained that the doctrines of their respective traditions are true and superior to competing claims. Thus Jews contend that they are God's chosen people and partners in a special covenant – their mission is to be a light to the nations. In this sense the Jewish people stand in a unique relationship with God. This does not lead to the quest to convert others to Judaism, but it does give rise to a sense of pride in having been born into the Jewish fold.

Within Islam, Muslims are convinced that Muhammad was the seal of the prophets and that through the *Qur'an* God revealed himself decisively to the world. This implies that while Muslims are obligated to recognize the veracity of the other Abrahamic traditions – and in some cases extend the Qur'anic concept of the People of the Book to other faiths as well – they none the less assert that the *Qur'an* has a unique status as God's final, decisive word. On the basis of this central dogma, they view themselves as the heirs of the one and only true religion.

Convinced that only those who belong to the true faith can be saved, the Christian community has throughout history sought to convert all human beings to the Gospel.

Hindus, on the other hand, believe that it is possible to have access to eternal truth as incarnated in human language in the Vedas. Although Hindus are tolerant of other faiths, it is assumed that in this life or in the life to come, all will come to the fullness of Vedic understanding. Further, in advaitic philosophy it is maintained that the theistic forms of religion embody an inferior conception of ultimate Reality. Thus, Hindus believe that their faith is uniquely superior to other religious conceptions.

Likewise in the Buddhist tradition, it is assumed that the true understanding of the human condition is presented in the teachings of Gautama Buddha. The Dharma, Buddhists stress, contains the full and saving truth for all humanity.

Each of these religious traditions then affirms its own superiority – all rival claims are regarded as misapprehensions of Ultimate Reality. From a pluralistic perspective, however, there is no way to ascertain which, if any, of these spiritual paths accurately reflects the nature of the Real *an sich*. In the end, the varied truth claims of the world's faiths must be regarded as human images which are constructed from within particular social and cultural contexts. Hence from a pluralistic perspective it is impossible to make judgments about the veracity of the various conceptions of the Divine within the world's religions. Neither Jew, Muslim, Christian, Hindu nor Buddhist has any justification for believing that his respective tradition embodies the uniquely true and superior religious path – instead the adherents of all the world's faiths must recognize the inevitable human subjectivity of religious conceptualization. A theology of religious pluralism thus calls for a complete reorientation of religious apprehension. What is now required is for Jews to acknowledge that their conceptual system, form of worship, lifestyle, and scriptures are in the end nothing more than lenses through which Reality is perceived, but the Divine as-it-is-in-itself is beyond human understanding.

Within this new theological framework, the absolute claims about God should be understood as human conceptions stemming from the religious experience of the ancient Israelites as well as later generations of Jewish sages: Jewish monotheism – embracing a myriad of formulations from biblical through medieval to modern times – is rooted in the life of the people. In all cases pious believers and thinkers have expressed their understanding of God's activity on the basis of their own personal as well as communal encounter with the Divine. Yet given that the Real *an sich* is beyond human comprehension, this Jewish understanding of the Godhead cannot be viewed as definitive and final. Rather, it must be seen as only one among many ways in which human beings have attempted to make sense of the Ultimate. In this light, it makes no sense for Jews to believe that they possess the unique truth about God and his action in the world; on the contrary, universalistic truth-claims about divine Reality must give way to a recognition of the inevitable subjectivity of beliefs about the Real.

The same conclusion applies to the Jewish belief about God's revelation. Instead of affirming that God uniquely disclosed his word to the Jewish people in Scripture and through the teachings of the sages, Jews should acknowledge that their Holy Writ is only one record of divine communication among many. Both the Written and the Oral *Torah* have special significance for the Jewish people, but this does not imply that these writings contain a uniquely true and superior divine communication. Instead the *Tanakh* and rabbinic literature should be perceived as a record of the spiritual life of the people and a testimony of their religious quest; as such they should be viewed in much the same light as the New Testament, the *Qur'an*, the Bagahavad Gita, the Vedas and so forth. For the Jewish people this sacred literature has particular meaning – yet it should not be regarded as possessing ultimate truth.

Likewise the doctrine of the chosen people must be revised. Although Jews have derived great strength from the conviction that God has had a special relationship with Israel, such a belief is based on a misapprehension of Judaism in the context of the world's religions. Given that the Real *an sich* transcends human understanding, the conviction that God selected a particular people as his agent is nothing more than an expression of the Jewish people's sense of superiority and impulse to spread its religious message. In fact, there is simply no way of knowing if a specific people stands in a special relationship with the Divine.

Again the pluralistic approach challenges the traditional conviction that God has a providential plan for the Jewish people and for all humankind. The belief that God's guiding hand is manifest in all things is ultimately a human response to the universe – it is not, as Jews have believed through the ages, certain knowledge. This is illustrated by the fact that other traditions have postulated a similar view of providence, yet maintain that God's action in history has taken an entirely different form. In other cases, non-theistic religions have formulated conceptions of human destiny divorced from the activity of God or the gods. Such differences in interpretation highlight the subjectivity of all these beliefs.

The Jewish doctrine of the Messiah must also be seen in a similar light. Within a pluralistic theology of the world's religions, the longing for messianic deliverance must be perceived as a pious hope based on personal and communal expectation. Although this belief has served as a bedrock of the Jewish faith through the centuries, it is inevitably shaped by human conceptualization. Like other doctrines in the Jewish tradition, it has been grounded in the experience of the Jewish people and has undergone a range of changes in the history of the nation. Because the Real *an sich* is beyond comprehension, there is simply no way of ascertaining whether this belief in a personal Messiah accurately mirrors the nature of ultimate Reality.

Finally, this new interpretaion of Jewish theology demands a similar stance regarding the doctrine of the Afterlife. Although the belief in the eschatological unfolding of history has been a central feature of the Jewish faith from rabbinic times to the present, it is simply impossible to ascertain whether these events will occur in the future. In our finite world – limited by space and time – certain knowledge about life is unobtainable. Belief in the Hereafter in which the righteous of Israel will receive their just reward has sustained the nation through suffering and tragedy, yet from a pluralistic outlook these doctrines are no more certain than any other features of the Jewish religious heritage.

The implications of this shift from the absolutism of the Jewish past to a new vision of Jewish theology are radical and far-reaching. Traditional Judaism, like all other religions, has advanced absolute, universal truth-claims about the nature of Reality – but given the separation between our finite understanding and the Real *an sich*, there is no way of attaining complete certitude about the veracity of these beliefs. The Real transcends human comprehension, and hence it must be admitted that Jewish religious convictions are no different in principle from those found in other religious traditions – all are lenses through which divine Reality is conceptualized. Judaism, like all other major world religions, is built around its distinctive way of thinking and experiencing the Divine, yet in the end the believer must remain agnostic about the correctness of his own religious convictions.

Redefining Judaism and Jewishness

Given the shift in orientation from a Judeo-centric to a theo-centric conception of the world's religions, it is possible to view Judaism in a new light. No longer should Jews regard their faith as the fullest expression of God's will. Rather in the contemporary world the Jewish community needs to adopt a more open stance in which the Divine – rather than the Jewish faith – is placed at the centre of the universe of faiths. Such pluralism would enable Jews to affirm the uniqueness of their own heritage while acknowledging the validity of other religions. The theology underpinning this shift of perspective is based on the distinction between Real *an sich* and the Real as perceived. From this vantage point, the truth-claims of all religions should be regarded as human constructions rather than universally valid doctrines. As a consequence, the Jewish faith should no longer be perceived as embodying God's final and decisive revelation for humanity. Instead, the entire range of Jewish beliefs regarding God's nature and activity as well as the role of the Jewish people in the unfolding of a divine providential scheme should be perceived simply as religious hypotheses. The Jewish religious system hence is in principle no different from the myriad of religious traditions, shaped by social and cultural circumstances, which have emerged throughout history.

Such a new vision of the Jewish heritage calls for a re-evaluation of the traditional commitment to both belief and practice. In the past the doctrines of the faith were regarded as binding upon all Jews. In his formulation of the principles of Judaism, for example, Maimonides stressed that those who ceased to subscribe to these tenets were to be deemed heretics. In his view, such individuals had departed from the body of Israel and should be despised by all true believers – religious belief was here conceived as determinative of true Jewishness. Similarly, through the centuries rabbinic authorities insisted that it is obligatory for all Jews to adhere to the Code of Jewish

Law since it is based on the Written and Oral *Torah* revealed at Sinai. Anyone who deliberately violates the *mitzvot* is guilty of transgressing against God's sacred word. Judaism as a monolithic religious system was thus grounded in the inviolate communication of divine truth.

No longer, however, is it possible to regard Jewish belief and practice in this way; a theology of religious pluralism in which Judaism is regarded simply as one faith among many, calls for an attitude of openness. If the Jewish faith is ultimately a human construct growing out of the experiences of the nation over four millennia, it must be susceptible to reinterpretation and change. Aware of the inevitable subjectivity of religious belief, each Jew should feel free to draw from the tradition those elements which he finds spiritually meaningful. In other words, the authoritarianism of the past should give way to personal autonomy in which all individuals are at liberty to construct for themselves a personal system of religious observance relevant to their own needs.

Unlike Orthodox, Conservative, Reform, Reconstructionist and Humanistic Judaism – all of which advocate varying systems of belief and practice – this new interpretation of Judaism would espouse a truly liberal ideology of individual freedom. Like Polydoxy, Open Judaism would seek to grant persons full religious independence. As we have seen, Alvin Reines in his exposition of Polydox Judaism formulated what he regarded as a Freedom Covenant. According to this concept, each member of a religious community possesses an inalienable right to religious authority; in his view, the freedom of each member ends where another member's freedom begins. So too, within the framework of Open Judaism, such freedom is paramount; individual liberty must be granted to all Jews given the ultimate subjectivity of religious belief.

The central feature of this new conception of Judaism is, therefore, the principle of personal liberty – Open Judaism would allow all individuals the right to select those features from the tradition which they find spiritually meaningful. This approach is not an innovation – it has always been a tenet of Reform Judaism, for example, that members of the community are at liberty to practise those observances which they find significant. Yet the principle of autonomy has not always been carried to its logical conclusion; instead, throughout the history of the Reform movement reformers sought to impose their religious views on others. Adherents of Open Judaism, on the other hand, would be actively encouraged to make up their own minds about religious belief and practice. No-one – no rabbi or rabbinical body – would be allowed to decide what observances are acceptable for the community as a whole. In other words, Open Judaism would foster personal liberty and freedom. In this context rabbis who subscribe to such an ideology would have the duty to instruct their congregations about the Jewish way of life, yet such teaching should be descriptive rather than prescriptive. All Jews should be able to choose for themselves which aspects of the tradition are helpful in promoting their spiritual development. Any return to centralized rules or regulations laid down by a small self-appointed body of rabbis would, in reality, be nothing more than Orthodoxy in disguise.

It might be objected that such extreme liberalism would simply result in chaos, leading to the dissolution of Judaism. Such criticism, however, fails to acknowledge the state of religious diversity within contemporary Jewish society. In all the branches of Judaism across the religious spectrum there has been a gradual erosion of centralized authority. Although many rabbis have attempted to establish standards for the members of their communities, there is a universal recognition that in the end each Jew will define for himself what aspects of the Jewish heritage are personally relevant – modern Jews are ultimately guided by their own consciences. Moreover, the rabbinic establishment is no longer able to impose sanctions on those who wish to ignore its rulings. In short, in the contemporary Jewish world there is a conscious acceptance of the principal of personal autonomy, even if in some quarters it is only grudgingly accepted. Open Judaism would hence be in accord with the spirit of the age; its endorsement of personal decision-making would be consonant with the nature of Jewish life in Israel and the diaspora. Open Judaism is thus grounded in an acceptance of the nature of contemporary Jewish existence; in this sense its philosophy reflects the realities of everyday life.

As a radical alternative to the more structured models of the Jewish faith represented by the major branches of Judaism, Open Judaism provides a non-dogmatic foundation for integrating Jewish belief and practice into modern life. Within this framework Jews are encouraged to chart their own path through the tradition. Such liberalism also offers a new orientation to current preplexities regarding Jewish identity. According to Jewish law, it is sufficient for someone to have been born of a Jewish mother for them to be regarded as a Jew. Conversely, a person born of a Jewish father and a non-Jewish mother is not Jewish – such an individual is a gentile. For millennia this has been the understanding of Jewish identification. This means that an agnostic or atheist as well as a nonreligious person born of a Jewish mother is Jewish. Correct belief is irrelevant.

As a result of this legal definition of Jewishness, there are many born Jews who though formally recognized as Jews are in no sense religious. Some of these individuals adamantly identify themselves as Jews; others refuse such identification. Yet, whatever their response, the Jewish community regards them as belonging to the Jewish fold and accords them religious rights (such as the right to be married in a synagogue or buried in a Jewish cemetery). Here, then, is a simple concrete criterion for Jewishness. In modern times, however, such a definition has been obscured for two major reasons. First, the gentile world has not invariably applied this legal criterion of Jewishness to the Jewish community. Frequently – as occurred in Nazi Germany – individuals were deemed Jews even if they did not qualify by their internal Jewish classification. During the Third Reich, for example, the Citizen Laws deemed someone as Jewish if they were simply of Jewish blood. This means that some people who were massacred by the Nazis would not have been regarded as Jews by the Jewish community.

The second difficulty concerns the decision taken in 1983 by the Central Conference of American Rabbis that a child of either a Jewish mother or a Jewish father should be regarded as Jewish. As noted previously, by expanding the determination of Jewishness to include children or both matrilineal and patrilineal descent, the Reform Movement defined as Jews individuals which other branches of Judaism regard as gentiles; this means that neither these persons nor their descendents can be accepted as Jews by the non-Reform religious etablishment.

In addition to the legal ruling about biological descent, Judaism also permits gentiles to become Jews by undergoing conversion. According to traditional Judaism, conversion is a ritual process involving immersion in a ritual bath, and circumcision for males. Conversion is to take place in the presence of three rabbis who compose a court of law. However, within the non-Orthodox branches of Judaism, there have been various modifications to this process. Conservative Judaism generally follows the traditional procedure, but it does not always follow the precise legal requirements. For this reason, most Orthodox rabbis do not recognize Conservative conversions as valid. Similarly, since Reform Judaism has largely abandoned ritual immersion and does not conduct circumcision in the required form, its converts are not accepted by the Orthodox community. Thus Reform and Conservative converts and their offspring are deemed to be non-Jews by the Orthodox establishment, and in consequence there is considerable confusion in the Jewish world as to who should be regarded as legitimately Jewish.

A simple solution to this problem is to redefine Jewishness. Given Open Judaism's reinterpretation of religious doctrine, there is no reason to regard the traditional legal definition of Jewishness as binding. Instead, Jewish identity could be defined along the lines suggested by Humanistic Judaism. As we have seen, Humanistic Jews are anxious to avoid any form of racism in their definition of Jewishness, nor do they wish to impose a religious test on converts. Instead, they seek to welcome within the Jewish fold, all individuals who wish to identify themselves with the Jewish people. Similarly, Open Judaism – with its emphasis on personal autonomy – could offer a similar definition of Jewishness. Distancing itself from either biological descent or correct belief and practice, Open

Judaism would welcome as Jews all those, regardless of ancestry, who simply wish to be identified in this way. On this basis, Jewish identity would be solely a matter of choice. In other words, Jewishness would be construed as an optional identification rather than the result of matrilineal or patrilineal descent or religious conviction formally accepted by a rabbinical body. Further, within the framework of Open Judaism, no conversion would be necessary in order to obtain this status. Being a Jew would be an option open to all. Although such reinterpretation of Jewish status would not be acceptable to the major branches of Judaism, it would eliminate the general uncertainty surrounding the question: 'Who is a Jew?'

Here then is a new vision of Judaism for the future. Liberal in spirit, Open Judaism would provide the foundation for individual decision-making, unfettered by the religious restraints of the past. Within the framework of this new philosophy of the Jewish heritage, each individual would be free to exercise his personal autonomy in determining which aspects of the tradition he wishes to retain or discard. Departing from the legalism of Orthodoxy as well as the prescriptive character of the various branches of non-Orthodoxy, Open Judaism would fully embrace the principle of self-determination. As a result, this new approach to the Jewish faith – though rooted in Jewish history – calls for a revolution in thinking about the meaning of Jewishness in the modern age.

Reinterpreting Jewish Belief

As we have seen, in previous centuries Jews were united by a common acceptance of fundamental precepts regarding the nature and activity of God. Thus, in the Middle Ages, a number of Jewish theologians attempted to systematize the principles of the faith; despite the variations in their formulations, there was widespread agreement as to the central features of Judaism as a religious system. Until the period of the Enlightenment there was a universal acknowledgement that God's revelation on Mount Sinai furnished a final and complete basis for religious life. In the wake of Jewish emancipation, however, the Jewish community fragmented into a variety of differing religious groupings with widely divergent interpretations of the tradition. Today, Open Judaism – as a new Jewish ideology – provides an alternative basis (different from that found in any non-Orthodox branch of Judaism) for the expression of personal autonomy in the sphere of religious belief.

According to Open Judaism, there is a distinction between the Real-as-it-is-perceived, and the Real-as-experienced. Here the different religious traditions with their various conceptual systems, modes of worship, and lifestyles constitute the lenses through which the various faiths conceptualize the Ultimate. As a result, Judaism must be viewed as simply one human construction among many. For those who subscribe to this divergent philosophy of Judaism, it is a mistake to regard the central tenets of the Jewish faith as absolute and universally valid – rather, they should be viewed as religious assumptions which have developed over the course of Jewish history and experience. Within such a theoretical framework, each adherent of Open Judaism is at liberty to select those elements of the faith that he regards as veridical. There is thus a broad range of alternative religious positions available within the structure of Open Judaism.

First, it is possible to adopt a traditional stance, embracing the major features of the Jewish belief system of the past. Here an advocate of Open Judaism would accept the conventional picture of God as a supernatural being who created and sustains the universe. Such a view would, in essence, be no different from what is found in Orthodoxy, or for that matter, Conservative and right-wing Reform Judaism. Yet, there is one crucial difference between traditional theism and theism as understood within Open Judaism. For the traditionalist, this view of the Godhead is accepted unhesitatingly – there is no question as to its validity. For a follower of Open Judaism, however, such a religious belief would be conceived as a working hypothesis. Aware of the tentative nature of all religious belief, he would acknowledge that his conceptualization of ultimate Reality is a humanly constructed lens through which the Divine is perceived. His theism would thus be tempered by agnosticism.

Some adherents of Open Judaism might, on the other hand, wish to advance a modified form of theism in which various features of the traditional understanding of God is revised. They might argue, for example, that it is no longer possible to believe in an all-good God in the light of the terrible events of the Nazi period. To account for the existence of evil, such believers might want to limit God's omnipotence. Such a view would be similar to the theological position adopted by the Jewish theologian, Arthur A. Cohen, who maintained that God is not an active agent in history, and in consequence it is a mistake to hold him responsible for the horrors of the Holocaust. Within Open Judaism such theological adjustments would be in harmony with an emphasis on personal independence. A cardinal feature of this new Jewish ideology is the appropriateness of religious modification to the traditional doctrines of the faith. This means that all divine attributes as well as theological concepts could be subjected to revision. Hence the various changes to traditional Orthodox teaching suggested by Reform, Conservative, Reconstructionist, Humanistic and Polydox Jewish thinkers would all be acceptable. Further, there could be no compulsion that such altered conceptions be accepted by all members of the community – it would be impossible for Open Judaism to authorize the creation of an Open Judaism statement of belief (akin to the Platforms produced by the Reform movement) or for individual thinkers to impose their views on others. Instead, each person would be encouraged to engage in the formulation of a personal philosophy of Judaism in accord with his own religious leanings.

Such liberalism would also permit an even more radical reconsideration of Jewish belief. Open Judaism would, for example, regard as acceptable the reinterpretation of the nature of God as proposed by Mordecai Kaplan and Alvin Reines. In both cases, there is an explicit rejection of supernaturalism and the substitution of a naturalistic understanding of the Divine. As we have noted, Kaplan defined God as 'the source of all the authority, organizing forces and

relationships which are forever making a cosmos out of chaos'
– for Kaplan, God must be understood primarily in terms of
effects. Similarly for Reines, God is 'the entire possibility of
meaning'. Such descriptions are far removed from traditional
theism or even a modified form of traditional belief. Yet Open
Judaism – with its stress on individual freedom – would permit
such naturalistic conceptualizations. Likewise, within Open
Judaism there would be be no hesitation about accepting an
atheistic Jewish perspective as propounded by Sherwin Wine.
For Wine and other followers of Humanistic Judaism, 'the
natural universe stands on its own requiring no supernatural
intervention – Jewish history is a human story'. With its stress
on personal decision-making, Open Judaism would accept
even such iconoclastic views. Religious options within this new
Jewish ideology thus range across the theological spectrum
from traditional belief to atheistic naturalism.

Despite their divergent views, the adherents of Open
Judaism should acknowledge that whatever beliefs they hold,
there can be no way of demonstrating the correctness of their
convictions. This is due to the inevitable subjectivity of
religious opinion. Given that human beings are only able to
experience Reality-as-perceived rather than Reality-as-it-is-
in-itself, it is impossible to know which religious beliefs are
valid. Religious convictions are inevitably based on interpretation. Such an understanding of religion was given by John
Hick who explained that religious belief should be conceived
as a form of 'seeing-as'. For Hick, there are two senses of the
word 'see'. If I am looking at a picture of a face, for instance, I
see what is physically present on the paper. But in another
sense of 'see' I see the parts of a face. This second sense of
seeing involves understanding and interpretation. The interpretive activity is particularly evident when we look at a
puzzle picture, such as the following illustration:

Looked at from one angle, this is a drawing of a duck; from another – when the paper is on its side – it is of a rabbit.

Related to the process of 'seeing' is the notion of 'experiencing-as'. In our everyday perception of our environment, we use several sense organs at once: 'experiencing-as' is an interpretive mode of cognition which operates even in commonplace situations. If, for example, a stone-age savage were shown knives and forks, he would not experience them as such because of his lack of the concept of eating at a table with manufactured implements. As far as religious belief is concerned, religious experience should be seen in similar terms. Throughout history human beings have displayed a tendency to experience individuals, places and situations as having religious meanings. Such 'experiencing-as' in religious terms is very much like the example of the puzzle-picture of a duck/rabbit. It is clear then that the way in which believers see the world depends on the system of concepts used. Such a view helps to explain why it is that the same features can be experienced in radically different ways. Furthermore, it illustrates why there is not simply one form of religious experience. Given the different conceptual frameworks of different religious systems, 'the world can be experienced as God's handiwork, or as the battlefield of good and evil, or as the cosmic dance of the Shiva' (Hick, 1985, 27). These are simply different forms of 'experiencing-as' which constitute the core of the religious response.

Such an understanding of religious belief illustrates the inevitable interactive nature of religious claims. For this reason it would be a mistake for those who adhere to Open Judaism to assert that they possess ultimate religious truth. In our earthly existence it is impossible to know conclusively that one's religious convictions accurately mirror the nature of divine Reality. None the less, although religious claims cannot be demonstrated to be true or false, religious assertions could in theory be susceptible to verification or falsification in an afterlife. If there is a hereafter, it is possible to conceive the sort of experiences which would tend to confirm religious beliefs. To illustrate this point, Hick tells a parable about two people who are travelling together along a road. One of them believes that it leads to a Celestial City; the other thinks it goes nowhere. But there is only one road; they must both travel on it. Neither has been this way before, so they cannot say what they will find around each new corner. During their journey they meet with moments of refreshment and delight as well as with hardship and disaster. The traveller who thinks of his journey as a pilgrimage to the Celestial City interprets the pleasant parts as encouragement and the obstacles as trials and lessons of endurance prepared by the sovereign of the city, and designed to make him a worthy citizen when he arrives there. The other disagrees – he sees the journey as unavoidable and aimless. For him there is no Celestial City, no all-encompassing purpose. During the course of their journey this disagreement is not an experiential one; nevertheless when they turn the last corner, it will be apparent which one of them has been right all along.

This parable points to the ambiguous character of our present existence. From our earthly standpoint the differences between believers cannot be resolved by an appeal to empirical features of the world. In the main they do not have divergent expectations of the course of temporal history. But they do expect that when human history is completed it will be seen to have led to a particular end-state and to have fulfilled a specific purpose. Thus, although experience of the world is religiously ambiguous, in the hereafter (if it exists), such ambiguity would be transcended (Hick, 1963, 103). Religious convictions then serve as fundamental presuppositions which profoundly shape an individual's life, and such all-absorbing dedication is frequently connected with the stories or parables which feature as central to particular traditions. Religious faith then, is a form of 'experiencing-as' – experiencing life as infused with a divine presence. In our present life this religious vision is inevitably based on a personal response to the features of the world which are themselves ambiguous and this ambiguity makes it impossible to determine with certainty which religious interpretation is valid. Such a recognition is fundamental to Open Judaism, which allows each person to formulate his own belief-system. Yet if there is hereafter, all will be revealed. Until that time, however, adherents of Open

Judaism must show tolerance towards those whose views conflict with their own.

Jewish Practice in a New Age

According to tradition, God revealed 613 commandments to Moses on Mount Sinai; they are recorded in the Five Books of Moses. These prescriptions, which are to be observed as part of God's covenant with Israel, are classified in two major categories: (1) statutes concerned with the ritual performances characterized as obligations between human beings and God; and (2) judgments consisting of ritual laws that would have been adopted by society even if they had not been decreed by God. These 613 commandments consist of 365 negative (prohibited) and 248 positive (duties to be performed) prescriptions. Traditional Judaism also maintains that Moses received the Oral *Torah* in addition to the Written Law. This was passed down from generation to generation and was the subject of rabbinic debate. As a result, *The Code of Jewish Law* contains innumerable precepts based on Scripture.

As we have seen, the major branches of non-Orthodox Judaism do not accept biblical and rabbinic law as binding; in their different ways these movements have redefined the scope of Jewish law. Yet despite such liberalism. Conservative, Reform, Reconstructionist and Humanistic Judaism are prescriptive in their approach to the legal tradition. Open Judaism, however, like Polydoxy would encourage each individual Jew to determine for himself which Jewish observances are religiously significant: as in the sphere of Jewish belief, personal autonomy is of paramount importance. Thus, more traditionally minded supporters of Open Judaism might wish to follow the Orthodox pattern of Jewish observance, including daily worship, attendance at Sabbath and Festival services, and a strict adherence to ritual law. In terms of outward appearances, their Jewish lifestyle would resemble that of pious Orthodox, Conservative or Reconstructionist Jews. Indeed such individuals might feel most comfortable as members of Orthodox, Conservative or Reconstructionist synagogues. Yet, as followers of Open Judaism, they would acknowledge that their personal religious choices are no more valid that those of the less observant.

Jews less conservative in approach, on the other hand, might wish to abandon or modify various features of Jewish law. Such individuals, for example, might desire to distance themselves from the vast number of prescriptions surrounding Jewish worship, home observance and personal piety – instead they would seek to formulate a Jewish lifestyle more in keeping with the demands of modern life. As we have seen, this has been the policy of Reform Judaism from its inception; for these less observant Jews, Reform Judaism would in all likelihood offer the most acceptable religious attitude. None the less, even if they were members of a Reform congregation, as followers of Open Judaism they would recognize that their individual decisions should in no way set a standard for others. Rather, as exponents of this new liberal philosophy of Judaism, they would respect the choices of all Jews no matter how observant or lax.

Open Judaism would also accept as valid the resolve of Jews who wish to express only a minimal acknowledgement of their Jewishness. Such persons, for example, might choose to ignore Jewish law altogether in their everyday lives and only attend synagogue on the High Holy Days, or for the *yartzeit* of a parent. Alternatively, they might simply wish to be married or buried under Jewish auspices without belonging to a synagogue. Open Judaism – as an all-embracing, fluid system extolling personal autonomy as a fundamental principle – would accept the legitimacy of even such a nominal form of Jewish identification.

Open Judaism then, as a philosophy of Judaism, does not set out to establish itself as another organized movement within the ranks of Jewry. Unlike the various branches of religious Jewish life with their own seminaries, rabbis, congregational structures, and educational facilities; Open Judaism should be understood as an ideology, a new vision of Judaism based on a revised conception of divine Reality. Liberal in orientation, it offers all Jews – no matter what their particular religious affiliation – a remodelled conceptualization of Jewish life more in accord with the realities of Jewish existence. As an overarching framework for Jewish observance, Open Judaism respects the manifold religious choices made by contemporary Jews: within Open Judaism, Jewish practice whatever its form is accepted as valid.

Open Judaism then, would encourage a spirit of tolerance concerning each Jew's choice of Jewish observance no matter how rigorous or lenient. In addition, Open Judaism with its emphasis on personal autonomy would be opposed in principle to the traditional *Code of Jewish Law* as an authoritative legal structure for all Jews or to the foundation of a contemporary system of Jewish law. As we noted, the major branches of non-Orthodox Judaism have at various times pressed for the creation of a modern code of law rooted in the Jewish heritage; such a legal system would differ from Orthodoxy in that it would need to be based on explicit criteria of selection – yet it is unclear what such criteria could be.

One common suggestion is that modern Jews should attempt to ascertain what God's will is. In this way they would be able to establish an ultimate, absolute authority for their adherence to tradition. But how can one ascertain with certainty what God has revealed? Is his revelation to be found in the Pentateuch, or the Prophetic books, or the rest of Scripture? Is God truly concerned if Jews eat lobster? Does he care whether they wear fringes, or seethe the kid in its mother's milk? Is he annoyed if they go out to work, drive a car to a synagogue or smoke on the Sabbath? Is he angry if they commit adultery or steal? In the past some non-Orthodox Jews have been anxious to distinguish between ritual and moral law, but is this distinction valid as far as God is concerned? These are ultimately unanswerable questions since there is simply no basis for determining the content of divine revelation. Although non-Orthodox rabbis state categorically that they have some sort of knowledge of God's revelation, an examination of the wide diversity of opinion among these rabbis illustrates that such claims are nothing more than subjective beliefs based on personal disposition and judgment.

If there is disagreement as to what constitutes revelation, what can be said about the claims of conscience? Frequently non-Orthodox rabbis assert that the demand of conscience is a reliable guide in formulating a modern system of law. But this criterion is also beset with difficulties. No doubt many of these rabbis do follow their consciences, but how can they be sure that what they are doing is right? The dictates of one person's conscience often differ from someone else's. To take a simple example: one person's conscience might urge him to see euthanasia as an inalienable human right, whereas another person might well condemn it as utterly sinful. Here there is a direct conflict, yet there is no way to discover which individual's conscience is on the right track. And if in trying to decide who is right, some external standard, like humaneness, is invoked, then conscience ceases to be the final arbiter for moral action.

Conscience then, like revelation, is undependable. But what if we ask whether particular laws are relevant for our time – this is an approach frequently advocated by non-Orthodox rabbis, but the notion of relevance is equally problematic. It is obvious that what one person considers relevant is an ambiguous concept. So too, is the notion of contemporary appeal. How is one to decide what is really of value when change is so constant? Most people have enough difficulty keeping up with modern ideas, much less employing them as criteria for deciding which traditional laws should be retained.

The same applies to such standards as ethical propriety, justice and aesthetic value. From everyday experience it is clear that what is morally offensive to one person can be totally acceptable to another. In such cases as the current debate about abortion, nuclear disarmament and genetic engineering, there is no consensus in society generally, or in the Jewish community in particular, about such issues. The concept of justice is equally unclear. Is it *just* that one individual receives higher wages than someone who works equally hard but at a different task? It is *just* that a limited number of people have private medicine, or are able to hire expensive lawyers? In all these cases some Jews think it is just and some do not. The concept of justice is thus as nebulous and ill-defined a notion as moral propriety. Aesthetic sensitivity too, does not provide the answer. Some laws, like ritual immersion, might commend themselves on such grounds. Yet some Jews view ritual immersion as aesthetically offensive because it involves the personal indignity of the convert who must be interrogated naked. This is just one example, but it illustrates that taste, like many other things, varies from person to person.

Some non-Orthodox rabbis have suggested that psychological considerations should be taken into account in framing a modern code of Jewish law. On this basis, certain observances could be ruled out because of a modern understanding of human psychology. But here again there is widespread disagreement. For example, the Bible explicitly forbids homosexuality. However, on humane and psychological grounds it is possible to take a lenient view of homosexual behaviour – yet a number of non-Orthodox rabbis would disagree. Thus, here too, an appeal to humaneness does not provide a clear basis for selection.

What then about common sense? A number of non-Orthodox rabbis have argued that it is important to consider whether traditional Jewish law undermines common sense. For example, some Reform rabbis have stated that the laws governing Sabbath observance transcend the boundary of common sense and that more room should be made for individual spontaneity. Yet there are other rabbis who advocate a strict observance of Sabbath law. It is common sense, they believe, for Jews to differentiate themselves in just this way so as to perpetuate Judaism as a civilization and to establish their identity as Jews in an increasingly secularized world. It is equally hopeless appealing to the notion of reasonableness as a criterion. How could Jewish ritual and practice be regarded as reasonable? It is reasonable for a secular man in the modern world to wear a prayer shawl and hat in synagogue, blow the *shofar* on *Rosh Hashanah*, eat *matzot* on Passover, light candles on the Sabbath, fast on the Day of Atonement, build a *sukkah* and so forth? Such traditional observances are a part of non-Orthodox Judaism not because of their reasonableness, but because they are viewed as spiritually meaningful.

Finally, it has been suggested that certain traditional laws should be retained because of commitment to the wider Jewish community. Thus, for example, some non-Orthodox rabbis

argue that circumcision and ritual immersion for converts as
well as the issuing of a bill of divorce is of vital significance in
furthering the unity of the Jewish people. Yet, given such a
commitment, where is one to draw the line? If ritual
immersion, circumcision and Jewish divorce are mandatory,
why not the food regulations? Or the laws of ritual purification? Or the Sabbath observances? Or the wearing of *tefillin*
and *tzizit*? Why indeed not all the law in the traditional *Code of
Jewish Law*?

What can be seen, therefore, is that there is no way to
determine which traditional laws should be included in a
contemporary system of law for non-Orthodox Jewry. Revelation, conscience, relevance, contemporary appeal, ethical
propriety, justice, aesthetic value, psychological considerations, common sense, reasonableness, the people-hood of
Israel – all these criteria which have been prescribed by
leaders of the various non-Orthodox movements – are so
nebulous and contentious as to be of little use. In the modern
world, although non-Orthodox Jews are heirs to a vast legal
tradition, they lack any well-defined, coherent and consistent
method for sorting out those traditional laws they should
adopt for themselves. Responding to this situation, Open
Judaism is opposed to the evolution of any Jewish system of
law. Rather, as a new philosophy of Jewish life, Open Judaism
would encourage all individuals to practise those observances
which they find spiritually significant. No one – no rabbi or
rabbinic body – should be allowed to decide what observances
are acceptable for others. What is currently needed throughout the Jewish world is a commitment to personal liberty and
freedom.

Open Judaism and Global Theology

Given the transition to Jewish pluralism in which the Jewish
tradition is perceived as simply one among many paths to the
Divine, the way is open to interfath encounter on the deepest
levels. In the past, Jewish theologicans asserted that Judaism
is the superior tradition – even the most liberal thinkers
maintained that in the future humanity will acknowledge the

truth of Jewish monotheism. In this sense Jewish theology throughout the ages was Judeo-centric in nature. Today, however, in our religiously diverse world, it is no longer possible to sustain this position – what is now required is a redefinition of the theological task. In the modern world, Open Judaism provides a framework for such theological exploration given the recognition that religious doctrines in all faiths are simply human attempts to comprehend the nature of Ultimate Reality.

The pursuit of religious truth now calls for a global dialogical approach. As Wilfred Cantwell Smith remarked:

> The time will soon be with us when a theologian who attempts to work out his position unaware that he does so as a member of a world society in which other theologians equally intelligent, equally devout, equally oral, are Hindus, Buddhists, Muslims and unaware that his readers are likely perhaps to be Buddhists or to have Muslim husbands or Hindu colleagues – such a theologian is as out of date as is one who attempts to construct an intellectual position unaware that Aristotle has thought about the world or that existentialists have raised new orientations, or unaware that the earth is a minor planet in a galaxy that is vast only by terrestrial standards. (Smith, 1962, 123)

The formulation of a Jewish global, inter-religious theology is based on two preconditions. First, Jewish theologians must learn about religious traditions other than their own. Global theology undertaken from within the context of Open Judaism requires religious thinkers to investigate what the world's faiths have experienced and affirmed about the nature of divine Reality, the phenomenon of religious experience, the nature of the self, the problem of the human condition, and the value of the world. Second, Jewish theologians should attempt to enter into the thought-world as well as religious experiences of those of other faiths; this can only be done by becoming a participant in their way of life. Paul Knitter argued, 'Theologians must "pass over" to the experience, to the mode of being in the world, that nurtures the creeds and codes and cults of other religions . . . (they) must imaginatively participate in the faith of other religions: "Faith can only be theologized from the inside"' (Knitter, 1985, 226).

Jewish thinkers must thus enter into the subjectivity of other traditions and bring the resulting insights to bear on their own understanding of religion: such reflection demands a multi-dimensional, cross-cultural, inter-religious consciousness. Open Judaism is most suited to such a multi-faceted approach in which all religions are conceived as interdependent. Given this quest for a global perspective, those who subscribe to this new Jewish philosophy must insist that the theological endeavour takes place in a trans-religious context. This enterprise requires an encounter in which Jews confront others who hold totally different truth-claims – such individuals can help Jewish thinkers to discover their own presuppositions and underlying principles. In this process Jewish partners should be able to acknowledge the limitations of their own tradition, and as a result make a conscious effort to discover common ground with other faiths. Such an interchange is vital to the formulation of a multi-dimensional theological outlook.

Given the possibility for this type of inter-religious exploration, there are a number of central issues which Jews and adherents of other faiths could fruitfully explore together:

1. *Symbols.* Jews and members of other traditions could profitably explore the nature of religious symbols as long as neither the Jewish nor the non-Jewish partner adopts the standpoint that the symbols in his respective faith are superior. Not very much is known about the logic of symbols: we do not understand why, for example, people use certain symbols, why they give up others, why they remain unmoved by symbols that members of other faiths find meaningful, and why they are moved by a symbol that others find objectionable. If discussion were to occur across religious lines, it might be possible to attain greater insight into what is involved in religious symbolism.

2. *Worship.* In most of the religions of the world, worship is a response to the Divine, an acknowledgement of a reality independent of the worshipper. Assuming that neither the Jewish nor the non-Jewish participant in interfaith dialogue maintains that his conception of Ultimate Reality is uniquely true, it would be helpful to discuss the ways in which various forms of worship provide some glimpse into the nature of

Divine Reality. Furthermore, it might be possible to investigate the ways in which the liturgical features of one tradition could be incorporated into the other. The Passover *Seder*, for example, is viewed by most scholars as the ceremony celebrated at the Last Supper. In this regard it is as much a part of the Christian as the Jewish tradition, and could become an element of the Christian liturgy. This is simply one example of the ways in which adherents of different faiths could enrich the liturgical dimensions of one another's traditions.

3. *Ritual*. Like worship, ritual plays a major role in the world's religions, and there are areas worthy of joint investigation as long as neither party adopts an attitude of religious superiority. First, an examination of formal and elaborate practices as well as simple actions could reveal the ways in which the believer sees his action as making contact or participating in the Divine. Second, a comparative study of ritualist practice could clarify the ways in which an outer activity mirrors an inner process – a relationship fundamental to the concept of ritualistic behaviour. Third, it might be beneficial to examine the contemplative and mystical activities in different traditions which allegedly disclose various aspects of the Divine and enable the practitioner to reach an altered state of con-sciousness.

4. *Ethics*. Traditional Jews believe that God chose the Jewish nation to be his special people and gave them his law on Mount Sinai. The moral law is thus embodied in immutable, divine commandments. In other faiths, however, ethical values are perceived in a different light. For the traditional Christian, for example, Christ is understood as the end of the law, thereby superseding the *Torah* as the mediator between God and man. Allowing that both Jews and Christians could adopt a more liberal open-minded stance to moral attitudes within their respective traditions, it would be worthwhile to examine Jesus' critique of Pharisaic Judaism; such an investigation could help illumine the tension between specific rules and general principles as well as the relationship between action and intention. As far as other faiths are concerned, the exploration of the foundations of alternative ethical systems could result in a deepening of ethical perception.

5. *Society*. Religions are not only systems of belief and practice; they are also organizations which have a communal and social dimension. Given that neither the Jewish nor non-Jewish

partner in dialogue assumes that their faith possesses a better organizational structure and a more positive attitude toward modern society, it would be of interest to examine the ways in which each religion understands itself in relation to the world. In addition, since many faiths contain religious hierarchies, an analysis of the nature of institutional structures, the training of leaders, and the exercise of authority could clarify the ways in which religious traditions reflect the non-religious characteristics of the societies in which they exist. In the face of modern secularism, such an examination would be of particular consequence, since more than ever before, religions find themselves forced to adapt to a rapidly changing world.

These subject areas by no means exhaust the possibilities for interfaith dialogue, but they do indicate the type of joint activity that could take place. In addition, those who subscribe to the ideology of Open Judaism could also engage in a new form of interfaith encounter on a practical level. No longer should Jews feel constrained to stand aloof from the worship services of other faiths. Rather a pluralist standpoint in which all faiths are recognized as authentic paths to the Ultimate would encourage adherents of all the world's religions – including Jews – to engage in common religious activities. In this regard, it is important to distinguish between three major types of interfaith worship:

1. Services of a particular religious community in which members of other faiths are invited as guests. On such occasions, it is usual to ask a representative of the visiting faith-community to recite a suitable prayer or preach a sermon, but the liturgy remains the same.
2. Interfaith gatherings of a serial nature. At such meetings representatives of each religion offer prayers or readings on a common theme. Those present constitute an audience listening to a liturgical anthology in which the distinctiveness of each religion is acknowledged, but everyone is free to participate as well.
3. Interfaith gatherings with a shared order of service. In such situations all present are participants, and there is an overarching theme. (Braybrooke, 1992, 151)

These different kinds of service possess their own particular characteristics. In the first type – where adherents of one faith invite others to attend their services – they are not seeking to make converts; rather, there is a conscious recognition of the integrity of other traditions. In such a setting, proponents of Open Judaism should feel completely comfortable: Open Judaism would encourage the process of learning and sharing, and ideally, Jewish guests at another faith-community's worship service should strive to enter into the experience of those praying. In this regard, advocates of Open Judaism should not feel hesitant to recite prayers or sing hymns whose truth-claims conflict with the truth-claims of their own faith. Given that the Real *an sich* is unknowable, the different liturgical formulations in the world's faiths should be understood as human constructions which attempt to depict the nature and activity of a divine Reality; as models of the Divine, they guide the believer to the Ultimate.

Similarly, in the second type of worship service – in which there is a serial reading by representatives of other communities – Open Judaism would welcome the opportunity to share the Jewish liturgical tradition with others. Those who espouse this new Jewish ideology should feel no reluctance in joining in the liturgy from other traditions when appropriate. In accord with a pluralist stance, such serial services are based on mutual respect and afford each community an equal role in worship.

Turning to the third type of worship service – in which there is a common liturgy – Open Judaism would encourage Jews to pray together in this fashion with members of other faiths. In such contexts, participants are frequently invited to worship the One Eternal One – the ultimate ground of being to which all religious dogma and ritual point as the Divine Mystery. This form of service is particularly amenable to a theology of Open Judaism in which final Reality is viewed as the unknowable Infinite that cannot be fully conveyed in any particular faith. In services of this type the distinctiveness of each religion is accepted – there is no attempt to replace the regular liturgy of the individual faith communities. Yet there is the implicit assumption that in worship, adherents of all faiths stand before the Ultimate which they have given different names. The third form of worship then, is consonant with the principles of Open Judaism – it affirms other faiths while simultaneously recognizing the limitation of all human conceptualizations of the Real.

Open Judaism thus not only provides a basis for reformulating the Jewish faith in the light of contemporary theological reflection, it also serves as a framework for interfaith encounter on the deepest level; here then, is a new vision of Judaism consonant with the needs of Jewry as it stands on the threshold of the twenty-first century.

Bibliography

Adler, Morris, 1964. 'The Philosophy of the Conservative Movement', *Review* (USA), 16, No. 4 (Winter).

Agus, J., 1959. *The Evolution of Jewish Thought* (Abelard Schuman).

Arzt, M., 1955. 'Conservative Judaism', in Theodore Friedman, *What is Conservative Judaism?* (Horizon Press).

Baeck, L., 1948. *The Essence of Judaism* (Schocken).

Bamberger, B., 1964. *The Story of Judaism* (Schocken).

Baron, S. W., 1952–76. *A Social and Religious History of The Jews* (Columbia University Press).

Ben-Sasson, H. H., 1976. *A History of the Jewish People* (Harvard University Press).

Bergman, S. H., 1963. *Faith and Reason: An Introduction to Modern Jewish Thought* (Schocken).

Berkovitz, E., 1983. *Not In Heaven* (Ktav).

Berkovitz, E., 1974. *Major Themes in Modern Philosophies of Judaism* (Ktav).

Berkovitz, E., 1973. *Faith after the Holocaust* (Ktav).

Bokser, B. Z., 1964. *Jewish Law: A Conservative Approach.*

Bokser, B. Z., 1941. 'Doctrine of the Chosen People', *Contemporary Jewish Record*, June.

Borowitz, E., 1983. *Choices in Modern Thought* (Behrman House).

Borowitz, E., 1969. *How Can a Jew Speak of Faith Today?* (Westminster Press).

Borowitz, E., 1968. *A New Jewish Theology in the Making* (Westminster Press).

Braybrooke, M., 1992. 'Interfaith Prayer', Dan Cohn-Sherbok, *Many Mansions* (Bellew).

Bulka, R., 1984. *The Coming Cataclysm* (Mosaic Press).

Cohen, Arthur A., 1981. *The Tremendum* (Crossroads).

211

Cohn-Sherbok, D., 1993a. *Judaism and Other Faiths* (Macmillan).

Cohn-Sherbok, D., 1993b. *The Jewish Faith* (SPCK).

Cohn-Sherbok, D., 1989. *Holocaust Theology* (Lamp).

Cohn-Sherbok, D., 1988. *The Jewish Heritage* (Basil Blackwell).

De Lange, N., 1986. *Judaism* (Oxford University Press).

Encyclopaedia Judaica (Keter Publishing House), 1972.

Epstein, I., 1975. *Judaism* (Penguin).

Fackenheim, E., 1982. *To Mend the World: Foundations of Future Jewish Thought* (Schocken).

Fackenheim, E., 1987. *What is Judaism?* (Collier).

Feuerlicht, R. S., 1983. *The Fate of the Jews: A People Torn Between Israeli Power and Jewish Ethics* (Times Books).

Finkelstein, L., 1948. 'The Things that Unite Us', in Rabbinical Assembly, *Proceedings*.

Freehof, S., 1960. *Reform Responsa* (CCAR).

Freud, S., 1981. *The Future of an Illusion. The Complete Psychological Works of Sigmund Freud* (Hogarth Press).

Friedman, G., 1967. *The End of the Jewish People?* (Hutchinson).

Goldstein, I., 1928. 'Inadequacies in the Status of the Synagogue Today', Rabbinical Assembly, *Proceedings*.

Goodman, S. L. (ed.), 1976. *The Faith of Secular Jews* (Ktav).

Gordis, R., 1970. *Conservative Judaism: A Modern Approach to Jewish Tradition* (Behrman House).

Graetz, H., 1891–8. *A History of the Jews* (Jewish Publication Society).

Grayzel, S., 1968. *A History of the Jews: From the Babylonian Exile to the Present* (New American Library).

Greenberg, I., 1981. *The Third Great Cycle in Jewish History* (National Jewish Resource Centre).

Greenberg, I., 1980. *On the Third Era in Jewish History* (National Jewish Resource Centre).

Greenberg, S., 1955. *The Conservative Movement in Judaism: An Introduction* (United Synagogue of America).

Guttman, J., 1964. *Philosophies of Judaism: The History of Jewish Philosophy from Biblical Times to Franz Rosenzweig* (Holt, Rinehart and Winston).

Hartman, D., 1985. *A Living Covenant.*

Hertzberg, A. (ed.), 1959. *The Zionist Idea: A Historical Analysis and Reader* (Atheneum).

Heschel, A., 1985. *God in Search of Man* (Harper and Row).

Hick, J., 1963, 1973. *Philosophy of Religion* (Prentice Hall).

Hirsch, S. R., 1960. *The Nineteen Letters on Judaism* (Feldheim).
Husik, I., 1958. *A History of Medieval Jewish Philosophy* (Jewish Publication Society).

Jacob Joseph of Polonnoye, 1954–5. *Told of Yaokou Yosef* (Israel Rev Publisher).
Jacobs, L., 1988. *Principles of the Jewish Faith* (Jason Aronson).
Jacobs, L., 1973. *A Jewish Theology* (Behrman House).
Jacobs, L., 1964. *Principles of the Jewish Faith* (Basic Books).
Jewish Encyclopaedia (Funk and Wagnalls, 1901–5).
Johnson, P., 1987. *A History of the Jews* (Weidenfeld and Nicolson).

Kaplan, M., 1967. *Judaism as a Civilization* (Schocken Books).
Kaplan, M., 1916. 'The Future of Judaism', *Menorah Journal*, June.
Kaplan, M., 1970. 'The Meaning of God for the Contemporary Jew', in A. Jospe (ed.), *Tradition and Contemporary Experience* (Schocken Books).
Kaplan, M., 1962. *The Meaning of God in Modern Jewish Religion* (Reconstructionist Press).
Katz, S. T., 1983. *Post-Holocaust Dialogues* (New York University Press).
Kaufman, W., 1976. *Contemporary Jewish Philosophies* (Behrman House).
Knitter, P. F., 1985. *No Other Name* (Orbis).
Kohler, K., 1968. *Jewish Theology* (Ktav).
Kreitman, B. Z., 1975. 'Conservative Judaism – The Next Step', *Review* (USA), 27, No. 3 (Winter).
Kurzweil, Z., 1985. *The Modern Impulse of Traditional Judaism* (Ktav).

Lenn, T., 1972. *Rabbi and Synagogue in Reform Judaism* (CCAR).
Levinthal, I., 1928. Rabbinical Assembly, *Proceedings*.

Mahler, R. (ed.), 1941. *Jewish Emancipation: A Selection of Documents* (American Jewish Committee).
Maimonides, 1881. *The Guide of the Perplexed* (Hebrew Publishing Co.).
Margolis, M. L., and Marx, A., 1965. *A History of the Jewish People* (Harper and Row).
Marmur, D., 1982. *Beyond Survival* (Darton, Longman and Todd).
Maybaum, I., 1984. *The Face of God After Auschwitz* (Polak and Van Gennep).
Maza, Bernard, 1984. *With Fury Poured Out* (Ktav).
Mendelssohn, M., 1969. *Jerusalem and Other Jewish Writings* (Schocken).

Meyer, M., 1988. *Response to Modernity: A History of the Reform Movement in Judaism* (Oxford University Press).

Meyer, M., 1967. *The Origins of the Modern Jew* (Wayne State University Press).

Nemoy, L., 1952. *Karaite Anthology* (Yale University Press).

Novak, D., 1989. *Jewish–Christian Dialogue* (Oxford University Press).

Parkes, J., 1964. *A History of the Jewish People* (Penguin).

Philipson, D., 1967. *The Reform Movement in Judaism* (Ktav).

Philo, 1949. *De Opificio Mundi* (Loeb Classical Library).

Plaut, W. G., 1965. *The Growth of Reform Judaism* (World Union for Progressive Judaism).

Plaut, W. G., 1963. *The Rise of Reform Judaism* (World Union for Progressive Judaism).

Raphael, M. L., 1984. *Profiles in American Judaism* (Harper and Row).

Reines, A., 1987. *Polydoxy* (Pantheon).

Rosenthal, G., 1980. 'The Foundations of the Conservative Approach to Jewish Law', in Rabbinical Assembly, *Proceedings*.

Rosenthal, G., 1973. *Four Paths to One God: Today's Jew and His Religion* (Block Publishing Co.).

Rotenstreich, N., 1968. *Jewish Philosophy in Modern Times: From Mendelssohn to Rosenzweig* (Holt, Rinehart and Winston).

Roth, C., 1970. *A History of the Jews* (Schocken).

Rubenstein, Richard, 1966. *After Auschwitz* (Bobbs-Merrill).

Rudonsky, D., 1967. *Emancipation and Adjustment: Contemporary Jewish Religious Movements – Their History and Thought* (Behrman House).

Sachar, A. L., 1967. *A History of the Jews* (Alfred A. Knopf).

Sachar, H. M., 1977. *The Course of Modern Jewish History* (Dell).

Sacks, J., 1993. *One People? Tradition, Modernity and Jewish Unity* (Littman Library).

Sacks, J., 1989. *Traditional Alternatives* (Jews College Publications).

Schechter, S., 1959. *Seminary Addresses and Other Papers* (Burning Bush Press).

Seltzer, R., 1980. *Jewish People, Jewish Thought* (Collier Macmillan).

Siegel, S., 1980. 'Approaches to Halachah in the Conservative Movement', in Rabbinical Assembly, *Proceedings*.

Simon, E., 1958. 'Torat Hayyim: Some Thoughts on the Teaching of the Bible', *Conservative Judaism*, Spring.

Sklare, M., 1972. *Conservative Judaism* (Schocken).

Solomon, M., 1954. *The Autobiography of Solomon Maimon* (The East and West Library).

Solomon, N., 1991. *Judaism and World Religion* (Macmillan).

The Condition of Jewish Belief: A Symposium Compiled by the Editors of Commentary Magazine (Macmillan, 1969).

Trepp, L., 1973. *A History of the Jewish Experience* (Behrman House).

Vital, D., 1990. *The Future of the Jews* (Harvard University Press).

Wine, S., 1985. *Judaism Beyond God* (Society for Humanistic Judaism).

Wouk, H., 1968. *This is My God* (Doubleday).

Wyschogrod, M., 1983. *The Body of Faith* (Seabury Press).

Glossary

Aggadah	rabbinic teaching
Aliyah	immigration to Israel
Aljama	Jewish community in medieval Spain
Amidah	the eighteen blessings
Anus	coerced
Ashkenazim	Eastern European Jews
Ayn Sof	infinite
Bakkashah	liturgical composition ('supplication')
Bar mitzvah	coming of age ceremony for boys at age 13
Devekut	mystical cleaving to God
Doenmeh	Judeo-Muslim sect of the seventeenth century
Elohim	God
Epiqoros	heretic
Erusin	stage in bethrothal
Exilarch	head of the Babylonian Jewish community
Galut	continuous wandering
Gan Eden	heaven
Gaon	head of a Babylonian Academy
Gehinnom	hell
Get	bill of divorce
Goyim	non-Jews
Habad	Hasidic movement whose name is based on the initials of the words *hokhmah* (wisdom), *binah* (understanding), and *daat* (knowledge)
Haftarot	prophetic readings
Haggadah	Passover prayerbook
Halakhah	Jewish law
Hannukah	Festival of Lights ('dedication')
Hashgagh	divine action

217

Hasidei Ashkenaz	German medieval mystics
Hasidism	mystical Jewish movement founded in the eighteenth century
Haskalah	Jewish Enlightenment
Havurot	prayer groups
Kabbalah	Jewish mysticism
Kabbalat hamitzvot	acceptance of the divine commandments
Kaddish	prayer for the dead
Kahal	congregation or community
Kehillah	Jewish communal body
Kelippah	evil realm
Kelippot	powers of evil
Ketubah	Jewish marriage document
Ketuvim	Writings (third section of the Hebrew Scriptures)
Kiddush	sanctification prayer
Kiddushin	stage in betrothal
Klal Yisrael	Jewish peoplehood
Malkhut	kingdom
Mamzerim	illegitimate children
Marranos	Jews who converted to Christianity (in Spain and Portugal)
Maskilim	advocates of Jewish Enlightenment
Masorah	tradition
Matzot	unleavened bread
Midrash	rabbinic commentary on Scripture
Mikveh	ritual bath
Minhag	customs
Minin	heretics
Mishnah	compendium of the Oral *Torah*
Mitnagdim	rabbinic opponents of the Hasidim
Mitzvot	commandments
Neviim	Prophets (second section of the Hebrew Scriptures)
Nissuin	second stage in the marriage procedure
Olam	eternity
Oleh	immigrant to Israel
Omer	barley offering
Pesach	Passover
Piyyutim	hymns
Purim	feast of Esther
Rebbe	Hasidic leader

Rosh Hashanah	New Year
Seder	Passover ceremony at home
Sefirot	divine emanations
Sephardim	Mediterranean Jews
Shabbat	Sabbath
Shavuot	Festival of Weeks
Shekhinah	God's presence
Shema	prayer ('Hear, O Israel')
Shemini Azeret	final day of the Festival of *Sukkot*
Sheol	place of the dead
Shofar	ram's horn
Shogeg	unwitting
Shulhan Arukh	Code of Jewish Law
Simhat Torah	Festival of the Rejoicing of the Law
Sitra Ahra	demonic realm ('the other side')
Sukkah	booth
Sukkot	Festival of Tabernacles or Booths
Takkanot	enactments or rules
Tallit	prayer shawl
Talmud	compilation of the legal discussions based on the *Mishnah*
Tanakh	Hebrew Bible
Tefillin	phylacteries
Teshuvat ha-kana	the penance of *kana* or fasting
Teshuvat ha-mishkal	the penance of weighing
Tikkun	cosmic repair
Torah	Law (or Pentateuch, the first section of the Hebrew Scriptures)
Torah MiSinai	Torah from Mount Sinai
Torah Mitoldot Ameniu	Torah from our generations
Torah She-Be-Al-Peh	Oral Law
Torah She-Bi-Ketav	Written Law
Tosafists	rabbinic commentators
Tzimtzum	contraction of the Godhead into itself
Tzizit	fringes
Viddui	confession
Yartzeit	anniversary of a death
Yeshivah	college
Yom Kippur	Day of Atonement
Zaddik	Hasidic leader
Zohar	medieval mystical work
Zugot	early rabbinic scholars

Index